D0821723

CHOMSKY

Language, Mind, and Politics

James McGilvray

Polity Press

First published in 1999 by Polity Press
in association with Blackwell Publishers Ltd.

Editorial office:
Polity Press
65 Bridge Street
Cambridge CB2 1UR, UK

Marketing and production:
Blackwell Publishers Ltd
108 Cowley Road
Oxford OX4 1JF, UK

Published in the USA by
Blackwell Publishers Inc.
Commerce Place
350 Main Street
Malden, MA 02148, USA

ISBN 0-7456-1887-1
ISBN 0-7456-1888-X (pbk)

A catalogue record for this book is available from the British Library.

Library of Congress Cataloging–in–Publication Data

McGilvray, James A. (James Alasdair), 1942–
    Chomsky: language, mind, and politics / James McGilvray.
      p. cm.—(Key contemporary thinkers)
    Includes bibliographical references and index.
    ISBN 0-7456-1887-1 (alk. paper).—ISBN 0-7456-1888-X (pbk.: alk. paper))
    1. Chomsky, Noam—Philosophy. 2. Philosophy of mind.
  3. Linguistics. I. Title. II. Series: Key contemporary thinkers (Cambridge, England)
  P85.C47M39 1999
  191—dc21   99-11074
                                                    CIP

Typeset in 10½ on 12 pt Palatino
by Best-set Typesetter Ltd., Hong Kong
Printed in Great Britain by MPG Books, Bodmin, Cornwall

This book is printed on acid-free paper.

Key Contemporary Thinkers

Published

Jeremy Ahearne, *Michel de Certeau: Interpretation and its Other*
Peter Burke, *The French Historical Revolution: The* Annales *School 1929–1989*
Michael Caesar, *Umberto Eco: Philosophy, Semiotics and the Work of Fiction*
Colin Davis, *Levinas: An Introduction*
Simon Evnine, *Donald Davidson*
Edward Fullbrook and Kate Fullbrook, *Simone de Beauvoir: A Critical Introduction*
Andrew Gamble, *Hayek: The Iron Cage of Liberty*
Philip Hansen, *Hannah Arendt: Politics, History and Citizenship*
Sean Homer, *Fredric Jameson: Marxism, Hermeneutics, Postmodernism*
Christopher Hookway, *Quine: Language, Experience and Reality*
Christina Howells, *Derrida: Deconstruction from Phenomenology to Ethics*
Simon Jarvis, *Adorno: A Critical Introduction*
Douglas Kellner, *Jean Baudrillard: From Marxism to Post-Modernism and Beyond*
Chandran Kukathas and Philip Pettit, *Rawls: A Theory of Justice and its Critics*
James McGilvray, *Chomsky: Language, Mind, and Politics*
Lois McNay, *Foucault: A Critical Introduction*
Philip Manning, *Erving Goffman and Modern Sociology*
Michael Moriarty, *Roland Barthes*
William Outhwaite, *Habermas: A Critical Introduction*
John Preston, *Feyerabend: Philosophy, Science and Society*
Susan Sellers, *Hélène Cixous: Authorship, Autobiography and Love*
David Silverman, *Harvey Sacks: Social Science and Conversation Analysis*
Geoffrey Stokes, *Popper: Philosophy, Politics and Scientific Method*
Georgia Warnke, *Gadamer: Hermeneutics, Tradition and Reason*
James Williams, *Lyotard: Towards a Postmodern Philosophy*
Jonathan Wolff, *Robert Nozick: Property, Justice and the Minimal State*

Forthcoming

Maria Baghramian, *Hilary Putnam*
Sara Beardsworth, *Kristeva*

James Carey, *Innis and McLuhan*
Thomas D'Andrea, *Alasdair MacIntyre*
Eric Dunning, *Norbert Elias*
Jocelyn Dunphy, *Paul Ricoeur*
Matthew Elton, *Daniel Dennett*
Nigel Gibson, *Frantz Fanon*
Graeme Gilloch, *Walter Benjamin*
Karen Green, *Dummett: Philosophy of Language*
Espen Hammer, *Stanley Cavell*
Fred Inglis, *Clifford Geertz*
Sarah Kay, *Žižek: A Critical Introduction*
Paul Kelly, *Ronald Dworkin*
Valerie Kennedy, *Edward Said*
Carl Levy, *Antonio Gramsci*
Dermot Moran, *Edmund Husserl*
Harold Noonan, *Frege*
Wes Sharrock and Rupert Read, *Kuhn*
Nick Smith, *Charles Taylor*
Nicholas Walker, *Heidegger*

Contents

Abbreviations   x
Acknowledgments   xii

Introduction   1
  A unified project   1
  Some aspects of Chomsky's rationalist intellectual project   3
  The basic observations   6

1 Common Sense and Science   8
  Chomsky's contributions: a quick overview   8
  How Chomsky's work has been received   13
  Common sense, science, and mind   17
  The science of mind and the perils of empiricism   28

2 Mapping the Mind   32
  Rationalist versus empiricist: who's the scientist of mind?   32
  Non-problems: access and mind/body   33
  Where and what is reason?   35
  A challenge to a science of the human mind   40
  The mind mapped and capacities enabled   46
  An illustration   57
  Enablement by limitation   60

Contents

3 Poverty, Creativity, and Making the World   62
Plato, rationalists, and Chomsky's nativism   63
The creative aspect of language use   78
Constructivism and the biological rationalist   89

4 Languages and the Science of Language   94
Some terms of the science of language   95
Locating Chomsky's theoretical approach to language:
   syntax, semantics, and pragmatics   98
Science, 'science', and common sense: I-language,
   E-language, and differences between languages   105
The natural way to count languages: UG, natural
   language, and I-language   113
Adequacy in linguistic theory and progress in linguistics   118

5 How to Make an Expression   125
Why transformational grammar?   127
How the P&P framework makes a sentence   133
Simplicity again and optimality   147

6 Meanings and Their Use   151
Perspectives   151
Deep Structure   153
Perspectives and the Minimalist Program   156
The shape of the lexicon   158
Naturalized meanings   162
Chomsky and Cudworth on interpretation: "innate
   cognoscitive power" and prolepsis   168
Meaning guides use   174

7 Anarchosyndicalism and the Intellectual   177
Getting into focus   177
The "liberal" economic conception of humans and
   US domestic and foreign policy   180
The anarchosyndicalist conception of the person   196
The manufacture of consent   203
The responsibility of intellectuals   216

8 Human Nature and Ideal Social Organization   221
   Language and politics   221
   The needs of human nature   224
   The relativist's challenge, the new social science, and
      projection   235
   Orwell's problem   239
   Socrates and Chomsky   244
   Rationalist philosophy and the new social science   247

Notes   250
References   264
Index   268

Abbreviations

APNM	*American Power and the New Mandarins* (New York: Pantheon, 1967)
ATS	*Aspects of the Theory of Syntax* (Cambridge, MA: MIT Press, 1965)
CG	*The Common Good* (Monroe, ME: Common Courage/Odonian, 1998)
CILT	*Current Issues in Linguistic Theory* (The Hague: Mouton, 1964)
CL	*Cartesian Linguistics* (New York: Harper and Row, 1966)
CR	*The Chomsky Reader*, ed. James Peck (New York: Pantheon, 1987)
DD	*Deterring Democracy* (London and New York: Verso, 1991)
KL	*Knowledge of Language* (New York: Praeger, 1986)
LGB	*Lectures on Government and Binding* (Dordrecht: Foris, 1982)
LL	*Letters from Lexington: Reflections on Propaganda* (Toronto: Between the Lines, 1993)
LM	*Language and Mind* (New York: Harcourt Brace Jovanovich, 1972)
LP	*Language and Politics*, ed. Carlos Otero (Montreal: Black Rose, 1988)
LPK	*Language and Problems of Knowledge: The Managua Lectures* (Cambridge, MA: MIT Press, 1988)
LR	*Language and Responsibility*, interview with Mitsou Ronat (New York: Pantheon, 1979)
LSLT	*The Logical Structure of Linguistic Theory* (New York: Plenum, 1975; originally 1955 and 1956)

LT   *Language and Thought* (London: Moyer Bell, 1993)
MC   *Manufacturing Consent*, with Edward Herman (New York: Pantheon, 1988)
MP   *The Minimalist Program* (Cambridge, MA: MIT Press, 1995)
NI   *Necessary Illusions* (Toronto: Anansi, 1989)
PEHR   *The Political Economy of Human Rights*, with Edward Herman (Montreal: Black Rose, 1979)
PKF   *Problems of Knowledge and Freedom* (New York: Pantheon, 1971)
PP   *Powers and Prospects* (Boston: South End Press, 1996)
RL   *Reflections on Language* (New York: Pantheon, 1975)
RP   *Radical Priorities*, ed. Carlos Otero (Montreal: Black Rose, 1981)
RR   *Rules and Representations* (New York: Columbia University Press, 1980)
SPE   *Sound Patterns of English*, with Morris Halle (Cambridge, MA: MIT Press, 1968)
SyS   *Syntactic Structures* (The Hague: Monton, 1957)
TNCW   *Towards a New Cold War* (New York: Pantheon, 1973)
TTGG   *Topics in the Theory of Generative Grammar* (The Hague: Mouton, 1966)
WOON   *World Orders Old and New* (New York: Columbia University Press, 1994)
Y5   *Year 501* (Montreal: Black Rose, 1993)

Acknowledgments

I am indebted to many individuals for encouragement, editing, discussion, comments, suggestions, and advice. To Norbert Hornstein and Andrew Winnard of Polity Press (and now at Cambridge University Press), thanks for getting me started. To Polity's Petra Moll and Lynn Dunlop, thanks for keeping me going. And to the press's editorial and production staff – particularly to Jean van Altena, whose editing greatly improved the text – thanks for helping to make the work presentable.

My intellectual debts in this project are many. Several bright and enthusiastic sets of undergraduates in my course on Chomsky have kept me on my toes. Some of my graduate students – Nick Adamson and Andy Burday in particular – provided helpful comments and criticism. Colleagues at McGill and elsewhere – Claude Panaccio, Melinda Hogan, Ann Mackenzie, Norbert Hornstein, Benjamin Shaer, and Paul Bloomfield – commented and made suggestions on this and related work on Chomsky. Special thanks go to colleagues who participated in three FCAR grant-funded seminars over the last few years – Sue Dwyer, David Davies, and Paul Pietroski in philosophy and Mark Baker and Brendan Gillon in linguistics. I am particularly grateful to Paul and a former colleague and friend, Harry Bracken; both carefully read drafts of the manuscript and commented on them (in Harry's case, twice), leading to many improvements. And to Harry, for helping me out of an earlier Wittgensteinian slumber, *muchas gracias*.

My greatest intellectual debt, however, is to Noam Chomsky. He read and critically commented on a draft of this book, and over the last few years has generously corresponded with me and set aside time to discuss a wide range of philosophical and linguistic issues. I am grateful for his attention and interest. Most important, though, is the example that he sets as a responsible intellectual worker in philosophy, linguistics, and politics. I am not alone in being very grateful to him for inspiration.

My greatest overall debt in the writing of this book is to my wife, Joan. Her sharp mind and insightful comments have improved much of its exposition and arguments. Her careful reading and editing have clarified several drafts and helped reduce a verbose manuscript. And her support and encouragement have made writing it possible.

I gratefully acknowledge that some funding for work that went into the project was provided by a Québec FCAR équipe grant.

Introduction

A unified project

In an interview on BBC3 some years ago, Cambridge University historian Jonathan Steinberg complimented Noam Chomsky on the excellence of the research behind a review he had written of one of modern historian Gabriel Jackson's books on the Spanish Civil War. He asked how Chomsky managed to find time to carry out such painstaking research. Chomsky, displaying uncharacteristic pride in his scholarship, remarked that he had done the research when he was about 12 years old and working on an article for his school newspaper.

Chomsky's intellectual career obviously had an early start. Even so, his output during the last 58 years is prodigious. He has published over 70 books and hundreds of articles. He has given thousands of speeches to audiences ranging from a few people gathered in a local meeting hall to thousands crowded into a large lecture theatre. He has found time to meet with hundreds of people a year, to read and respond to thousands of letters, and to read hundreds of articles and books, often writing to the author and commenting on the work. Despite his busy schedule, he is legendary for his attention to the work of students: a philosophy graduate student at McGill University – not Chomsky's MIT – recently sent some 80 double-spaced pages of her dissertation to him for his comments. Within weeks, she received 27 pages of comments in return, single spaced and in small type. There are similar stories. Yet Chomsky also manages to maintain a private life.

At least as remarkable, Chomsky's intellectual productivity spans several fields, some apparently remote from others. A quick look at his works reveals an intriguing collection of articles, speeches, and books that include at one pole a large number of extraordinarily sophisticated and, to many, incomprehensible works in mathematical linguistics and, at the other, scores of political works that are so easy to understand that it takes determination to fail to comprehend them. His work appears, then, to be divided between a narrow science for the few and broad political discussions for all. But a closer look hints at a way in which these apparently disparate intellectual interests are parts of a more general project. Both his linguistic and his political works discuss and advance a view of human nature that suggests how his work as scientist is connected to his work as political analyst and advocate. This view of human nature may provide a way to forge a single, coherent intellectual project that ties together the two poles. I say "may," because, while Chomsky hints that human nature provides the link, he is diffident about claiming that there is a close connection between his linguistic and political work, and is sometimes reluctant even to pursue the question of just how a connection might be forged. There is no a priori reason to assume that Chomsky's intellectual work must be coherent, of course: Sakharov's scientific work in physics bore no discernible relationship to his political views. But Chomsky's political and linguistic works do seem to be part of a unified project.

That project is a philosophical one. By placing his work within a reasonably coherent scientific research paradigm that began with Descartes and continued in the work of a group of seventeenth- to mid-nineteenth-century philosophers and linguists who developed a rationalist and Romantic conception of language and the powers of the human mind, Chomsky provides a philosophical framework for thinking of him as engaged on a single intellectual project that integrates linguistics and politics. Chomsky calls these thinkers – among others, Descartes, Cordemoy, Arnauld, Cudworth, A. W. Schlegel, and Humboldt – the "Cartesian linguists." They are Cartesian because Chomsky thinks that Descartes identified the basic issues and data that needed to be dealt with, and in so doing initiating a revolution in the study of mind. They are linguists because they were as a rule naturalistically or scientifically inclined and sought to construct a theory of the universal features of language in a way that respects basic observational data and the norms of science as understood at their time. This is not to say that they all acknowledged Descartes' basic contribution, or that they recognized that they were working within a single research paradigm. But there was enough in common in their assumptions, their understanding of the nature of the problem and their task, and the views of mind and language they developed that one can usefully think of them as working within a coherent research paradigm, particularly when one contrasts their assumptions and their developed views of mind and language with those of a contrasting rival paradigm, the empiricist one. Crucially, none of them shied away from trying to link their views of morality and politics to their views of the nature of human beings, minds, and the physical world. There were differences in how they chose to do this, often correlating with the state of scientific investigation of humans at the time they were working. But none of them thought that moral and political issues could be divorced from scientific efforts to understand the human mind.

Chomsky aligns himself firmly with the rationalists and their view of mind and language. The biological and computational twist he introduces to the science of mind would probably have surprised (but perhaps pleased) some of the earlier rationalists. But it also advances their aims to a degree that they could not have anticipated.

Some aspects of Chomsky's rationalist intellectual project

Rationalism and the Enlightenment values that are characteristic of it might be thought outmoded, wrong, even silly. They can seem unscientific. They are certainly unfashionable. But the rationalist strategy for understanding mind, Chomsky argues, represents the only viable naturalistic, scientific approach available. Far from being 'unscientific', rationalist assumptions and strategies lead to sciences of the mind, whereas empiricist ones do not.

To guide the reader through what may be unfamiliar territory, I outline here five central aspects of Chomsky's rationalist views. All can often be found – in some form – in works of other Cartesian linguists. First, Chomsky is what philosophers call an *internalist*. With respect to his linguistic science, this is reflected in his view that the science of language is a science of a specific mental faculty that operates inside the head, not of any linguistic phenomena outside the head, such as linguistic behavior. The external phenomena of

4
Introduction*Introduction*

language observable in linguistic behavior – the varied and complicated ways that people use language to deal with their world – play a role in constructing a theory of what goes on in the head, of course; they provide one source of information and evidence. But they are not the subject matter of the linguistic theory. So when Chomsky constructs a computational theory of language, he is concerned with the computations (linguistic mental/neural processes) that relate one set of linguistic mental events to another, *not* with what is outside the head, or with any relationships between these mental events and things or situations outside the head. Indeed, since the theory deals with linguistic mental events alone and supposes that these occur in relative isolation from other mental events (at least until after they "interface" with other mental events), his linguistic theory is also *modular*: it supposes that the "language faculty" in which these events take place is relatively isolated from other mental faculties. Internalism, however, is primarily a matter of maintaining an inside the head/outside the head distinction; it does not require modularity. Chomsky's internalism about language applies also to what he has to say about the meanings of words and sentences. His account of meaning in natural languages is not a theory of how language is related by people to the world through reference or truth, but a theory of the intrinsic meanings of words and expressions themselves.

As political thinker, Chomsky's internalism appears in his view that a person's mind cannot be controlled, although his or her actions sometimes can. It also appears in his belief that any morally defensible view of social organization must encourage human freedom – that is, human self-development and self-expression.

The second aspect is *nativism*. A nativist in language assumes that human beings are born with a capacity for language that need only be allowed to develop. It is not learned: it is not impressed on the mind from outside the head by culture, community, parents, or nation. Chomsky assumes, that is, that natural languages are *innate*. For Chomsky, innateness is grounded in biology – our languages are products of our genes – and one can think of the language faculty in which linguistic processing takes place as a biological organ that takes some time to develop (as do vision and other cognitive capacities) but that develops more or less automatically, given minimal supporting input. This nativism has important repercussions for an understanding of the mind, because language plays such an important role in so much of what we take to be distinctive about humans. For instance, Chomsky sees the difference between common sense and scientific understanding as depending on the fact that common sense is itself largely unlearned: that is why it is massively shared across the human population. Specifically, common sense understanding depends heavily on the knowledge that is innately specified in language. Science, in contrast, owes much less to innate natural language. The different degrees of dependence on innate concepts of these two forms of understanding help explain why common sense is available without difficulty to everyone, whereas science takes work and special instruction. It also makes sense of why Chomsky thinks that political issues and arguments (and decisions) are well within the competence of everyone, while scientific issues and arguments are not.

The third aspect is *universalism*. In Chomsky's linguistics, this appears in what he calls Universal Grammar: if language is largely innate, it must, at one level, be the same across the human population. In his politics, universalism appears in the idea that there is a nature that all humans have and that this nature is morally and politically relevant: it bears on the actions of creatures with this nature and on their needs and goals. If, for example, there are some needs that humans have as a part of their fundamental natures, then these should be satisfied within any form of social organization that can count as ideal.

The fourth is *individualism*. In Chomsky's linguistics, this appears in the idea that every individual has his or her own individual language or languages (technically, "I-language," for an *i*ndividual, *i*nternal, and *i*ntensional language; all I-languages are particular "states" of Universal Grammar).[1] In his politics, it appears in his constant insistence on allowing free rein to individual self-expression. It is represented in his proposed ideal form of social organization, anarchosyndicalism – a form of political organization which affords a way to satisfy both the need for self-expression and that for community.

Fifth, Chomsky is a *constructivist*. This stems from his internalism and nativism and amounts to the idea that the things and the "world" of common sense understanding and, in a different way, of science are in large measure products of our minds. As Chomsky says in an interview that appears in *Language and Politics*, "You could say that the structure of our experience and our understanding of experience is a reflection of the nature of our minds, and that we can't get to what the world really is. All we can do is develop constructs, and if they happen to work, more or less, and to provide what we might regard as insight and understanding, then we're satisfied with them" (*LP* 468). Common sense understanding is anthropocentric and serves our interests. The sciences try to be objective, but they and, in a different way, the phenomena they deal with are human constructs or artifacts, made by us in order to understand. In this respect, their worlds are still products of our minds.

I comment in the text primarily on Chomsky's internalism, nativism, and constructivism. The universalism and individualism will, I think, be obvious enough.

The basic observations

Interacting in various ways with these five aspects of Chomsky's biological rationalism are two sets of basic observations that play a central role in the rationalist tradition's view of the mind. Chomsky's science of language honors them scrupulously; many other 'sciences' and 'theories' of language do not. One set, the so-called poverty of stimulus observations, amounts in the case of language to the fact that language is acquired quickly and in a regular way by all children at approximately the same age, without training and on the basis of a very limited and impoverished set of data. These observations indicate that language and other mental faculties (to which similar poverty of stimulus observations apply) are unlearned and universal (nativism, universalism). As a consequence, they constitute an essential part of the definition of explanatory adequacy for a science of language. Basically, no theory of language can be adequate unless it shows how to explain these poverty of stimulus facts – which turns out to eliminate, as we shall see, any theory of language that tries to deal with linguistic behavior.

The second set of observations Chomsky labels "the creative aspect of language use" facts. The facts are (1) that the sentences used by people to deal with their world or for other purposes are stimulus-free (no specific stimulus, or any stimulus at all, is required for the utterance of a specific sentence); (2) that the set of sentences that can be produced is unbounded (there is no way to limit the set of sentences, whether the set is made relative to a specific circumstance or not); and (3) that sentences actually produced are typically recognizably coherent and appropriate to the circumstances of speech, whatever they might be. This set of facts supports internalism, individualism, and – of course – the idea that people are free in their actions (at least their linguistic actions), a form of free will. So it lends support to the idea that human moral choices are real, not merely epiphenomena of some form of deterministic processes.

1

Common Sense and Science

Chomsky's contributions: a quick overview

During his career Noam Chomsky has contributed immensely to the ways in which human beings understand their languages, their minds, their actions, and even themselves as persons. His writings and speeches have had an impact on linguistics, cognitive science, philosophy, intellectual history, the social sciences, and politics. A considerable part of Chomsky's work has focused on two different intellectual projects. The results of one of these projects are found in his books, articles, and speeches on formal (mathematical) linguistics. His goal in these is obviously to produce a good science of natural languages. A survey of these works shows that this project has been progressing towards an answer to the question of how a child is able to quickly acquire one or several of any of the thousands of natural languages. (His science of language and the progress it has made are outlined rather informally in chapters 4 and 6; chapter 5 has some formalism.) The results of the second project are found in a large and definitely nonformal corpus of incisive and highly topical social and political commentary that – while it displays underlying themes that do not change – is constantly updated to speak to changing government policies and world problems. Here Chomsky's aim seems to be to provide everyone who is willing to listen with massive amounts of information that are relevant to any moral person's political and social goals and choices – in effect, relevant to the ways people choose to live their lives. (Some major themes of this political work and Chomsky's political project as a whole are discussed in chapters 7 and 8.) The work on each project individually is extraordinary; the full corpus of works in both areas may be unprecedented. But his accomplishments in these two areas pose a puzzle. Chomsky's science of language seems irrelevant, at least at first glance, to his political commentary and to the Enlightenment political and social ideals he endorses, and vice versa. Faced with works that seem to represent two different projects, it can be difficult to see how and why they would be so vigorously pursued by a single individual. It is not just that the amount of work that Chomsky has devoted to each project would represent a very good life's effort for most individuals, but that the projects seem so different from one another that it is difficult to understand how they might be related.

Yet there is a way to understand how these projects complement one another and are perhaps even more closely connected than that. It lies in Chomsky's naturalistic (biological) rationalist philosophical position and the specific claims it contains. Central to that position is a view of the nature of the human mind – its structure and capacities – and of a person's ability to freely choose a course of action. If Chomsky's science of language is seen as contributing to a developing, biologically based science of mind, there is a connection between his linguistics and politics. If that developing science of mind provides the core of an account of what is distinctive about human nature, then it can be seen as a contribution to a science of human nature.[1] If it can, the science of language, along with other sciences of the mind, might then provide insight – and perhaps more than just insight – into the forms of social organization that creatures with minds like ours and with free choice would find satisfying. And, as it turns out, the form of social organization that Chomsky endorses – one which embodies humanistic Enlightenment ideals such as the right to the free development of one's talents and abilities in one's labor – constitutes a reasonable and at least partially justifiable answer to the question of what creatures with our minds and natures would find satisfying. At least, that is what I argue in this book. My aim is to outline Chomsky's work on language and politics and show that his linguistic and political works can be seen as aspects of a single, more fundamental philosophical (and perhaps eventually, scientific) project in which the science of language and other mental sciences tell us about what the mind is, so that we can then envision an ideal form of social organization based on rational and reasonable grounds. Chomsky's science of language plays a central role in this overall project. If it is on the right track, and if something like the connection sketched here is plausible, his Enlightenment humanistic ideals may have some justification in a science of what it is to be human.

Chomsky himself is not confident that there is a firm connection between his linguistic and political work, or that such a connection provides a foundation for what he takes to be the ideal form of social organization. Nor does he express anything like certainty in the correctness of his linguistic work. But he does think – on the basis of reasonable evidence – that his linguistic work is on the right track. And he thinks that there are at least "tenuous," "suggestive," and "abstract" connections between the linguistics and the politics. He said in 1977, "I wish it were possible, as it obviously is not, to deduce from our understanding of human nature that the next stage in social evolution ought to be such and such. That we can't do; at most we can draw very loose, tenuous connections that may be more or less suggestive to people" (*LP* 245). I assume that Chomsky is not here ruling out the possibility of a firm connection, perhaps even a 'deduction', between human nature and what ought to be; he is pointing out that, as things stand, it is obvious no one can manage anything more than a loose connection. I also assume, as the quote suggests, that he would *like* to see a firm, or at least firmer, connection. Like some other Enlightenment intellectuals, he would like some justification for being at least guardedly opti-mistic about humans developing (using their unaided reason and without appeal to authority) a view of what it is best for people to do. That calls for more than a tenuous and merely suggestive connection. Chapter 8 discusses the prospects of establishing some-thing stronger.

Chomsky's political and linguistic intellectual projects have been carried out in remarkably coherent and consistent ways. His polit-ical views (he admits to "anarchosyndicalism" and "libertarian socialism" but in general dislikes labels) and the ways in which he presents and defends them seem to have changed little, if at all, since he wrote his first article for his school newspaper at the age of ten. (It was a lament on the fall of Barcelona in the Spanish Revolution.[2]) His political works are easily understood, virtually empty of political 'theory', and far from being tracts. They typically consist of carefully researched and well-organized compilations of facts interlaced with irony. They invite listeners and readers to draw their own conclusions.

To appreciate the coherence and consistency of Chomsky's linguistic works, it is important to recognize that they represent various stages of a *developing* science of the natural phenomenon of human language. No one should expect Chomsky or anyone else to present a fully adequate science in their first attempt. In fact, one of the hallmarks of successful science is that it progresses by constructing hypotheses concerning a specific domain, refining them, and, often, rejecting them. So it is hardly surprising that Chomsky has changed his linguistic theories, sometimes in major ways. His scientific project's coherence and consistency lie not in a specific set of hypotheses or in an unchanging theory, but in persisting and apparently valid conceptions of what a science of language must speak to and the resources on which it can rely. These conceptions play a crucial role in determining the scope and limits of a science of language, and they determine whether a science of language is successful or not. They help determine what counts as progress in linguistic science.

Chomsky's understanding of the goals and resources of linguistic science is based on his view that linguistics must speak to certain basic observational facts concerning language and its use. Labeled the "poverty of the stimulus" and "creative aspect of language use," accommodating these observational facts leads Chomsky – among other things – to assume that much of human language is innately fixed, to hold that a basic goal of linguistics is to explain how any child can acquire any natural language readily on the basis of a rather thin set of data, to provide generative theories that deal with infinite sets of sentences, to *avoid* dealing with the ways in which people use language, and to locate language in a relatively modular part of the human mind. These accommodations of the poverty and creativity facts, as well as his distinctive mathematical (formal) approach to the science of language and his effort to meet the usual ideals of science (simplicity, elegance, and so forth), have characterized Chomsky's linguistics from the beginning.

Significantly, these observations and their nativist, internalist, and constructivist implications for the sciences of language and mind also have a central place in the works of the rationalist tradition of philosopher-linguists whom Chomsky calls the "Cartesian linguists." Chomsky quotes the work of Cartesian linguists much more often – and far more approvingly – than the work of contemporary philosophers. He quite clearly thinks that the rationalists were on the right track while most contemporary philosophers are not. To judge by the works of Descartes, Cudworth, and Humboldt, to name a few, this rationalist framework offers a way to relate language and mind to the goals and actions of human beings, promising a way to link what Chomsky has to say about language with his political views. And Chomsky not only endorses the rationalist framework and its effort to accommodate the poverty and creativity facts but clearly conceives of his own work as contributing to, filling out, and advancing that framework. Chomsky has always pointed out that there should not be a divide between science and philosophy. If his linguistic work not only makes the rationalist framework more plausible but adds to its promise of linking a science of language to action, his linguistics makes progress towards *answering* crucial questions such as "What is human nature?" and "What, given human nature, are the fundamental human needs?" These are questions that anyone hoping to link a science of mind to action should be able to answer.

Chomsky discovered the Cartesian linguists and their rationalist framework early in his academic career. There is an obscure mention of them in his earliest major work, *The Logical Structure of Linguistic Theory*,[3] a chapter of which constituted his PhD thesis, but that reference was apparently due to reading secondary sources. Chomsky started reading the relevant works only at the end of the 1950s, continuing into the early 1960s and later.[4] But while it was not until then that he began to explicitly use a Cartesian rationalist framework, his already formed formal linguistic and political views fit together so well in the framework that one could argue that his apparently separate interests in formal linguistics and politics must have been coherently (but not explicitly and systematically) related to each other from the beginning. It does not matter much if his political views guided the linguistic ones, if there was a single but not articulated set of principles from which both developed, or even if things just fell into place serendipitously. The important point is that at an early stage of Chomsky's career both his linguistics and politics began to be related through a rationalist philosophical framework. Within a decade of completing *The Logical Structure of Linguistic Theory* and *Syntactic Structures*, Chomsky had written *Current Issues of Linguistic Theory* (1963), *Aspects of the Theory of Syntax* (1965), and *Cartesian Linguistics* (1966), all of which – particularly the last – explore the rationalist framework. By the mid-sixties, then, Chomsky had a good start on a science of language, a clear and detailed grasp of political issues (he had just begun his career of political activism), and was working within a framework which will allow us to see how his science of language could be related to his politics. The years since have brought extraordinary progress in his science of natural language, to the point that it can now be argued that it can handle the poverty and creativity facts (particularly the former). They have also brought hundreds of thousands of pages of updated and always topical political commentary, as well as Chomsky's development of, and contributions to, the rationalist framework. Unlike one of Chomsky's political heroes, Bertrand Russell, Chomsky has never undertaken a radical change of course in his science, his politics, or his philosophical framework. And, again unlike Russell, his philosophical framework at least appears to offer a tie between his science and his politics.

In describing Chomsky's linguistics and political projects and what I see as the unified intellectual project that incorporates both, I will not detail all the terminology he has used in his linguistics and all the changes his linguistic theories have undergone. Nor will I discuss all of the many aspects of his political views. Instead, in my discussion of Chomsky's linguistic work I emphasize how it has progressed in being able to speak to the poverty of stimulus observations – to solving "Plato's problem," as Chomsky calls it – and to becoming a formally simple science like physics. In discussing his political work, I emphasize his views of US domestic and foreign policy, his own contrasting anarchosyndicalist views, and his discussion of intellectuals and their responsibilities. I also propose some terminological clarifications and suggest that the terms "mental faculty" and "mental capacity" – which he sometimes uses interchangeably – might better help provide a picture of the mind as conceived by a biological rationalist if they were given distinct referents. And in order to establish a firmer connection between a biologically based science of human nature and what people ought to do, I make more of Chomsky's early suggestion concerning a new form of social science than he has himself. The result is, I hope, a fair representation of how Chomsky conceives his intellectual projects, accompanied by suggestions and re-emphases that are, I think, consistent with his views. The suggestions and different emphases may – even if misguided – help clarify and aid discussion of the crucial issues they address: the nature of mind and how a science of language that contributes to a science of human nature could bear on what we ought to do.

How Chomsky's work has been received

Chomsky's work in linguistics, politics, and philosophy has been received very differently. Most of his colleagues in linguistics and related areas now acknowledge that his contributions to the science of linguistics and mind have been spectacular. In the 1950s a few talks before linguists, mathematicians, and information theoreticians, plus the publication of *Syntactic Structures* (and the underground circulation of his massive *Logical Structure of Linguistic Theory*), set the study of language on a new mathematically and formally inclined course, effectively making what was a taxonomy of human linguistic behavior into a science of the internal processes of the human mind/brain. In setting linguistics on this course Chomsky virtually invented the field of mathematical linguistics, while at the same time providing good motivations for revitalizing a rationalist view of the study of language as the study of mind, a view that had been almost abandoned by the mid-nineteenth century. Since the 1950s he has continued to develop a formal (computational) theory of natural languages. That theory has undergone several changes, some of them major, but there is a clear sense in which the changes have been improvements representing progress towards goals that were set very early in his work. His current form of Universal Grammar may be sufficiently close to fulfilling the goals of a theory of language and mind that it represents one of the few real successes among many efforts to construct a science of at least a part of the human mind. Moreover, his early contribution to a science of language is now acknowledged to have been a vitally important part of what is sometimes called the cognitive revolution in various sciences of, and approaches to, the mind, including psychology, linguistics, philosophy, and forms of computational theory. Chomsky himself is less than enthusiastic about the idea that his work began a cognitive revolution, in part because he suspects that the real cognitive revolution took place in the seventeenth century with Descartes' work and that the basic principles of that revolution have yet to be understood or appreciated by most of those who now call themselves cognitive scientists. If not revolutionary, at the very least his work helped reawaken interest in certain approaches to mind and gave the study of mind a mathematical, formal, and biological cast that it lacked for Descartes and his seventeenth-, eighteenth-, and early nineteenth-century co-rationalists. And the current popularity of computational and generative approaches to mind and mental capacities is surely due in some measure to Chomsky's work in formal linguistics.

If the importance of Chomsky's formal linguistic work is acknowledged, although sometimes a bit grudgingly, by a group of scientists, his political commentaries get a good reception from a very different audience. His political works and speeches are typically *not* welcomed by those in positions of authority and power ('managers'), including the academic establishment in the social sciences, such as in political science.[5] But they get a surprisingly warm reception from much of their intended audience – workers, unionists, students, and so on. Given Chomsky's views about illegitimate authority, about academics as a "secular priesthood," about the very limited political spectrum allowed expression in the USA, and his arguments against the control of government and media by corporations, the negative reactions to his political commentary by those in positions of authority is hardly surprising. What is remarkable is the resonant chord he seems to have struck with others – remarkable not because he reaches people without using any of the trappings of a star or a media personality (and can hardly be considered a great stylist in his writing), but because he seems to have captured something of deep concern to most people.

Speaking as an academic philosopher, it is, I think, fair to say that Chomsky's contributions to philosophy are only rarely received with warmth by established philosophers. There is a small group of philosophers of language who adopt much of his linguistic work (but often only that), and there is a handful of individuals who are sympathetic to his political and social views, along with his attempt to develop a philosophical framework based on human nature that will link language and politics. But for the most part his contributions to philosophy are little recognized and, when they are, are rejected. Perhaps one reason for this is that Chomsky chooses to present his views by appealing to the Cartesian rationalist tradition. Although he makes sure to emphasize that he defends a Cartesian position that is unlike Descartes' own (for example, he has no use for substance dualism or for Descartes' conception of matter) and very much unlike official – stereotypical – Cartesianism (for example, Chomsky rejects "privileged access" to the mind), Descartes' views on mind and its difference from 'matter' have too long been a favorite target when contemporary philosophers want to present what they think of as a patently wrong and perhaps even silly approach to the mind. Another more important reason is that many contemporary philosophers are heavily committed to a picture of the mind that is very different from the one that both Chomsky and Descartes endorse, relying instead on various versions of the idea that the human mind is plastic and shaped by world or community. Few would call themselves behaviorists – an obvious example of a view that insists the mind is plastic – but there are plenty of other variants on the theme in both analytic and continental philosophical communities, including the idea that our minds and concepts are shaped by our environments and the idea that language's rules are normative and that these norms are maintained by a linguistic community. Calling these and related plastic-mind views "empiricist" (with good historical justification), Chomsky, as a rationalist, has tirelessly attacked the assumptions on which the empiricist/plastic mind view is based, and he has argued against many philosophers of repute who adopt behaviorism or various other forms of "environmentalism," such as Quine, Dummett, and Putnam.[6] Because doctrines of the plastic mind are very popular, and acceptance of the innate ideas that are crucial to naturalistic (biological) rationalism anathema, he has won few friends in the academic philosophical community.

One lesson of all this is that even though it may be tempting – given the degree of acceptance that Chomsky's work enjoys among many linguists – to take acceptance by those in the field as the measure of the correctness of the views advanced, the reactions of academics in the social sciences and philosophy suggest that it is wiser to look for a better measure of whether Chomsky's political and philosophical work and – for a more objective appraisal – his linguistic work, is plausible or correct. Fortunately, that measure is not hard to find. As suggested above, it consists in whether the view advanced makes sense of the 'poverty of the stimulus' and the 'creative aspect of language use' facts. The poverty facts have to do with how only a relatively short amount of time and some impoverished information are needed to develop certain very complicated and rich cognitive capacities, such as the use of language, aspects of mathematics, and vision. The creativity facts were clearly stated by Descartes; they have to do with the fact that what we say in using language – the words we produce in speech and thought – need have little to do with our environment, and when we do say something that deals with the environment, we can say any number of things and still have them be appropriate. The creativity facts seem to support the idea that if one hopes as a scientist to say something sensible about the human mind and its capacities, one had better stick to the internal operations of the mind. Relations between internal states and processes and things in the outside world seem to be subject to the operations of human freedom. So the creativity facts seem to support what in the introduction I called "internalism" for a science of mind and free will to boot. The poverty facts seem to demand that the human mind bring to experience a massive stock of innate concepts that are highly specific to our cognitive capacities and so support what I called "nativism" in the introduction. And the creativity and poverty facts taken together strongly suggest that one's view of the mind and its relation to the world be constructivist: we have to use internally and natively provided concepts to make sense of our world, and it is therefore better to see experience of the world and the world as configured by internal concepts, rather than the world as configuring experience and concepts. Chomsky's developed biological rationalist position on language and mind is specifically designed to make sense of the poverty and creativity observations and, since at least the scientific part of his developed rationalist position seems, by respecting these facts, to be making progress, the science that respects them lends support to the rationalist framework that takes them to be of fundamental importance. A lot is at stake here; it's not just a matter of "I like Quine" (or Foucault, Putnam, Habermas, Hegel, etc.) rather than "I like Chomsky" (or Descartes, Cudworth, etc.). Chomsky remarks, "there's historically a quite interesting connection between approaches to human nature which have stressed its alleged malleability, and certain social attitudes as to what would be a proper organization of society. . . . [I]f the mind is extremely plastic, if we take an extreme empiricist view, if we say there is nothing to human nature apart from the sum of historically given conditions and that, at each point in time, human nature is simply the residue of whatever contingent cultural patterns exist; . . . then, if that is the case, there really are no moral barriers whatsoever so far as I can see, no moral barriers, to manipulation and domination and control. . . . My own view is . . . that one of the reasons why these empty organism [plastic-mind] theories have such appeal in our intellectual tradition is that they do in a sense eliminate the moral barriers to coercion and control and domination" (*LP* 244).

Common sense, science, and mind

If we hope to understand how to relate the science of language to ideals for human action, we had better start with a good diagnosis of the difference between these domains and what this says about the human mind. One key to the difference is found in the apparently trivial differences in Chomsky's audiences and styles when he does linguistics as opposed to offering political commentary. The audience for Chomsky's political commentary is, in principle, everyone, including the linguist and the physicist. Chomsky's political discussions require no expertise on the part of the audience; they rely on a shared (common sense) understanding of the issues and of how to discuss them. Everyone knows what kinds of evidence to appeal to – what is relevant and what irrelevant. They know how to reason in this domain where human interests are crucial. And to make sure that his points are understood by everyone, Chomsky uses very basic argument techniques. For instance, to show that mainstream media in the United States, particularly the 'elite' newspapers (and especially the *New York Times*), present coverage in a way that supports the interests of power in government and corporations, he compares newspaper coverage of the Khmer Rouge atrocities in Cambodia in the late 1970s with coverage of the Indonesian East Timor invasion and atrocities which took place at approximately the same time (*NI* 155f, *MC*, *PEHR*). The case is discussed in chapter 7; for the moment, it is enough to note that Chomsky's argument consisted of nothing more than well-documented and fair comparisons of how the two incidents were covered. The bias is clear to anyone who comes to the evidence without prejudice.

By contrast, the audience for his formal linguistic work is a group of individuals who have the background and training in formal symbol systems and techniques to understand the concepts and how to use them – a form of expertise. They know, for example, what a phrase structure grammar is, how a particular theoretical approach to language deals with a phrase structure component, and what is at stake in dealing with phrase structure in a different way.

This is not to say that political discussions and arguments are easy. Since they lead to decisions that balance competing interests, they can be very difficult – sometimes painfully so – and can require massive amounts of information that, while readily understood, can be hard to gather. Nor is it to say that the linguist's discussions are always abstract and theoretical. One source of evidence that a linguist might appeal to when trying to defend one theory against the claims of another is evidence that anyone can recognize (even if they do not appreciate its theoretical significance), such as the difference between "John is easy to please," "John is eager to please," "It is easy to please John," and "It is eager to please John," and the difference between the English-sounding /tik/ and /bik/ and the obviously foreign /pfik/. Any speaker of English can appreciate these differences, as speakers of other languages appreciate similar differences in their languages. But, on balance, politics lies within the understanding of anyone, while mathematical linguistics does not. A difference in audience correlates with a difference in the kinds of understanding that are required and applied when discussing politics as opposed to doing linguistics.

The same point and an important related one emerge when Chomsky's style in politics is compared to his style in science. In his political work he makes extensive use of the rhetorical device of irony; it rarely appears in his linguistic arguments. Irony requires that a person have the cognitive machinery needed to recognize that what is said is not the correct story. Irony presupposes, then, not just that a person has the concepts involved but that he or she can apply them, comprehending enough of what is going on to recognize that what is being said is false, misleading, or perhaps evasive. For example, when Chomsky speaks of the driving force behind the USA's often-repeated claims to defend freedom in developing economies, he sometimes speaks of what is defended as the "fifth freedom." Given the context of the discussion, it is clear to anyone who is not morally inert that in defending the fifth freedom, the USA does not defend the opportunities of the residents of the country to develop themselves and to pursue their interests, but instead contrives to maintain unconstrained access by corporations to that developing economy and its labor and resources. (He does the same with "free" in "free trade" and "free world.")

His style in his mathematical linguistic works is preponderantly formal and abstract. Only occasionally does one find an insider's joke or a tongue-in-cheek suggestion – irony of a sort, perhaps, but relatively rare and requiring considerable sophistication on the part of an audience to appreciate. The rarity is easily explained: it is inadvisable to employ irony in theoretical discussions, for too many people will lack sufficient background knowledge to see the humor, so will misunderstand.[7] This underscores the earlier point about difference in audience correlating with difference in understanding. A related point also emerges: that Chomsky can make extensive use of irony even in complex and charged political discussions because he can presuppose that everyone has the concepts and is able to deal with the issues without explicit instruction. The background knowledge needed for this feat, which everyone manages routinely, is massive. It is also sufficiently flexible that it can apply to a very broad range of cases. Yet it seems to be available to virtually anyone *without schooling or preparation*. Nothing like this can be supposed for a science.

Chomsky thinks that these differences in understanding and what is involved in them are sufficient to place science and politics in different intellectual universes (1995: 32).[8] The basis for these two different forms of understanding is found in fundamentally different mental capacities that yield the different cognitive domains of science and common sense. That is, Chomsky explains the difference in intellectual universes in terms of his biological account of the mind and of the cognitive capacities it affords humans. This point is central to his thinking. To see how and why he sees a difference and explains it this way, let us look for differences in the *concepts* found in the domain of science and – the basis of political argument – the domain of common sense. It helps to map these differences; I suggest the following

	Common sense concepts	Scientific concepts
1	Intrinsically rich	Austere
2	Anthropocentric	Objective
3	(Apparently) domain-general	Domain-specific[9]
4	A priori (innately specified)	Artifacts (created)

The major differences between politics and science – the extensive use of irony in discussions in one and not the other, for example – can be traced to differences in the natures of, one's use of, and the sources of the concepts of common sense as opposed to those of science. These differences are in turn explained by Chomsky by appeal to the biology of the human mind.

There is little doubt that many of the concepts that figure in common sense understanding – in the way in which we ordinarily understand ourselves, our affairs, and our world – are drawn from those provided by natural languages. To appreciate the point, think of natural language "words" as somehow *containing* concepts. (Chapter 6 shows why this is plausible if natural language words are defined in Chomsky's technical way – as lexical items containing semantic and formal features.) If words contain concepts, varieties of concept correlate with varieties of word (nominal, adjectival, verbal, and prepositional), of phrase, and of sentence. A glance at a list of such concepts shows that they often appear in our everyday thoughts, judgments, attempts to persuade, speculations about what someone is going to do, etc. Using the convention of indicating reference to its concept by underscoring the orthographic representation of a word,[10] virtually all of the thousands of nominal (box, trace, tree, widget), verbal (wash, rinse, persuade, intend, choose), prepositional (to, for, under), and adjectival (good, lousy) concepts commonly occur, as do any number of phrasal (under the chestnut tree) and sentential (He's looking for the widget) concepts. No doubt common sense relies on other concepts too, such as those provided by other cognitive capacities such as vision (colours and shapes) and taste (salty, bitter). But those provided by natural languages are surely crucial to the complex of ways of understanding ourselves and our world that we take so much for granted.

Scientific concepts do not figure in common sense understanding. Adopting the underscoring convention again and assuming for purposes of argument that scientific symbols "contain" concepts too, scientific concepts include 'noun' (kaon, H_2O, lepton, phonological feature), 'verb' (bond, reduce, Spell-Out), and magnitude (n Hertz, m electron volts) ones, plus some 'sentence' ($E = mc^2$) ones.[11] It would be difficult to argue that these terms ever figure in ordinary speech. More important, they are understood by very few people. A three-year-old might be encouraged by misguided parents or older siblings to utter sounds like "kaon" or "meson," but the concept would not be understood; in all likelihood, they would not be understood by parent or sibling either. So these individuals do not have the concept. Even more important, those that *do* have the concept rarely, if ever, use it to understand themselves and their world. There may be some crossover or hard-to-place concepts too, but fewer than might be thought, I suspect. Internet does not require familiarity with a theory and scientific training to comprehend; nor do many technological concepts (X-ray tube, alloy, transistor, refrigerator), at least so long as no one is asked to provide the principles of electromagnetic radiation on which X-ray tubes work. These are common sense concepts.

Let us start with a contrast in source. The concepts of the sciences are quite clearly made by us, or are artifacts. This is not completely obvious; arguably, for example, primitive mathematical concepts and whatever it is that generates the natural numbers are innately specified. But the concepts of elementary particle physics, such as kaon, quark, and electron, are not. The sciences are hard-won bodies of knowledge that took centuries and the work of thousands to develop, and the concepts that embody this knowledge are the products of this effort on the part of human beings. Moreover, it is difficult for children to acquire this knowledge: no child comes into the world with built-in kaon-knowledge. While talent and aptitude for learning science may differ, it takes time, effort, and preparation for anyone to put themselves in a position in which they can honestly say that they know what "kaon" means and can routinely apply the concept <u>kaon</u>. By contrast, the concepts that natural language lexical items provide come virtually for free. The thousands of concepts embodied in nouns, verbs, prepositions, and adjectives come automatically: children acquire them without instruction, often at an astounding rate. The only plausible assumption is that these concepts are (biologically) innately specified, requiring only apt occasions to come into use.[12] If they were not, they could not come to be parts of active vocabularies so early and so readily.

There is also a difference in use or application. The concepts of natural languages seem to be domain-general, while those of the sciences are clearly domain-specific. In the sciences, one deals with a particular set of carefully circumscribed phenomena: elementary particle physics deals with just its domain, not with the supply of wheat in Russia this winter or Kate's revelations. To attempt to make the concepts and laws of elementary particle physics responsible for dealing with matters that are irrelevant to them and their domain would produce nonsense. By contrast, the concept <u>house</u> seems to have a virtually unlimited range of application. We apply it to toys and movie images, imagine trolls living in houses, feel nothing amiss when we speak of an ant house, wonder whether to have a house built, distinguish between commodious houses and inconvenient ones, move houses and think about doing so, and so on. Unlike the concepts of elementary particle physics, there is no predetermined set of circumstances to which a natural language concept is taken to apply, or restrictions on the uses to which such concepts can be put. Moreover, if one takes the thousands of concepts provided by natural languages and then takes into account the fact that they can be combined in various ways to provide a potential infinity of sentential concepts, natural language seems to be able to 'anticipate' virtually every circumstance one can imagine. Natural language concepts are not really completely domain-general, of course, for it is difficult to imagine anything but whimsical applications of them to the domain of elementary particle physics (and similarly for the domains of the other sciences). But they appear to be so, no doubt because *our* world contains houses, tyrants, puppies, and wombats and pays no heed to kaons and event horizons.

There are also differences in the nature of the concepts in common sense and science. The objectivity of scientific concepts seems to be the product of hard intellectual labor. It took centuries of work to eliminate anthropocentric and teleological elements from the concepts of science. This effort indicates that objectivity is a goal sought by humans, but it does not make the concepts so produced anthropocentric. The concepts of natural languages, by contrast, while not manufactured by us, are virtually designed for use by humans. Many, perhaps all, nouns have a kind of Aristotelian explanatory structure built into them that indicates clearly that the things that these nouns can be used to refer to are seen by us in the light of human needs and interests. Water (stuff described by the concept <u>water</u>) is not the scientist's H_2O but stuff that slakes thirst, becomes tea when operated on in a particular way, can be frozen into an ice cube, falls from the sky as rain, and looks blue under blue skies. The verbal concept <u>give</u>, when used to describe a procedure, relates an agent person who gives something to another person, in the process changing the ownership of the thing. No object of science gives a gift in this sense to another thing. In effect, the concepts of natural languages divide up the world and the things in it in ways that suit our interests; they are anthropocentric.

Finally, the concepts of natural languages are intrinsically rich and can be combined by the generative processes that natural languages include to yield even richer concepts. Richness is not a matter of ambiguity; ambiguity is found where a single sound has different concepts associated with it, such as "bank." Richness is a matter of the structure and textured 'grain' of individual concepts. Nouns have a built-in structure that invites questions about where the things a noun might be used to describe come from (their origin), what they're for (their function), and what they're made of (their composition). A house, for example – as everyone who speaks a natural language knows – is the sort of thing that we conceive of as built of suitable materials by humans to serve as a place to live. Water comes from wells and taps, slakes thirst, is used for cooking, and is water all the way through even if it has various impurities. Chomsky nicely illustrates this when he points out that if a town filters its water through tea bags, what comes from the taps in this town is water, even if it has exactly the same composition as water into which a tea bag has been inserted (which is tea) (1995: 42); in effect, dropping a tea bag into water with the intention of making tea is crucial to making that water into tea. (Similar points are discussed in chapters 3 and 6.) Note that – given the fact that these concepts are innately specified – the concept <u>house</u> and other nominals in natural languages do not have their structures given to them by the uses to which they are put (the questions raised about houses, for example). Their structure and the specific features that distinguish one concept from thousands of others are built into the concepts themselves. (Note too that this structure is *not* something that children (or adults) learn or are trained to recognize. It *must* be built in, for even the small child at play displays knowledge of the explanatory structure of a great many nouns.) The point is made in a different and perhaps more obvious way by verbs. A causative verb like "persuade," for example, has a built-in *argument structure* that demands that someone do the persuading and someone be persuaded (to do something). It also requires that if it is true that a person persuades another, the person who is persuaded has at least the intention to do what the other has caused him or her to have the intention to do. In general, by having a particular lexical item or word in your vocabulary, you have in its concept a built-in implicit, rich store of knowledge. This knowledge is in part like knowledge of other concepts (all verbs have *some* argument structure, and classes of verbs have very similar specific structures) and in part unique to the concept itself (wash and rinse have the same argument structure, but are very different concepts). The thousands of natural language concepts one finds in nouns, verbs, prepositions, and adjectives are each individually structured and richly specified in ways that, while they may only be revealed in the uses to which they are put, are intrinsically richly specified in ways that suit human interests. Moreover, they are combinable in various ways in accord with general principles that are themselves innately specified to – potentially – yield an infinity of sentences. So they offer a boundless array of woven concepts, much richer still than the already rich lexical stocks that go into them. Chomsky speaks of these rich and interest-laden concepts as *perspectives* that people can use to characterize their world and other worlds, or use in any number of other ways.

Scientific concepts, in contrast, are relatively austere, extrinsically specified by appeal to their roles in the theories of which they are a part, and limited in their combinatorial properties by the theory. The 'noun' concepts kaon and muon for example, are deliberately thin: the theory provides each a unique place in the panoply of basic particle concepts, and each is fully specified by its place in the panoply (meson or lepton), charge, and weight. In a way, the theory answers where kaons and muons come from (perhaps particle collisions) and what they 'do'; but this is not part of the intrinsic specification of the concept. The science as a whole answers questions like this, no doubt because physicists do elementary particle physics to find out these things. But because the theory as a whole can be used in this way does not make the concept <u>kaon</u> rich. As for verbs in the sciences, such as <u>bond</u> or <u>decay</u>, these are quite unlike those of natural languages, such as <u>give</u>, which often demand that agents (persons with intentions, etc.) carry out an action. They are thinner, their definitions come extrinsically by their places in a theory, and the theoretical 'sentences' in which they can appear are limited to those that the theory provides for.

This discussion of Chomsky's contrast between common sense and science should make it easy to see why Chomsky thinks his political and his linguistic work are in different intellectual universes. Politics turns out to be within the intellectual range of all people, because political discussions rely on the resources of common sense understanding, and common sense understanding depends heavily on the largely innate conceptual resources of natural languages. This suggests – as Chomsky intends – that everyone has the equipment needed to discuss political matters and political issues. They acquire it early. Even two-year-old Gerald, who understands a lot of English although he rarely says anything, has a good grasp of the principles of folk psychology on which political issues rely. He also has a good grasp of folk physics – which with folk psychology makes up an important part of common sense understanding. He knows what will happen when he pushes his dish of mashed peas off his tray: it will make a satisfying mess on the carpet and bring welcome, if unfriendly, attention from the babysitter. This surprisingly early understanding of agent causality, intention, affect, impact, and so on becomes more sophisticated in its application as Gerald gets older. But it is not long before he can present and defend political views, even when dealing with the intentions of those in authority and the rights of individuals. Chomsky, recall, managed it well at ten, and the research he did in his early years was good enough to provide the basis for a review of a book by a distinguished historian many years later.

Notice that we have a plausible explanation of why Chomsky can use irony in political discussions with everyone, whereas he can afford to use it with only a few individuals on the 'inside' in science. If political discussions lie within the competence of anyone with common sense understanding and common sense relies heavily on the conceptual resources of natural languages, which everyone has, then everyone has the competence, so everyone can recognize when a speaker or writer is ironic – particularly when it is made obvious as Chomsky takes pains to do.

   The contrast also makes it easy to see how an account of the mind could explain *why* there is a difference between common sense and science, an issue taken up in chapter 2. Briefly, Chomsky provides good evidence that there is a *language faculty* in everyone's mind that can generate the infinite set of perspectives mentioned above. (Chomsky's science of language is a science of this faculty.) Common sense understanding is shared and has the richness and subtlety it does precisely because it relies so heavily on this innate language faculty. The same cannot be said of science. (In fact, science seems to progress towards its goal of objectivity only when scientists abandon the concepts of common sense understanding and with considerable difficulty invent others.)

   We have enough now to clear up some possible confusions about what Chomsky has in mind by common sense and science. Common sense is sometimes understood in too localized or sectarian a way, as when someone in a particular culture at a particular time identifies common sense with what he or she and his or her community think is obvious. But common sense as Chomsky intends it really is common: it is a form of understanding that all normal humans have, without regard to their backgrounds, cultures, training, general intelligence, or wit. Furthermore, while for Chomsky common sense understanding is certainly relevant to human action and to the strategies that people work out to deal with friend and foe, it is not just a form of prudence or 'wise action'. You might advise a friend that it is "just common sense" to observe certain politeness conventions or to be cautious (watch your step, stay away from the hard stuff). But this is not what Chomsky has in mind either; this is the wisdom of parents, friends, and horoscopes. The concept of common sense understanding as Chomsky employs it appeals to principles that are culture-independent – that are held in common by all human beings. The set of these principles is rarely articulated or stated by anyone. Only some linguists, philosophers, and anthropologists try. And it is not learned or obtained through instruction and training. Instead, it is largely innately specified, and young children pick it up at a very young age indeed. It amounts to – as Chomsky puts it in "Language and Nature" (1995: 28) – "how people interpret [understand] object constancy, the nature and causes of motion, thought and action, and so on ("folk science," in one of the senses of the term)." It is the basic cognitive capacity we all have and rely upon to get along in our world. Chomsky sometimes speaks of "Cartesian common sense," pointing to Descartes' notion of *good sense*, which Descartes takes to be a gift from God to *all* people, a form of understanding that serves for human affairs and needs and is a good practical guide for life that no one learns but that comes automatically. Take away "gift from God" (or perhaps reinterpret it in biological terms),[13] and you have Chomsky's conception of common sense.

Of course, there are some – in fact, many of those who consider themselves enlightened intellectuals – who deny that there could be anything like common sense understanding that is shared across the human population. Every culture has its own beliefs, they say, or there are differences in "standpoints" or "frameworks" or "perspectives," so there cannot be uniformities. This response misses the point. No one is denying that there are cultural differences: to talk of culture at all is virtually to invite talk of difference. But the inference from cultural differences to no shared common sense knowledge depends upon – among other things – the assumption that culture is the sole source of belief and knowledge. The assumption might seem natural to those who want to think of human beings as products of their environments, and it is congenial to all sorts of relativists, including racists; but it is wrong. We will see later that Chomsky reverses matters: innately aided common sense understanding is a condition for cultural development and cultural difference.

Some of the remarks above might lead one to think that scientific understanding is concerned solely with the 'material world' or the 'physical world', while common sense understanding is concerned with human practical affairs. But that too is wrong. Think of both forms of understanding as dealing in different ways with both mental and physical aspects of reality. Common sense understanding includes *both* "folk physics" and "folk psychology." It includes, that is, the principles and beliefs we need to deal with Kate's snits (and the intentions and beliefs she has that lead her to have them, etc.) and those we need to deal with what plates of peas do when infants push them off their trays. Scientific understanding also deals with both the physical and the mental – it does not come with a restriction to the material world, whatever that is. Think of scientific understanding as resting on a set of tools (formal reasoning, including mathematics, certain notions of elegance and simplicity, and certain conceptions of what counts as a good explanation) that apply as readily to mental phenomena as to physical. Mental sciences can be just as scientific as nonmental ones. Choosing a label to remind us of his point, Chomsky suggests that anything described and explained scientifically counts as "naturalistic."

Since (Chomsky demonstrates) his linguistic program leads to successful science even in the domain of meaning, even meaning is 'naturalized'.[14]

We have seen enough to see why Chomsky speaks of common sense and science as two intellectual universes. He also speaks of different *pictures* of the world: "the search for theoretical [scientific] understanding pursues its own paths, leading to a completely different picture of the world, which neither vindicates nor eliminates our ordinary ways of talking and thinking [common sense]" (1995: 8).[15] This imagery raises all sorts of difficult philosophical questions, such as whether a claim that is true in the common sense picture – "Harriet scraped the door of her red Volvo", for example – would have to be true in the scientific picture, where there are no colors – or doors or Harriets, for that matter (the answer is no). But these questions would take us too far afield. It is enough to recognize that Chomsky's basic position is that our mental biology is the basis of a cognitive split that no philosophical it-cannot-be-that-way can deny. That said, linguistics offers an important scientific tool – perhaps the most important we have – for investigating the nature and scope of common sense understanding, for it tells us what natural language's contribution to common sense can be. That is why scientific investigation of the human mind can – in principle – bear on politics.

The science of mind and the perils of empiricism

One way to get a grip on Chomsky's view of the science of mind is to contrast it with what he thinks of as a class of failed efforts. His 1959 review of psychologist B. F. Skinner's *Verbal Behavior* helped make the curious phenomenon of psychological behaviorism disappear, or at least go underground. But Chomsky thinks that the assumptions about the mind and the science of the mind that allowed behaviorism to pretend of offer sciences of 'higher mental processes' such as thought and the use of language remain: behaviorism is a form of a more general disease, empiricism, which preceded behaviorism and thrives in other forms. In a preface to a 1967 reprint of his Skinner review, he says:

> I had intended this review not specifically as a criticism of Skinner's speculations regarding language, but rather as a more general critique of behaviorist (I would now prefer to say "empiricist") speculation as to the

nature of higher mental processes. My reason for discussing Skinner's book in such detail was that it was the most careful and thoroughgoing presentation of such speculation, an evaluation that I feel is still accurate. Therefore, if the conclusions I attempted to substantiate in the review are correct, as I believe they are, then Skinner's work can be regarded as, in effect, a *reductio ad absurdum* of behaviorist assumptions. My personal view is that it is a definite merit, not a defect, of Skinner's work that it can be used for this purpose, and it was for this reason that I tried to deal with it fairly exhaustively. I do not see how his proposals can be improved upon, aside from occasional details and oversights, within the framework of the general assumptions that he accepts. I do not, in other words, see any way in which his proposals can be substantially improved within the general framework of behaviorist or neobehaviorist, or, more generally, empiricist ideas that has dominated much of modern linguistics, psychology, and philosophy. The conclusion that I hoped to establish in the review, by discussing these speculations in their most explicit and detailed form, was that the general point of view is largely mythology, and that its widespread acceptance is not the result of empirical support, persuasive reasoning, or the absence of a plausible alternative. (1967: 142)

The harshness of Chomsky's view – that in behaviorism and empiricism one finds mere mythology and speculation about higher cognitive processes – is supported by the care with which he dissects Skinner's claims and, for the more general case of empiricist assumptions about higher cognitive processes, by his efforts from the early 1960s on to reveal the emptiness of empiricism's assumptions about how to construct a science of mind.[16] Keep in mind that empiricism's aim is a science of the higher cognitive processes. It is not always made clear what these are, but most of those who think that they are dealing with them include among them thought, reasoning, and perceptual judgment. They include, that is, all those cognitive things we 'do' when we think and reason about the world and ourselves, everything that plays a role both in common sense understanding and in science, and perhaps more besides. It is obvious that natural language must play a key role in common sense thought and judgment, at least. Constructing a science of language is thus central to constructing a science of higher cognitive processes. That is why Skinner thought language his greatest challenge and why he was so proud of what he thought he had accomplished.

Empiricism can be identified with three assumptions about what higher cognitive processes do, what the mind must be like to have them, and how the principles by which they operate arise. First, the higher cognitive processes are supposed to be devoted to dealing with the world. This may be put – these days it often is – as the idea that the mind is a device that constructs theories that strive to mirror the world, and higher cognitive processes are a person's efforts to apply this theory. A perceptual judgment, for example, takes a concept (<u>horse</u>) within a theory of the world and applies it to sensory input ("That is a horse"). This is a *representational* claim: the mind's processes mirror the structure and properties of the world by conforming to a theory that mirrors the world's structure and properties. Second, an assumption about the initial state of minds: they have little prior cognitive structure and "content," so that most of the structure to which higher cognitive processes conform and most of the content (concepts) that they contain must be 'derived' from experience or "learned." This is empiricism's (almost) *empty mind* claim. The third assumption is that what little prior structure there is in the mind provides for some kind of generalized learning procedure that builds structure, or "learns." The procedure is rarely specified fully; it might involve a device that associates mentally similar sensations (for example, orange-red sensations) to make up "general ideas" or concepts (of orange-red) and joins these to other general ideas to yield object-concepts (orange-red and hot might be <u>fire</u>) plus a hypothesis formation and testing device that forms hypotheses – from what and how is rarely clear – and tests them inductively. This is empiricism's *general learning procedures do it all* (or most of it) claim. A general learning procedure bootstraps concepts and the causal and inferential connections between concepts that make up a theory of the world out of similarities and associations: smell smoke, so fire. Except for what is needed to bootstrap and maybe a little bit more besides, however, mind is basically plastic. Its structure comes from 'outside'.

There are well-known problems with this picture of mind. For one, 'analytic' connections between ideas – such as that if it is true that Mary has persuaded Mort to go to university, Mort at least intends to go – seem to require mental structure that cannot be obtained from associations. A typical strategy to deal with the difference between these and "smoke, so fire" is to introduce a distinction, such as Hume's between connections of ideas (the analytic ones) and connections of matters of fact (smoke, so fire). Where do analytic ones come from? "By convention," the empiricist might say – usually with little but hand waving to explain what conventions are and how they come to be impressed on the mind. Another problem lies in what a generalized learning procedure is supposed

to consist in. Unless the empiricist says what the mechanism is –
what device enables people to gain the structure they need to judge
and use language – he or she has no science of mind. Empiricists
with pretensions to offering a science of mind must provide the
mechanism that bootstraps concepts and connections from something thought of as "experiential input."[17]

Chomsky argues against empiricism – the arguments are taken
up in the next two chapters – by showing that any account of
language or its use in "higher cognitive processes" that respects
empiricist assumptions fails to account for the poverty and creativity observations. The arguments are powerful and, supplemented
as they are by a science of language that respects the observations
and *also* provides good answers to the issues which give the empiricists difficulty, they back up the harshness of his criticism.

2

Mapping the Mind

Rationalist versus empiricist: who's the scientist of mind?

Chomsky's version of rationalism, like that of other rationalists from the seventeenth to the early nineteenth century with whom he aligns himself, differs strikingly from empiricism. Not only does he hold that there are innate ideas of a sort that no empiricist would accept, but he insists that these ideas are necessary to develop the kinds of experience that play such an important role in human efforts to understand self and world. Where the empiricist is convinced that our ideas of the things of the outside world as conceived in common sense must develop from our experience of these things, Chomsky holds that we could not experience them without innate ideas. Our innate ideas enable us to perceive and understand as readily as we do and as early as we do – to develop common sense knowledge of the world and, in a different way, science. This is one aspect of Chomsky's constructivism: the idea that having the minds we do, we can develop only certain cognitive capacities and conceive only of certain things. But, says Chomsky, this is to our advantage. To see why he thinks so, we must first get a grip on the mind as he construes it.

The label "empiricist" used to speak of an approach to the study of mind should not be confused with "empirical methods" and "empirical science." When Chomsky rejects empiricism, he is not rejecting the methods, and particularly not the aims, of empirical science. Like any other empirical scientist, he wants to produce a theory of a part of the natural world – specifically, of a part of the mind. Being an empirical scientist is not committing oneself to a picture of the mind; it amounts only to committing oneself to the aims of naturalistic science – to investigating the things and phenomena of the natural world. Perhaps to avoid confusion, Chomsky often speaks of his work as that of a naturalistic scientist, rather than an empirical scientist (1994). And when he constructs a theory of language, he does so as a naturalistic scientist. As we will see, the theory-construction techniques behind his science of language/ mind are not different from those in the naturalistic sciences; the difference is only the subject matter. And, just as other scientists seek to accommodate their sciences to others (chemistry to physics and vice versa represent successful efforts), he hopes a way will be found to accommodate linguistics to the sciences of the brain. But it is possible even now to see Chomsky's computational linguistics as a branch of biology: it describes biological processes that can assume only certain biologically determined configurations. So he is a *biological* rationalist, but one who has a different picture of the mind than Descartes and others in the Cartesian tradition – one which leads to some interesting differences in how he conceives of relationships between mind and world, as we will see.

The naturalistic/empirical scientist of the mind cannot, Chomsky holds, accept the empiricist picture because of the massive amount of evidence against it and in favor of the rationalist. If he is right, then, ironically, the empiricists are *not* empirical about what a mind is. The reason for this, mentioned before and explored in the next chapter, has to do with the empiricists' apparent refusal to take the creative aspect and the poverty of stimulus observations seriously, or even into account, in contrast to the rationalist tradition, which routinely did and does both. So, locating himself with a group of rationalist philosopher-scientists who lived centuries ago is not putting himself among a bunch of mystics, astrologers, and soothsayers but rather with rationalists who take seriously observations that any naturalistic theory deals with.

Non-problems: access and mind/body

Chomsky's associating himself with Descartes does not mean he agrees with Descartes in all particulars. One major difference lies in Chomsky's view of access to the mind. Official Descartes – Descartes' views as construed by (and typically attacked by) con-

temporary philosophers[1] – holds that individuals have direct access
to their minds. It is also sometimes taken as a corollary of official
Cartesianism that only the individual whose mind it is has access
to it. No one constructing a science of the mind can accept the corollary; nor does Chomsky. He holds that the linguist can and does
describe and explain the operations of that part (or those parts) of
the mind that carry out language processing. Access to the mind is
not easy. It is gained by a lot of hard work in constructing an internalist science of language that deals with how any of an infinite set
of linguistic expressions is generated from the set of *features* that a
person has in his or her lexicon (mental dictionary). The details
come later; for now the point is that the science is successful, so it
provides objective access.

The claim of direct access is also rejected, at least for the kinds of
mental states and processes that are of concern to the linguist:
perhaps people have direct access to their pains and to what they
happen to be thinking right now, but they do *not* have direct access
to the states or processes a linguistic theory (or any similar mental
theory) describes. A complicated set of issues accompanies this
claim; some crop up later, such as whether people have tacit or
implicit knowledge of innate ideas (cf. *RL* 217; *KL* 244f, 249). But for
the moment it is enough to see that the linguist can say that people
have all sorts of mental states and processes in their heads of which
they are unaware. For example, there is good scientific reason to
hold that you have the principle *An anaphor is bound in the minimal
domain of a subject* in your head, and even know it. It is hardly likely,
unless you are a linguist, that you would have been *aware* of that
before, and it is impossible for you to have direct access to it. The
only kinds of states/processes the linguist is interested in that you
might have even *some* access to are the "interface" states of sound
and meaning that constitute a linguistic expression. There is not
really direct access to these, but at least they interact with other
systems in the head and may lead to effects of which one is aware.

Language is not unique in these respects: computational sciences
of vision also reject claims of direct and privileged access. Theories
of vision derived from Marr's seminal *Vision* (1982) explain mathematically how the mind/brain constructs any of an infinite set of
color-position spaces (visual spaces) from a set of arrayed numbers
that represent the intensity of firings of the cones in the human
eye. One can think of the theory as describing the computations
involved in constructing a six-dimensional spatial array that
provides theoretical representations of colors and positions: hue,
brightness, and saturation for colors and altitude, azimuth, and

depth for positions in visual space. Marr's theory holds, among other things, that somewhere in the mind/brain's visual system there are devices that solve Gaussian equations yielding what we can think of as representations of lines. The theory allows the scientist to say that those devices and the processes they carry out are in your head, thus denying privileged access, and it is hardly likely that *anyone* has direct access to them under this description or any like it. But these devices and processes operate to produce the visual cognitive states that we use to navigate in our world.[2]

Chomsky also rejects Descartes' views of matter or body, his contact mechanics, and his mind/body substance dualism. It is hardly surprising that he rejects Descartes' contact mechanics; the idea that things must be in contact to act on each other has been a dead horse since Newton's law of gravitation, which introduced action at a distance.[3] Rejection of contact mechanics should be enough to lead to rejection of Descartes' view of matter or body: if his contact mechanics makes no sense, neither does his view of matter nor physical substance. It should also lead to rejection of Descartes' mind/body substance dualism. Once Descartes' conception of matter is dead, and forces such as gravitation, which Descartes would have considered mysterious, become a part of the physical world, it is no longer possible to exclude mental features and operations from the physical or to make a coherent distinction between mind and matter (*PP* 6; *LPK* 145). Given that there are no other plausible ways to distinguish mind and body, Chomsky suggests, the mind–body problem so much discussed by philosophers should no longer be taken seriously. "One can doubtless devise artificial distinctions that allow . . . problems to be formulated, but the exercise seems to make little sense, and indeed is never undertaken apart from the mental aspects of the world. Why it has been commonly felt that these must somehow be treated differently from others is an interesting question, but I am aware of no justification for the belief, nor even much recognition that it is problematic" (*PP* 6). There is no problem to solve unless it is discovered that something about the natural world rules out the operations that various sciences today show us take place in our minds.

Where and what is reason?

With this as background, let us look at how Chomsky, the biological rationalist, conceives the human mind. This will help us draw a picture of the mind and then, with picture in hand, we can return to the unfinished business of the first chapter – making sense of why we seem to have two such different cognitive capacities as science and common sense understanding.

It is useful, I think, to begin by asking what *reason* is in Chomsky's view of the mind. It might be thought that a scientific rationalist's sketch of the mind would have to include a mental mechanism called "Reason" assigned the task of doing reasoning. While some rationalists may have held this, Chomsky does not. Unlike the syntactic processing within a computational system in the head that is characteristic of language and the intensity-position computation that is characteristic of vision, reason is not a mechanism with fixed operations. Because it is not, it cannot be the subject matter of a science; thus it is not assigned a place in a scientific rationalist's sketch of the machinery of the mind. But it *can* be seen as a well-founded and distinctively human attribute which is provided to us by common sense understanding and the science-forming capacity.

Chomsky, like other rationalists, certainly thinks that we should rely on reason when we deal with the world, whether through science or common sense. This is not because he has faith in reason. In an interview with James Peck, he said, "I don't have a faith in that or anything else"; but, he continues, "it's all we have" (*CR* 48). Rational enquiry, discussion, and decision offer us the only ways we have to decide the truth of matters, whether in affairs where common sense understanding prevails or in our scientific efforts to come to understand the natures of things. But holding this is not committing oneself to anything like a faculty or part or region of the mind that is to be labeled 'reason'; it is only to say that we should rely not on faith, unjustified loyalties, and prejudices, but on evidence and argument.

The fact that one can be reasonable both in doing science and within common sense points to why we cannot expect there to be a science of reason. There does not seem to be an overarching common system of good reasoning of which science and common sense are different instances, or aspects. In fact, there need not be a single truth at which both kinds of enterprise aim. There is, of course, some overlap in general methodological rules, and the vigilant attention to strict standards of evidence that is more characteristic of scientific practice can often be applied to common sense affairs. The good social scientist's use of care and statistical techniques in gathering information is an example. But there is no reason to think that there is, or need be, a single set of rules and principles whose observance makes inquiry and decision reasonable. Furthermore, while there is a degree of uniformity in how good science proceeds – Chomsky points out, for example, that linguistics is much closer to physics and chemistry in its invention of concepts and the way it proceeds than it is to social sciences or other efforts to be systematic within the domain of common sense understanding – and while there may be an explanation of sorts for this in our capacity to construct sciences, the flexibility and context-dependence of common sense reasoning confounds all efforts to regiment reason into a single system in that domain. So, not only is there no uniformity between domains, but within at least one domain there are no grounds for hoping that we will be able to capture reason. Many philosophers do not like this, for it eliminates a single, uniform, stable logic or set of principles of correct reasoning that one can appeal to anywhere. But it is difficult to deny a distinct lack of success in efforts to regiment reason.

The nonuniformity and unmechanical nature of reason undoubtedly have something to do with the fact that reasoning is essentially a *normative* exercise carried out by *persons*. Persons reason and are assigned praise or blame for reasoning well or poorly. And the evaluation of reason is context-dependent and can (and often does) change over time: what counts as good reasoning in bird watching need not count as good reasoning in chess strategy, and what counts as good reasoning in bird watching changes once a few 'birds' are discovered to be fakes. Given this, reasoning is obviously not carried out by a dedicated part of people's minds, operating unconsciously and automatically.[4] Reasoning is basically judgment making (often involving inference), and to the extent that making judgments is, or essentially involves, language use, we should not expect that there will ever be a complete systematic account of it, for language use lies within the domain of human freedom. So, however plausible it is to say that the mind is where reasoning takes place, and however tempting it might be to think that therefore minds must include a reason-box, or faculty of reason, where this reasoning takes place, Chomsky holds that there is no evidence to think that the mind *thought of as an object of natural science* has a special part that 'does reasoning' or 'is reason'.

It is no accident that Chomsky makes similar points about a philosophers' favorite topic, the notion of reference. Like reason, reference involving natural language terms is a phenomenon that no serious science can contend with.[5] Philosophers often think of reference as far more tractable to science than the notion of meaning

(Chomsky thinks exactly the opposite), and they produce what they call "theories of reference" that purport to tell us what reference consists in. They might, for example, try to make reference depend on a "natural" relationship, such as information flow. But these efforts completely miss the point, perhaps because philosophers tend to construe reference as being much simpler than it actually is. They usually think of it as a dyadic (two-term) relationship between a word and a thing, such that a word refers to a thing ("goosebump" refers to goosebump(s)) But, Chomsky points out, two terms are not enough. We need at least a tetradic (four-term) relationship between a natural language word, a person who uses the word, some circumstances, and some thing or things (existing or not) (1995: 43). The problem here is the person needed to use a word and apply it to something. People's actions are not determinate and never will be – unless, perhaps, they are coerced. If referring is something that people do – and it is difficult to conceive of what else it could be – it is not something a serious science can contend with.

Both reasoning and reference are normatively governed. Visual and linguistic processing are not. No one assesses the excellence or frailty of Jane's visual or linguistic processing. And Jane does not 'do' what happens in her head when producing visual spaces or linguistic expressions. They are automatic processes. Development (which is virtually automatic) and late second-language acquisition aside, visual and linguistic processes are also not modifiable by the person who has them in his or her head (they are "cognitively impenetrable"). Nor are they modifiable by the community. They are automatic and unconscious. These facts make them apt subject matters for serious science. But if persons as agents play a role, all wagers on the possibility of a serious science are off.

The point about modifiability leads to an important caveat concerning what Chomsky means by a computational theory. It is often assumed these days that the mind can be thought of as something like a machine that runs various programs. Serious problems arise, however, if one thinks of language as a set of 'rules' that are 'programmed into' a 'universal' machine that is largely unprogrammed at birth. The metaphor of programming makes it clear what is wrong. Whether programming is conceived of as provided by society, community, or culture (or perhaps an evil genius), or whether it is supposed to depend on a form of bootstrapping, operating with (say) sensory inputs and a generalized learning procedure provided at birth, the metaphor of programming a device that can run any number of different routines virtually demands that one think of the mind as a plastic medium, formed by society and/or the world. Empiricism's three assumptions (representationalism, empty mind, and general learning procedures explain all) then appear plausible, and Chomsky's claim that the language faculty is a computational device is all too easily misunderstood. It is important to emphasize, then, that a condition for constructing a computational theory of a part of the mind is that that part be universal in its operations and, surely as a condition for this, innately preconfigured. This can be put – although again with the danger of being misunderstood – by saying that language and vision are "hard-wired" and it is because they are that it is possible to construct sciences of them. It is better, however, to use traditional terminology and say that theories of vision and language deal with their respective *faculties*, making "faculty" a technical term for an innately configured mental device that operates automatically and blindly.

A related way to see the point is to recognize that vision and theories of linguistic expressions, like other successful theories of the mind, deal with *modular* domains that operate in distinct ways; a theory of vision, for example, deals with very different features and principles (arrayed intensities and Gaussians) than a theory of language (lexical features and "Merge" and "Move"). Nor is there a single computational device that carries out both; they do not follow the same algorithms, or formally definable procedures. If they occur at the same time, they proceed largely in parallel, working independently as two different physical organs do. Chomsky often uses the metaphor of a "mental organ" to characterize the language and visual faculties: like physical organs, they are independent and develop over time. There are dangers in this, because it might suggest that mental faculties have distinct, readily located parts of the brain carry out their operations. But, while so far as we can tell at the moment, this is true to an extent, it is not crucial that it be so. The important consideration is that what we know about visual and linguistic processing as revealed by theories of them shows that they are clearly distinct.

All of this leads to a useful distinction between language and its use, which reflects Strawson's (1950) distinction between what can be said about words and what can be said about uses of words. Like Strawson, Chomsky points out that in order to make sense of how words are used (in reference and reasoning), one must speak of persons as users of words. Another motivation behind Chomsky's distinction is not found in Strawson. It is that the distinction helps bound a domain where science can get a grip – the domain of words or language (or what they become in formal linguistic theory) – by distinguishing it from the domain of human action, where people use words and language.

A challenge to a science of the human mind

Chomsky's placing reason and reference outside the language faculty leads to a challenge to his approach that needs to be addressed before we draw a picture of the mind as he sees it. The challenge insists that unscientific (so far as Chomsky is concerned) concepts of common sense understanding are sufficient and necessary for understanding the human mind, so they had better be included in any science of the mind. Those who present this challenge argue that if we do not include common sense concepts like <u>intend</u>, <u>think</u>, <u>thought</u>, <u>reason</u>, <u>refer</u>, and <u>infer</u> in our efforts to understand the mind, we lose our grip on what the mind is. What Chomsky comes up with when he provides an arcane-looking formal computational theory of what he tells us are processes in our heads does not inform us about what matter to us in our mental lives – our reasoning, thinking, and intending. So his computational theory is irrelevant to the mind as we understand it and (it is suggested) as it must be understood. As Tyler Burge (1988; quoted in Chomsky 1995: 31–2) poses the challenge, any psychological science or science of the mind ought to "refine, deepen, generalize, and systematize some of the statements of informed common sense about people's mental activity." A science of psychology or mind ought to extend folk psychology, and psychologists ought to tell us what thoughts and reason are, deal with intentions, wishes, and musings, and construct systematic accounts of mental entities like these. Chomsky's science of mind, unlike this other project, threatens to eliminate these crucial ways of understanding ourselves.

Some contemporary philosophers feel that this threat to our understandings of ourselves was best expressed by Wilfrid Sellars in his "Philosophy and the Scientific Image of Man" (1960b). Sellars claimed that in the description and explanation of the phenomena of the world, what he called the "scientific image" could replace and eliminate the "manifest image" (the common sense framework) and its central figures, persons. To mollify offended intuitions, he suggested that important aspects of the manifest or common sense image, norms and values thought of as governing human actions, could and would remain. Choice, action, or what philosophers call "agency," would not be eliminated, even if persons as things disappeared in the eventual succession of the scientific image.[6] No science would speak of persons, and from the point of view of the sciences persons would be fictions, but they would not be complete fictions in the way the troll under my doorstep is. Thus the manifest image's concept of a person would remain at the center of our normatively governed practical affairs. However, Sellars's appeal to a normative dimension to limit the capacity of the sciences to supplant folk-psychological concepts has usually not been seen as sufficient to remove the threat of "eliminationism" – the threat, as Burge put it, that "mentalistic talk and mentalistic entities [will] eventually lose their place in our attempts to describe and explain the world" (1992; quoted in Chomsky 1995: 31). Surely, the response holds, no science can eliminate persons and their mental lives, made up of willings, intendings, and referrings. Any correct description and explanation of the species human being and of what happens in the heads of human beings must deal with persons and intendings.

Chomsky responds to this perceived threat dismissively, seriously, and constructively. The *dismissive* responses – they take several forms – agree with the objectors that 'our' understanding of persons comes in common sense concepts but reject the idea that these understandings are under threat. He has often remarked that in the past we have learned, and no doubt will continue to learn, more about people from novels than from all of psychology – perhaps even the biologically based psychology to which his work contributes. If the concept of a person is found, as it seems to be, in the domain of common sense, it is better explored by artistic works such as novels and poems that can cope with the context-sensitive and interest-dependent aspects of that domain than by an enterprise committed to formal description and explanation within modular but universal domains. Science is just not suited to the way in which the concept of a person is dealt with in common sense understanding. Some parts of science – in particular, lexicology or lexicography as Chomsky understands it – will take the natural language *concepts* person and intend as subject matter, but that is not a threat. In fact, once we discover what is in these and related concepts (intention, need, . . .), we may perhaps come to understand better how different people and different cultures play out the different themes that such concepts must obviously allow. If anything, this will aid coming to an understanding of ourselves.

A related dismissive response is found in Chomsky's expression of puzzlement that a project that is committed, as his is, to producing a naturalistic science of human beings should be thought to be a challenge to common sense understandings of persons. As he points out, those who worry about this aspect of his work do not feel any threat to common sense understandings and explanations of things like waves and wind, house and table, horse and shrub, although none of these have survived challenges from the sciences over the last few centuries. In effect, if the anti-eliminationists think that a science of human beings is such a serious threat to "our understandings of ourselves," they should also sense a threat to claiming that the wind blew down a tree, that the water became tea when a tea bag was put in it, that the mail box has faded blue paint on its surfaces – claims which can obviously be true in the domain of common sense understanding, but not science. The anti-eliminationists' practices show that they are perfectly comfortable with common sense *and* sciences that do not deal with the blue surfaces of mail boxes. As Chomsky put it (1995: 32), "no one really expects ordinary talk about things happening in the "physical world" [the world of folk physics] to have any particular relation to naturalistic theories; [their] terms belong to different intellectual universes." Underlying both of these dismissive responses is the idea that common sense description and explanation have served their purposes very well for millennia and, judging by the ways they are used and the purposes they serve, they are in no danger of being eliminated in favor of scientific descriptions and explanations that have no discernible hope of serving these purposes. The anti-eliminationists' sense of threat seems to be highly selective.

Chapter 1 laid the groundwork for what is needed for a *serious* response. It consists in showing that you cannot somehow make science continuous with common sense, so there is no challenge. Science and common sense are different intellectual universes and do not encroach on each other. Science does not explain human action. Far from it. Nor can you turn folk psychology into serious, naturalistic psychological science by stating generalizations, finding 'laws', and generally 'refining' common sense descriptions and explanations of human actions. The concepts just do not serve. This point is to an extent like that made by the philosopher Donald Davidson in "Psychology as Philosophy" (1980). He argued that rational choice theory, often presented as a paradigm case of how to proceed to construct a serious theory of human choice and action by appeal to common sense concepts such as <u>choice</u> and <u>interest</u>, fails in the simplest of cases. But that does not mean that there is no common sense explanation of human action; it is obvious that there is. Unlike Davidson, though, Chomsky sees no reason to then go on to say that, because within the common sense framework we speak of people *causing* their actions, this common sense concept of cause must have some mirror form of causality which links events within a brain science. That kind of move invites back in the question of which form of causality – common sense or scientific – is paramount, and the (supposed) threat gets new wind.

Chomsky's *constructive* response to the anti-eliminationist relies on innateness and on the fact that the human mind is limited in the sets of capacities it has available and in what they provide. It also brings us closer to the goal of mapping the mind by revealing a reason to map it the way Chomsky does. The strategy in the constructive response is to show that folk-psychological notions use concepts that are not just items that we have invented for our convenience and could dispose of; rather, they are concepts that are innately specified and that seem to be central to our capacity to survive and thrive. This is part of a more general strategy to show that certain limitations on the range of the human intellect and the expressive capacities of the human mind, imposed by innate concepts provided within certain faculties, are in fact great advantages. To see the force of this strategy, recall the empiricists' picture of the mind as having no, or only a very thin set of, innate capacities, with the rest of the contents of the mind coming from outside, "by experience." Having to learn almost everything would pose a real threat: humans could not acquire the necessary cognitive capacities in time to survive, much less thrive. Nor would they acquire them uniformly across the human population. Another problem is that, on the empiricist picture, one could actually make sense of losing the concepts used in folk-psychological descriptions and explanations and substituting others, perhaps even scientific ones that do not provide for the concept of an agent acting in accord with intentions. The *empiricist* picture allows for elimination; Chomsky's does not. But if Chomsky is correct, the empiricist picture is then wrong in still another particular; for the concepts will not disappear even if a scientific theory of mind is developed and accepted. We might choose to stop using them, but the chances of that are slim.

Imagine finding an empiricist who is willing to allow that folk psychology has not, and probably will not, change and wants to say why this is so. If such a person is smart, he or she will not argue that folk psychology persists only because people find it convenient to have it do so. If the stability of folk psychology is only a matter of convenience, then it is not clear why things have *not* changed; for what is convenient at one time for one person is not necessarily convenient for others (or even that same person) at a different time. Chomsky can too easily reply that convenience could explain stability only if there were a fixed human nature with fixed human interests. Folk psychology has to be convenient for Plato and Skinner, and for Quine and a six-year-old child, and the only way to show that it is convenient for all of them is to argue that there is a basic human nature with fixed concepts and basic needs that make the use of these concepts that are 'convenient'. This is not an explanation that empiricist doctrine welcomes. But there are no viable alternatives.

The empiricist might try this: continuity and basic similarity of culture explain stability, for people's minds are made by their societies, and if they agree in these respects, it must be because there are common threads to our culture.[7] This move tries to make an artifact of a stable, continuous folk psychology (continuity and basic similarity of culture) explain folk psychology's stability, making what is explained the explainer. But even if it were possible to show that basic similarity of culture (whatever that might be) is somehow more primitive than the psychological explanatory and descriptive concepts of the individuals who "have" a culture, it would have to be shown why, on empiricist grounds, culture is stable. Neither similarity nor continuity of culture is a simple datum. Chomsky, in contrast, has a ready answer to the stability of folk psychology in the concept of a fixed human nature made up in part of various cognitive faculties and capacities, and he has no difficulty with circularity: there are sciences of these faculties in place that cannot proceed except on the assumption of the innateness that constitutes a fixed human nature.

The empiricist might then try something like this: the concept of a fixed human nature is really just an artifact of a fixed *physical* world which changes very little indeed. Because human beings have to deal with this fixed physical world all the time, it is no surprise that they converge in the theories each learns that allow him or her to deal with that world. The idea seems to be that a supposedly uniform environment constrains the ways in which human beings interact with it, and thus constrains how they understand it and their place in it. Realist philosophers take this kind of argument very seriously, and as there are lots of realists around, it appeals to a fairly wide audience. The problem, however, is that it at best delays the inevitable. Assume, reasonably, that the 'constrained by the world' argument requires that the things and events of such a world be understood at least in part by those who are constrained by it. Chomsky then need only point out that the sole concept of a physical world that one could possibly think of as fixed over times, places, and people would have to be the one understood in common sense – the world with which folk physics deals. It cannot be the one or ones described in the sciences: the sciences as we understand them are recent inventions and could hardly have played a role in the culture of ancient Greece, to take one culture among many.[8] It is hard, in fact, to understand how any serious scientific concept of a world *could* play the constraining role that the empiricist wants it to. Very few people are competent at science, and those who are, are not necessarily competent in more than one, so it is difficult to conceive of how a world or worlds understood in this way could play any role in a child's 'learning' concepts such as <u>intention</u> and <u>choice</u> at, say, three years of age. Moreover, and more important, if it is the common sense concept of a world that is at stake, this attempt to somehow have a physical world constrain our under-standing of ourselves again begs the question. The empiricist offers no explanation of why the folk-physics concept of a world should stay fixed. The anti-eliminationists seem quite comfortable with conceding that there are no shrubs or mountains. But if this is the case, why have our concepts of the world made no attempt to take this into account? Chomsky's explanation for the stability of the common sense world is exactly like his explanation for the stability of our notion of a human being in folk psychology. The concepts we use for describing and explaining the 'physical world' are innately specified – the features that make them up are part of a fixed human nature. The right explanation of a fixed common sense, including folk physics and folk psychology, lies in a fixed human nature with the relevant concepts provided at birth and requiring only an ex-periential trigger to activate.

If Chomsky hopes to have this kind of explanation stick, he must show how innately specified concepts in the head bear on (common sense) experience and somehow constrain it. The empiricist talks vaguely about a "fixed world" outside the head determining what is inside the head and is taken seriously. Chomsky points out with careful argument that the empiricist story is myth and magic and is ignored. Perhaps nothing will change the empiricist's mind, but a strong positive account of how innate concepts figure in our experience of the world and ourselves might help. Additional details appear in chapters 3–6, but we have enough already to appreciate that the biological rationalist's map of the mind must make the cognitive capacity of common sense understanding depend on innate faculties. It should also suggest why only humans can 'do science'. Adapting one of Chomsky's informal terms, it should suggest how innate faculties *enable* the cognitive capacities of common sense and – in a different way – science. For enabling both enables reason.

The mind mapped and capacities enabled

The successes of linguistics and the science of vision show that we should look to these sciences in order to say what is in the mind, even if what they show does not satisfy philosophical intuitions about what must be in the mind. The point applies both to mapping the general areas of the mind and to providing a detailed account of the 'contents' of each faculty – saying what phonological, formal, and semantic features there are and what features make up human visual colors. Allowing that there could well be other successful sciences of the mind, Chomsky (following others in the rationalist tradition) calls the area each science deals with a *"faculty* of *x,"* where "of *x"* classifies the set of operations, features, and outputs that a particular science of the mind deals with. He calls the outputs of each faculty "interfaces"; the idea, intuitively, is that each faculty contributes to the cognitive functioning of mind by producing a unique set of internally defined products that can interact with other systems in the head. The faculty of vision is that area of the mind that carries out the various processes (described in part by a set of mathematical operations called "Gaussian functions") involved in human vision. Its interfaces – the various "faces" that it presents to other systems in the head – are mental hue-brightness-saturation-altitude-azimuth-depth positions, or positions in six-dimensional visual spaces. These six-dimensional visual spaces model what is in the head when our eyes are open and we are looking, but the 'positions' in this space, specified by assigning values to the six coordinates, are *not* color-spatial positions of 'things' in a space outside the head. A particular set of six values, defining a position in visual color-space, can be *used* by a person to present or represent things outside the head, and in the case of vision, they typically are used (almost automatically) in this way. But a visual 'space' of this kind is defined in terms of features inside the head and has the characteristics that the correct theory of the visual faculty assigns to it – for example, a particular mental color. In a broadly similar way, the language faculty, through the operations "Merge," which places lexical items together, and "Attract/Move," which moves features about – both operating over the phonological, formal, and semantic features of groups of lexical items – produces (if the computation is successful, or does not crash) two different interfaces, which always occur as paired outputs. The paired outputs are, informally speaking, *sounds* and *meanings*. Specific sounds are paired with specific meanings to yield what Chomsky calls "expressions." The point of a computational theory of the language faculty is to say how, in any person's head, sounds are paired with meanings in the production of expressions. Notice that while the faculty of vision and the faculty of language operate independently over their own sets of features, using their own 'rules' or principles, the theories that deal with them have broadly similar characteristics. Both theories are internalist, for they deal only with what happens in the head, and both are nativist, for they deal with machinery and features that seem to be innately specified – that are due to our biological heritage. Moreover, both call for a constructivist interpretation: in both cases, their outputs, while typically (in the case of vision) and sometimes (in the case of language) used to deal with the world 'outside', provide their own, internally generated properties and concepts. Colors, linguistic sounds, and linguistic meanings might be used to see and describe the world, but they are defined over, and have their origin in, the mind. We see a colored object, but its colors (and boundaries/lines, etc.) are mental entities, found in the head.

To introduce a few of Chomsky's technical terms and points, the sound side of the paired elements that make up an expression is what Chomsky calls a "PHON" – an acronym for "phonetic interface," sometimes also labeled "PF." The meaning side of an expression is called a "SEM" – an acronym for "semantic interface" or what Chomsky also sometimes calls "logical form" (LF). (PHON is the technical term for linguistic sound, and SEM the technical term for linguistic meaning.) Thus, expressions are PHON–SEM pairs (⟨PHON, SEM⟩s). It is important to keep in mind that these are not relabelings of folk-psychological concepts (linguistic sound and linguistic meaning) but well-defined theoretical ones. They are defined within a theory that provides for the generation of all the sound–meaning pairs of all natural languages, existing or not. In other words, the theory tells us what a possible natural language is, given our biological heritage. It is also important to keep in mind that the interfaces PHON and SEM do not figure directly in human efforts to communicate: PHONs do not come out of people's mouths. Instead, they interact with other systems in the head that produce signals (what happens when someone speaks, involving the larynx and the tongue) and that 'decode' signals (what happens when we listen to – involving the ears' tympani – and understand others speaking). In Chomsky's terminology, each interface defines a set of "instructions" that the language faculty gives to other systems inside the head; these other systems produce signals from mouths and perceive signals produced by others – what we call "communicating in language." Chomsky calls what the language faculty itself does (what happens on the language faculty side of the interface) a matter of linguistic "competence." He calls the other systems with which the language faculty interacts "performance" systems. His science of language is a theory of linguistic competence.[9]

While theories of linguistic expressions and visual spaces are broadly alike in the ways indicated, they are very different from each other, as are the processes that produce them. So the faculties themselves are separate, or modular. As Chomsky remarks, "it would be astonishing if we were to discover that the constituent elements of the language faculty enter crucially in other domains" (*LPK* 159). As suggested above, it has been shown that the processes that take place in visual computation and those that take place in linguistic computation occur in different "mental organs" located in different places in the brain,[10] although it is not necessary that one demonstrate this to show that the faculties of vision and language are different modules. There can be interactions, plausibly after the interface stage, when the visual or linguistic computations that produce a visual space or an expression are complete. One observation that suggests this is that we use sentences to provide linguistic descriptions of something that is presented within a visual field. It is not, however, the responsibility of the theories of the language faculty and the visual faculty to speak to such interactions, nor to others like them. At least until we know a very great deal more about the mind, and maybe even then, descriptions of such interactions are likely to proceed within folk psychology alone and will involve a person using a language to deal with something that is presented visually, where the thing presented visually is (thought to be) outside the head.

In addition to the faculties that carry out computations blindly, the mind also contains *capacities*. We are already familiar with two human capacities: common sense understanding and the capacity to produce sciences – what Chomsky calls the science-forming capacity. It is, as he says in compressed form, "a certain conceptual apparatus, certain ways of formulating problems, a concept of intelligibility and explanation, and so on" (*LPK* 156). It clearly involves mathematics – various forms of formalization (*RR* 8f). And it depends on some sense of what a good explanation is. But, while it differs in ways we have seen from common sense understanding and relies on different resources in the mind, it is, like common sense, a problem-solving capacity. Capacities provide ways to deal with and gain understanding of the things of the world.

Chomsky does not always distinguish capacities from faculties, no doubt because normal use of the English word "capacity" allows it to apply also to what he calls "faculties." I suggest, though, that it is important to Chomsky's view of the mind that he not place these two capacities (or any others) among the faculties (*LPK* 157; cf. *RL*: ch. 4) as defined above. One reason has to do with the fact that the capacities typically depend on contributions from more than a single faculty – the contributions that various interfaces provide. Science, for example, rests in part on numerical mathematics, which Chomsky tends to trace to the language faculty (because both numbers and language involve discrete infinities) and on geometry, which he traces to the vision faculty. Common sense obviously involves cooperation between vision and language – a simple case in which both operate is linguistic-perceptual identification of an animal as a wombat or a facial expression as a wince – and language must cooperate with touch, etc., too. Many of the sub-capacities that are found in common sense also rely on multiple faculties: the capacity for facial recognition seems to (*RL*: ch. 4), as does that for recognition of a person's place in a social hierarchy. In effect, both science and common sense understanding are far too complex in their operations to be captured by computational theories that call on a fixed set of features and detail a set of inputs and outputs produced by well-defined procedures or principles. (This recalls points made earlier about reason. Whether scientific or common sense, reason is no faculty.)

A second reason is that the capacities are, to an extent, cognitively penetrable, whereas faculties are not. On the assumption that faculties are parts of the mind for which there are – or one can expect to find – computational theories, if common sense and science *were* faculties, it could be supposed that they operate unconsciously and without interference (see *LPK* 156–8); they would have to be cognitively impenetrable (*KL* 261–2). In effect, they would have to be modular parts of the mind that operate beyond our conscious intervention, functioning relatively independently of other parts and providing specific interfaces to other parts of the mind. They would have to proceed in accordance with well-defined biologically determined algorithms over biologically determined features and produce determinate outputs. But this makes no sense of science or common sense, for they are basically capacities for solving problems. Humans rely upon them (in different ways and to serve different purposes) in ways that involve choice, selection, and improvement. Science can be refined: techniques and procedures can be changed and improved, and new concepts invented. Common sense allows – to name some areas of penetrability – flexibility in application through the infinity of perspectives it can rely upon, subtlety and nuance, and development of themes. In important ways, then, it too can be 'tuned' by the individuals who depend on it.

A related (and telling) point is that if these capacities *were* faculties, we would have to conceive of them as inflexible cognitive engines that for a particular input yield either a single correct (fitting, appropriate, etc.) judgment or 'answer', no answer at all, or a wrong answer – with no alternatives and no opportunity to consider them. If correct, we are lucky. If no answer, it is a matter of chance. If wrong, we are unlucky. If any of these, we have no choice as to which perspective to choose, and this makes no sense at all of the ways in which we exercise either science or common sense understanding.

The result so far is that the mind seen as the subject matter of science includes a cluster of faculties for which there are, or plausibly will be, sciences that treat that particular faculty as carrying out computations over determinate sets of features. By "computational procedures" I mean procedures that produce determinate outputs from particular inputs in a way that can be captured by a formalized (mathematical) theory of the relevant domain, in which all inputs, outputs, and procedures (algorithms) are well-defined. Very likely the other sensory faculties, such as audition, touch, and taste, can be included among the faculties; it would be surprising if computational sciences of them were not developed in the not too distant future. Even now it is possible to show that they have "interfaces" which are systematic in the interrelationships of the various "perspectives" provided by the sensory faculty. Just as vision's perspectives are possible configurations of a six-dimensional hue-brightness-saturation-altitude-azimuth-depth visual space and linguistic meanings are computationally possible configurations of formal and semantic features, so tastes are possible configurations of a sweet-sour-salt-bitter space (Clark 1993), showing that taste has outputs with a particular structure. What has not been shown in the case of taste, so far as I know, is how to produce these perspectives. But the easily mapped and structured outputs provide a reason to think that it must be possible: *some* regular and automatic faculty has to produce them. In addition, there is reason to add a faculty of facial configurations that underlies the capacity to recognize faces: both humans and other apes have fairly large parts of their brains devoted to producing whatever kinds of representation the capacity of facial recognition relies on when it takes into account fine-grained features (and differences in features) of other members of one's species. These representations provide a highly textured species-specific mapping of facial pattern in what seems to be an automatic and unlearned (or innate) way. This is what one would expect: only a creature that had these kinds of 'perspectives' innately available could develop as readily and quickly as we do the cognitive capacity to discern very fine differences in human faces.

If a scientific map of mind must include regions for faculties, though, it is not clear that it should also include any indications of capacities – prominently, common sense and science. Chomsky's view seems to be that it should (*RL* 144f; 1997: 1f; 1995; cf. Chomsky 1974). He holds that capacities can be placed on a scientific map of the mind because, unlike the cognitive *powers* I mention later, the capacities seem to be universal and relatively uniform. People seem to have them even if they do not, have not, and will not exercise them. No doubt few human beings have managed to live for long without exercising common sense understanding, but it is not unusual to find people who have not exercised the science-forming capacity, except in the most primitive of ways. On the other hand, it is plausible that any human being alive today, yet to be born, or who lived in 5,000 BC has the capacity to 'do science' and make at least elementary mathematical judgments, even if he or she has neither opportunity (occasion), nor interest, nor particular talent to do so. So there can be a capacity without its exercise. Presumably that is because science and the other capacities depend heavily upon the faculties which clearly are lodged in everyone's mind, no matter when they are born, and no matter with what opportunities they are provided. The faculties are universal, and this suggests strongly that the capacities that rely heavily on them are too.

As with faculties, there may be unrecognized and/or unused capacities. Capacities rely on faculties, but they need opportunity and occasion to be exercised. Common sense understanding develops in everyone, because there is so great a need for it; the science-forming capacity – at least in developed form – takes some time. Other capacities include aesthetic judgment and particular forms of it – music, for example (Jackendoff and Lerdahl 1983) – and the particular species of moral judgment we have, as well as, perhaps, our form of social cognition (Jackendoff 1994, 1997).

Some of our faculties might be the same as those of other creatures – our visual faculty at least is very much like that of the macaque monkey, for example. The language faculty is not shared, of course. Because of that it is arguable that our visual capacity – to the extent that it relies on language and our specific facial configuration faculties too – differs from that of the macaque. The macaque might see another creature when it looks at one of us, but not a human being, agent, or friend with a concerned frown on its face.

What is the relationship between capacities and faculties? Adapting a term Chomsky uses in a narrower context, I suggest speaking of capacities – specifically, judgment-making capacities – as being *enabled* by faculties. This terminology attempts to capture an important aspect of Chomsky's suggestion in *Language and Mind* (*LM* 13) that while the explanation of (intelligent) behavior is not part of the rationalist project, explaining how intelligent behavior is possible is. The idea, basically, is that innately specified faculties provide human beings with what is needed to develop the kinds of capacities we all share – common sense understanding and the capacity for science. Enabling is not exercising: the science-forming capacity is enabled by various faculties, even if not exercised. And there is no unique mapping from faculty to capacity: the human visual capacity no doubt requires the visual faculty, but it relies on the faculty of facial configuration as well. Indeed, the mapping is likely to be very complicated. In the case of common sense, it is likely that one would need to base it on vision, language, audition, and just about all the other faculties that human beings have – although, as I suggested earlier, language might play a predominant role. We should take into account that common sense is not a single, monolithic capacity. It is plausible to think of it as including various sub-capacities, such as facial recognition and the capacity to recognize position in a social hierarchy. And we should recognize that a single faculty might enable various capacities: the language faculty (partially) enables common sense, of course, and Chomsky has suggested that it enables at least basic mathematics by providing the number system (*LPK* 169). The visual faculty partially enables common sense too, and Chomsky has suggested that by providing straight lines, triangles, dimensions, and the like (*LPK* 159–60) it enables geometry. It is less clear in some cases which faculty or faculties enable which capacities. Take, for example, what Jackendoff calls "social cognition." Undoubtedly language would have to play a role, for it provides the intentional concepts and perhaps the hierarchical structures needed. I assume the same of moral and aesthetic judgment. The capacity for aesthetic judgment would also depend upon vision, audition, and, in the case of unusual media, other faculties. Clearly, saying what enables what might be difficult. In the case of social cognition, for example, it is unlikely that language would be sufficient: apes seem to have some of the same hierarchical and intentional notions that we do, and they do not get them from language. There are many open questions. But the point is clear: one has to have the faculties in order to develop and exercise the capacities. They make the capacities, and their exercise in judgment, possible.

Given enabled capacities, it is plausible that, when exercised, they provide for domains of experience. Take the science-forming capacity. In anything but the most rudimentary form, it comes late to children. But they can develop it (because they are enabled to do so), and when they do, they gain a rich, structured domain of experience. The same point, although with different kinds of structure and much greater richness, applies to common sense understanding. So we come closer to making sense of how 'innate ideas' could bear on experience.

The idea of a domain of experience available to a species only when enabled by one or more mental faculties is easily understood by thinking about how difficult it is to explain the development of such domains *without* appeal to an innately specified, automatically developing mental faculty or faculties and the rich and structured concepts they provide. The most spectacular case is common sense, for humans – as we know – at a very early age have no difficulty in coming to an understanding of the wishes and motivations of human beings, of hierarchies and equality, of sympathy and trust, of rights and obligations, and any number of other things having to do with people. The two-year-old has no difficulty in predicting that the plate's contents will fall and make a satisfactory mess on the carpet, in predicting the reactions of babysitters and other agents with intentions and desires, and in integrating the two predictions. The two-year-old has, then, a good appreciation of folk physics and psychology – two "domains of experience" within a capacity that integrates these and any number of other more specialized domains within common sense (facial recognition, social status, etc.). It is extremely unlikely that children could have access to virtually the whole of common sense understanding and its integrated domain of experience (revealed in perception, judgment, and action) by age six if they had to gain it without being able to rely upon those innate ideas that provide the detailed conceptual structure and texture that common sense needs. The only alternatives that have ever been proposed amount to gesturing – the proposals are never worked out – towards some kind of "generalized learning procedure" such as association (of what?), hypothesis formation (using what, and on what basis?), and inductive testing (over what relevance classes?). This empiricist proposal sets a child a daunting task, for however much innate machinery even the enlightened empiricist is willing to provide to aid the task of explaining how a child has common sense understanding by six, no empiricist who wants to keep his or her credentials can allow that children have the conceptual structure and texture that the biological nativist can take for granted. So there is no innate persuade, intend, house, person, or thousands of other concepts. If so, though, the empiricist cannot make sense of how a child readily gains access to the rich and flexible domain of experience we think of as common sense.

It is important to recognize, moreover, that the empiricist must also explain acquisition (and limits on acquisition) for the sciences, and must do so while recognizing that in doing science, we rely on at least some aids that are difficult to account for except by appeal to innateness. Doing science at all would be impossible if we had to construct and test what could well be an infinite set of hypotheses for a domain. Recognizing this and accounting for the narrow range of permissible hypotheses by appeal to Peircean abduction (but without Peirce's rather confused machinery), Chomsky suggests that we have innately available "a certain concept of explanation" that – luckily for us – happens to work in at least some domains, including physics and linguistics. We also have, of course, numerical mathematics and geometry and a capacity to formalize (cp. *RL* 155f), concepts of simplicity and elegance, and so on. To be sure, since the sciences depend to a much smaller extent than common sense on innate conceptual structure, empiricists might be able to convince themselves that they can at least deal with *this* domain of experience. But they have to keep in mind that even here they are going to have to speak to the difference in time of acquisition between common sense and science, the fact that most people do quite well without any science at all, and that there seems to be such a gulf between common sense and science. The prospect that they will be able to, given the machinery they are willing to accept, is nil. If so, it is plausible to hold that (as things stand) only the (biological) rationalist map of the mind will make sense of the full range of human domains of experience, the differences between various ranges, and the flexibility without regimentation of the common sense domain.

Incidentally, one would expect that where human beings *do* have to rely on generalized learning procedures, their problem-solving abilities are reduced to little better than chance. This seems to be the case. Other things being equal, human beings are no better at running mazes than rats. Human beings can, of course, figure out how to run a maze that requires turning left at each prime-number corner, and no rat can do that. But that is because, unlike rats, human beings have a guided domain of experience in very elementary mathematics – counting.

Faculties and capacities have now been placed in the mind and related by the relation "enables by," where the various faculties enable the capacities. And capacities have been said to provide for domains of experience and differences between them. What, then, of various cognitive *powers* – cognitive talents (for acting, for seeing the point, for painting), abilities (to ride a bicycle, walk a tightrope), skills (at manipulating a plow, at dancing the tango), habits (of bluffing when losing at poker, of rinsing the toothbrush under hot water), and any number of other cognitive and near-cognitive or mixed-cognitive powers that have been assigned to, or claimed for, the human mind? Undoubtedly the development or learning of most of these powers depends on having human cognitive faculties, and capacities too. No doubt, also, when some of these powers have been developed, a person can be said to have a kind of knowledge: people know how to ride a bicycle even when they are not actually riding one. But while these powers are in some sense enabled by faculties and capacities, and while some, when developed, involve a kind of knowledge that remains fixed within the individual, in spite of loss of ability, there is no compelling reason – unlike with faculties and capacities – to place them among the machinery of the human mind as science sees it. One reason for this is that, unlike the faculty language and the capacity common sense ("Grammar and common sense are acquired by virtually everybody" (*RL* 144)), these powers are not universal: they can differ quite markedly among various people. A second reason is that skills, abilities, and powers (although perhaps not the knowledge associated with some of them (*LPK* 11)) are changeable; they can improve, and they can even pass away. This is unlike a capacity, which is to a reasonable approximation unchanging. These two points are underscored when we notice that powers are attributed to individual persons, not to minds. People may need the faculties and capacities that their minds afford them, but they are not themselves individually responsible for them. But they, and not their minds, can, and often will, be held responsible for acquisition or elimination of their powers.

In essence, Chomsky's view of the mind is that of a set of faculties and capacities, but not powers or skills, with – assuming a distinction between them – capacities taken to depend upon faculties. His aim is to provide a universalizable picture of the mind. The sketch is tentative, of course. It includes the faculties for which there are good sciences in place – vision and language – and some which are anticipated, although there may be others (or, conceivably, some about which we now know little might be combined). It also provides for a set of capacities that seem reasonably firm. But one must remember that even the sciences of faculties that are in place are still young, and that the boundaries between the faculties are not completely settled. Nor, really, is the boundary between capacities and powers. And no empirical (naturalistic) commitment can be completely certain. With these caveats in mind, it is still clear that Chomsky's scientific sketch is of a universal form of human mind. It portrays what philosophers call an essential cognitive nature – a nature that people have, no matter what kind(s) of environment(s) they may be in. And the only plausible way to make sense of how the human mind could have this essential nature is to presume that what humans can conceive and think is largely predetermined. In Chomsky's view, it is biologically fixed.

We have, now, an answer to why common sense and science represent "different intellectual universes." They do so because the overall domain of experience characteristic of common sense relies on the conceptual repertoire offered by the language faculty, which is heavily anthropocentric and focused on persons and agents. The different capacity science does not. Not coincidentally, the empiricist cannot explain this difference (or why other domains of experience are unavailable).

An illustration

It might help to focus on a specific innate idea and how it could provide for a (very limited) domain of experience. A good way to do this is to speak to how innate concepts help address why we agree as much as we do – why there is agreement in the ways we have developed to deal with the world. The empiricist has problems with this phenomenon. It raises not only the issue of how people form concepts, but how they come to form very similar concepts and apply them in like ways.

The empiricist has strategies to deal with agreement. One is to say that we develop similar concepts because they are brought about by the same world. As we saw, this route has problems. Another is to try to explain agreement via social regimentation, typically thought of as administered through training of the young by individuals in a community who know what "correct linguistic usage" is and induce it in the young by praising and punishing their efforts. This is a version of the "continuous culture does it" theme; we will find several more reasons to reject it.[11] Where the empiricist appeals to world and conforming community, the biological rationalist starts with innate faculties and the concepts they provide and has them play a role in enabling capacities and providing for a domain of experience. To see how this works in a particular case, let us help ourselves to Hume's two categories of truth: truths of reason and truths of fact. Let us also restrict our truths of fact to descriptive and explanatory uses of natural language sentences within common sense understanding – sentences used to make judgments, such as "Harry is chasing his beagle," but not "Anaphors are bound in the minimal domain of a subject." (The truths of fact of naturalistic or empirical science 'sentences' – whether of physics or linguistics – are a different matter, for they receive little if any aid from natural language concepts.) And let us restrict truths of reason to those underwritten by the structures of natural language concepts. The aim is to make it clear that natural language conceptual structure somehow provides for a domain of experience. Begin with the observation that any English speaker knows, without thinking about it or being told, that if the sentence "Harry is chasing his beagle" is true, so is "Harry is following his beagle." The explanation of why Harry chasing is also Harry following is found in the fact that this connection is an instantiation of what philosophers call an "analytic a priori truth" of the form "y chase $x \rightarrow y$ follow x," where the term "a priori" is intended to indicate that the principle that warrants the inference from chasing to following is known "before experience," and the term "analytic" to suggest that knowing it is due somehow to "analysis of the words alone" – in this case, by the structure of the concept contained in the verbal lexical item "chase." If that inference is underwritten by the concept <u>chase</u> – specifically, if the principle is somehow contained in the structure of the concept <u>chase</u> – not only is the traditional technical notion of analytic a priori truths on the mark, but, more important, we can see how the structure of that concept provides for a domain of experience. A connected (and in this case rather small) domain of experience in the form of what one sees, anticipates, and watches out for when one sees Harry chasing his beagle depends for its structure and organization on a "connection of ideas" that underwrites a Humean truth of reason. Intuitively, by applying in a judgment the perspective provided by a sentence that contains the concept <u>chase</u> to describe something you see, your mind effectively constitutes a connected domain of experience that includes (in this case) Harry with certain intentions making an effort to accomplish something unspecified that involves his beagle. Principles of folk psychology and folk physics are brought to bear on a visual scene, and that scene is assigned a structure – simplified for emphasis in this case, of course.

This sort of story depends on showing that the concept <u>chase</u> has the relevant structure. There is, however, evidence from lexical studies that it does. And there is massive evidence that other lexical concepts contain structure that can underwrite analytic truths that can organize experience. For example, the verb "persuade" – another of Chomsky's favorite examples – is a "causative" verb, so that if it is true that x persuades y to A, then y must at least intend to A, because y's intention was brought about by x's efforts. It may of course be that y is thwarted or prevented from doing A, but it seems clear that he or she must intend to do it. So when someone is described as persuading another, the persuaded person is seen as standing in a specific causal relation to the persuader who brings this about.

Assuming that concepts are biologically innately specified and provided within a language faculty with which all humans are endowed, the explanation of why there is a strong degree of uniformity in concepts among a group of speakers comes *gratis* – or almost. Concepts are by assumption innately specified, but this does not guarantee that all individuals will have the same ones in their repertoires, or active vocabularies. Explaining why their repertoires will nevertheless overlap to a large extent is part of the job of an account of how various concepts are triggered and activated by circumstances that "invite" them (to use Cudworth's (1731) term). This is taken up later. In addition, something must be said about why concepts tend to be applied in similar ways. Not the whole story, but part of it, comes from an account of how concepts 'guide' their use. I say more about this too later, although the point may be clear already. Finally, if one wants to speak to how people communicate, something must be said about how people within a population often choose to pair sounds with meanings in the ways in which others in their population or speech community do. That is a trivial task: it is prudential to do so.

The biological rationalist's strategy deals with other issues too. Empiricists often recognize that it takes interconnections between concepts to make sense of experience, and, to deal with this, they favor the idea that one's dealings with the world are mediated by a *theory* with an interdefined set of concepts. In effect, they treat common sense understanding as a theory. Then they have to say where this theory comes from, and, once they think they have it in hand, they have to deal with the familiar problems that theories bring with them, including 'meaning holism', or (adapting a remark of Wittgenstein's (1953)) the idea that you must have the whole theory in place before you can understand the meaning of a single term in it (so before you have a single concept). By turning things around and making common sense – which is obviously not a theory but a flexible framework that can deal with multiple domains – depend on innate endowment, the biological rationalist handily undercuts the assumptions that create the 'problem'. Biological rationalism provides for interconnected concepts, but without requiring created theories to define them. And, in the domain of science, where theories really are to be found, biological rationalism suggests that human beings have innate resources that give them the capacity to develop theories and invent concepts (although with various degrees of difficulty).

Enablement by limitation

To summarize some of the themes of this chapter and anticipate later ones, let us look at what I call Chomsky's "enablement by limitation" thesis. He says that the "specific scope and limits of the various faculties of the human mind are matters of fact, matters in principle amenable to human inquiry, unless they transcend the limits of the human mind" (*LPK* 150)[12] and continues by saying that these natural limits are *not* a disadvantage; we should not regret that we can "readily deal with certain problems – learning of human language, for example – while others, which are neither 'harder' nor 'easier' in any useful absolute terms, are beyond our reach, some of them forever." We should not regret this – indeed, we "are fortunate that this is so" (*LPK* 151) – because in the domain of aesthetic experience and judgment, for example,

> Work of true aesthetic value follows canons and principles that are only in part subject to human choice; in part, they reflect our fundamental [and limited but in some areas very rich] nature. The result is that we can experience deep emotion – pleasure, pain, excitement and so on – from certain creative work, though how and why remains largely unknown. But the very capacities of mind that open these possibilities to us exclude other possibilities of mind forever. The limits of artistic creativity should . . . be a matter of joy, not sorrow, because they follow from the fact that there is a rich domain of aesthetic experience to which we have access. (*LPK* 152)

He continues: "The same is true of moral judgment. What its basis may be we do not know, but we can hardly doubt that it is rooted in fundamental human nature. It cannot be merely a matter of convention that we find some things to be right, others wrong. Growing up in a particular society a child acquires standards and principles of moral judgment. These are acquired on the basis of limited evidence, but they have broad and often quite precise applicability" (ibid.). Later in the discussion he adds theory construction, or "the science forming capacity" to the list (*LPK* 156–7). Common sense understanding must be added, obviously; it is perhaps the central case, but difficult to illustrate just because it is so rich, includes other capacities, and deals with so much.

The enablement by limitation thesis seems to amount to this: the various highly specific innate biologically based faculties that make up the core of the human mind provide infinite sets of 'outputs' that can be used by a human being to deal with the world in various 'problem-solving' ways, and it is only because the faculties are both limited and unlearned or innate, yet offer perspectives (1995: 20; *LT*; 1997) that can serve human interests, that we can develop various problem-solving capacities. In this way, the limited faculties enable various cognitive capacities.

The enablement by limitation thesis is another way to put the points I have been making about how innate faculties provide the perspectives that are needed for people to develop capacities and the domains of experience that come with them. Why, however, speak of limitation? The faculties can provide, in principle, infinite numbers of outputs. The language faculty can provide an unbounded number of sound–meaning pairs; the visual faculty can provide infinite numbers of space–color configurations. But each faculty can provide only the kinds of perspectives that are unique to it. The limitations lie in this fact. Although our minds can generate, in principle, an infinite number of meanings, they can come only in certain configurations, and they can contain only the semantic features available in a lexicon that relies on the innately fixed set of possible semantic features. This might seem to be an undue restriction on our cognitive capacities. Empiricists like to say so, suggesting that the bootstrapping of concepts and principles that they must rely on even for common sense understanding offers much greater potential for creativity and invention. But, Chomsky points out, the restriction is really an advantage. For without this extraordinary native endowment of items that serve human interests, we could not develop the rich, structured domains of experience we do. We would not be able to develop, individually or culturally. We would not be able to create unless we had this endowment. The empiricists' picture of a virtually empty mind, or even of a mind that has some endowments, but not those highly specific and anthropocentric ones offered by the language faculty, makes no sense at all of human achievement. The rationalist picture does.

3

Poverty, Creativity, and Making the World

We have seen how a biological rationalist maps the human mind. In this chapter we look at the basic observations – the poverty of stimulus and creativity observations – that justify this picture of the mind and also set the task for a science of language. The way the science of language solves the task set for it by the observations is dealt with in chapters 4–6. The overall result is an internalist, nativist, and constructivist view of mind and its relationship to the world. This is an unusual, perhaps even a heretical, combination today. But it was not always so.

A caveat: I call them "observations," but really the poverty and creativity facts are observational generalizations – simple general-izations from easily observed and observable instances. Some would dispute calling them observations at all, usually because they want to save the term "observation" for something that is reported through a very restricted set of terms, such as color and shape terms. (Some empiricists are examples of this.) By observation I mean something that anyone with common sense, with no special training or instruction, could easily make. They are obvious facts that any serious theory of a mind or a natural language must account for, on pain of failing to be a serious scientific theory at all. No one assumes, of course, that dealing with these observations is the *only* thing that a theory must do to be an adequate theory of a natural language, or of mind with language in it. A theory must also completely describe its domain, be articulate, economical, formal, and so on – standard conditions on anything that goes by the name of science. Not every theory of every domain will always have some easily made common sense observation(s) that the theory must deal with: a theory of bonding in chemistry, for example, does not (or the connection with common sense observations is so circuitous that it is not worth mentioning). But when the subject matter of the science is language and mind, and if minds affect the ways people think and behave, it is not surprising that such observations exist.

It is important to emphasize that they are both observations and relevant. Empiricists, perhaps upset that such observations make nonsense of their views, might claim that they are not common sense observations but artifacts of the developed theory – that they are theory-laden claims selected by Chomsky to make his approach look like the right one. It might also be claimed that there are, or could be, other observations that should be taken to be more basic clues to the nature of mind. The second claim can be dismissed. No one has come up with other observations and shown that they somehow trump the ones Chomsky focuses on, and saying that there "might be" more fundamental observations is, as it stands, a desperate maneuver. As to the idea that these are not observations but theory-laden claims – in effect, denying Chomsky a reason to appeal to them to rule out other approaches – I say more below. But it is *prima facie* difficult to think of them as 'theoretical'. Making them does not require familiarity with recondite theory or instrumentation. Anyone can do it. Only common sense – with which all human beings are endowed – is needed, plus a couple of hints about where to look. These are not the educated observations of the specially qualified scientist-expert. It helps, of course, to have no prior commitment to the idea that they *must* be wrong because they undermine fondly held externalist and anti-nativist (empiricist) views.

Plato, rationalists, and Chomsky's nativism

Relying upon poverty of stimulus observations to support arguments in favor of innate ideas and innate capacities is as old as Plato. In the *Meno* Plato portrays a slave-boy who, without explicit instruction in arithmetic or geometry but with prompting from Socrates, comes to understand – that is, apply correctly to the relevant instances – concepts used in the Pythagorean Theorem, such as <u>right triangle</u>, <u>line</u>, <u>right angle</u>, <u>area</u>, <u>hypotenuse</u>, and the like. The boy did not understand, and had not been instructed in the use of, these concepts beforehand; he had had no training in their application in the theorem, or in other geometric principles. Nor was he explicitly instructed in them (and he did not have the prior training to understand such instruction anyway). Socrates' diagrams and questions thus constitute an impoverished stimulus for what the boy learned or came to understand. Yet Plato points out that, despite all this, it took the boy a very short time, with no more guidance than Socrates' questions, to understand. Plato's aim is to show that the slave-boy did not *learn* the theorem or the concepts required to understand it, but had in some way already known them. All that Socrates did in the way of 'instruction' was to trigger this implicit knowledge and make it come to apply. ('Trigger' is modern terminology, intended to suggest that Socrates' questions were only the occasion for the boy to develop his understanding; they did not somehow impart the knowledge.) As Socrates put it, he did not place the concepts in the slave-boy's mind but served as midwife to concepts already there. Midwifery is not creation, but encouragement and aid.

To convince his audience that these concepts must be innate, Socrates counts on surprising it with the rapidity with which the slave-boy manages to understand, without instruction or any other form of "learning procedure." For rhetorical reasons, this surprise is easiest to elicit in a case that seems to require a rich, highly specific, 'abstract' kind of knowledge; the Pythagorean Theorem is clearly a good case. It requires knowledge of the concept of a right triangle (but not use of the *sounds* "right triangle") and also these concepts: <u>side</u>, <u>right angle</u>, <u>line</u>, <u>length</u>. ... It also requires knowledge of how these concepts apply to instances, for it is a specific claim about *triangles* that *have a right angle*. And these triangles are *abstract* "objects of knowledge." They seem to be beyond the range of an untutored slave-boy.

To see why richness, complexity, and abstractness are important, consider a case in which Socrates tries to convince an audience that because the slave-boy could discriminate things in terms of their colors, his color concepts must be innate. If the task set the boy were to discriminate between a yellow and a blue triangle, few would be prompted to think "Oh, you're right. He did not know about color discrimination before, so it must be innate." That is because color concepts are (incorrectly) assumed to be simple and non-complex. This may be one reason some empiricists are willing to concede, correctly, that color concepts are innate. Plato wants to say that *triangle* is just like colors are.[1] Chomsky wants to add: so are <u>chase</u>, <u>persuade</u>, <u>water</u>, and <u>for</u>.

The move from "Notice how short a time it takes to bring the slave-boy to understand the theorem" to "the concepts must be innately specified" does not follow the traditional form for an argument from observations to support for a hypothesis. There is no hypothesis, "Aha, maybe all ravens are black," followed by supporting evidence, perhaps in the form of instances ("This raven is black," "That raven is black"), and the conclusion, ". . . and so, in all probability, all ravens are black." It is closer to what philosophers call an "inference to the best explanation," but it is not that either. It is more like this: "Here's a very swift case of coming to understand and apply a concept that, given the structure and texture included in it – in this case, the concept of a right triangle and a lot more besides – is really quite surprising. Surely the only way to make sense of what occurred is to *assume* that the subject (the slave-boy) already knew the concepts he 'learned'." Innateness and the accompanying idea of implicit knowledge of a concept are assumptions needed to explain or make sense of the short-time poverty of the stimulus observation.

Jumping forward more than two millennia, Chomsky's favorite case of an innate idea is not a specific concept such as <u>right triangle</u> but natural language as a whole, with all its structure and detailed texture. The surprising fact is that by age five or six children are capable of what is virtually adult use of language. This change of example has several effects, two of which apparently reduce the force of the move from "observe this" to "we had better assume this" – although this can be remedied – but the third increases its force considerably and clearly offsets any attenuating effect of the others.

The first attenuating effect arises because there is so much confusion about what language is that Chomsky cannot count on an audience being surprised at a child's grasp of the highly abstract structure and extremely rich texture necessary in order to be said to know how to speak a language. Someone might think that languages are really quite simple and unstructured ("If I can understand it, . . ."), and hence that it cannot be *that* much of a problem to make sense of how a child comes to use language or understand a natural language. The remedy, of course, is to get people to recognize what a language is and what it contains. This need not be a matter of explaining what a language is in full in theoretical terms, but can involve making some simpler points about natural languages: for example, that they are structured ('abstract'). Most people will grant that languages have a phrasal structure, and that there are very few kinds of phrases: noun phrases ("the dog under the good table"), verb phrases ("scratches itself every few minutes"), prepositional phrases ("under the table"), adjective phrases ("good table"), and inflectional phrases, clauses, or sentences ("Albert is scratching the door"). There are no arbitrary parsings of sentences: "Albert door" is out, as is "hing the." And every clause in every language comes in one of a very few alternative forms; in some languages, the "head" of the phrase (a noun in the case of a noun phrase) is at the beginning of the phrase, in others, at the end. If a language allows relatively free variation in word placement, it has to indicate which words belong in a phrase in some other way. In Latin, for example, this is done with markings on the words. Chomsky often makes these points by using simple examples that show how obviously structure-dependent the principles and rules that relate one phrase or clause to another must be. That no child makes the mistake of saying "Is Albert who my dog is under the table?" indicates that a child's rich and specific implicit/innate knowledge must include the concept <u>main clause</u>, because the grammatical construction "Is Albert who is my dog under the table?" takes an 'is' from the *main* clause of "Albert, who is my dog, is under the table," not from just any clause, and not from the first. This and other cases bear out innate (but intrinsic) knowledge of linguistic structure, for otherwise children would produce (perhaps randomly) at least some non-grammatical constructions.[2] Phonology and phonetics, branches of linguistic science that deal with linguistic sounds, provide similar structural points and their lesson. Any English speaker, including the young child, recognizes that /pik/, /tik/, and /bic/ are possible sounds in English, even if they do not all have meanings associated with the sounds (/bic/), while also recognizing that /ftik/ is impossible (*CILT* 30). Indeed, there is evidence (Mehler and Christophe 1994) that infants a few days old who have been given minimal exposure to a particular language, such as Japanese or English, know that language's sounds and have already begun to develop that natural language rather than another. Since it is very difficult to claim that these infants have been taught a language, been 'socialized', or instructed, this is strong evidence in favor of phonological/phonetic innateness.

In addition to remedy by appeal to structure, one can appeal to richness. One can, for example, elucidate particular concepts: "Here is a particular lexical item [word], here is what you know about it, now let's see how long it took you to acquire it and thousands of others equally rich." One of Chomsky's favorite examples is the word "house" (1995: 20; *PP* 20–1). Aristotle used the same example (*Metaphysics* VIII, ch. 2), as did Cudworth. Chomsky points out that we all know that this and a large number of other terms are "container words," because we all know that when George tells us he is painting his house, our initial reaction is to think that he is painting the outside surface of the house. Moreover, the concept <u>house</u> has built into it the explanatory structure mentioned in chapter 1 (and outlined below). Similar moves can be made with virtually any lexical concept: such concepts are surprisingly rich.

The second attenuating effect of the shift to natural languages lies in the fact that it takes five or six years before children count as fully competent – that is, before they approximate adult competence – and it might seem that five or six years is plenty of time for a child to acquire a language without assuming that most of it is innately specified. Remedy again lies in pointing out how rich and uniquely structured language is, emphasizing how daunting a task learning a language in this time really is: the child needs the necessary concepts, and there is no plausible non-innate story to be told about how they could be learned in the relevant period.

To get a grip on the third effect of the move from one or a small number of concepts to a whole language, recall the *Meno* case. There we were dealing with a single person who in a short time and on the sole basis of impoverished stimuli came to understand the concepts required to make the calculations summarized by the Pythagorean Theorem; despite impoverished conditions, the boy quickly acquired understanding of a rich, abstract subject matter. When we shift the example to natural language, we move beyond a single example of a slave-boy on one occasion to all humans over the history of the species. Not all these individuals can be observed, of course, but many have been, and others can be. So we can make generalizations. We find that all children come to understand a (first) language or languages in a short time and proceed through various stages of development in the same order and at approximately the same rates. Specifically, if we look to see whether children acquire different languages at different rates, some acquiring a language by four, and others by ten, we find that they do not. If we explore whether children acquire different languages by going through stages of acquisition in different orders, we find they do not. If we check to see whether children of differing social status, differing IQ, and differing amounts of training acquire languages any faster or any differently, we find that, as a rule, they do not. We

can introduce other age-related, readily observable factors concerning development, such as when a child seems to lose the ability
to acquire a second language easily (at around nine or ten). And we
can provide crude generalizations concerning how much vocabulary a child acquires each day (a word per waking hour, from age
two to eight (1995: 15).[3]

The upshot here is that while shifting to the example of acquisition of natural languages requires saying something about what a
natural language is and calling attention to some facts about all
humans that, while easily discerned, people seem to overlook or
ignore, the richness and highly structured nature of the 'innate
idea' involved, and especially the fact that it develops in such a
uniform fashion across the human population, makes the argument
that such acquisition must be assumed to be innate all the more
compelling.

In the *Meno*, the poverty of the stimulus is apparent – Socrates
did not instruct the boy, but only elicited or triggered his responses
by questioning. He served as the occasion for the birth of the 'ideas'
right triangle, area, line, right angle, etc. The same is true in the case
of language, despite the widespread myth that children learn a language by associating a sound with a thing. According to the myth,
in the presence of Fido a parent says "dog," and the child learns the
word "dog" by being encouraged by the parent to associate it not
just with this three-dimensional, four-legged, furry experience, but
with similar Roveroid and Spotoid experiences, when "dog" is said
in the presence of Fido, plus Rover and Spot. That this view of learning is a myth becomes clear later in this chapter when I provide a
fuller understanding of what Chomsky's constructivism amounts
to and, in particular, its implications for relationships between
words and world. It will also be seen to be nonsense when we take
up Chomsky's view of a word. But none of this heavy machinery
is needed to see that it must be wrong. Let us assume that by the
time a child is six or so, he or she has a vocabulary of 13,000 words.[4]
(Words here are stems, such as "intelligible," not various affixed
forms ("unintelligible," "intelligibility," "unintelligibility," etc.);
children know, in principle, an infinite number of these.) Now ask
yourself how many times parents or others sit down with children
and go through the routine I described above with "dog." It would
be very surprising if anyone could honestly answer, "Several thousand." But if the myth made sense, even several thousand might
allow for only a few hundred words; no one who thinks that
"dog" – Fido training correctly describes how children learn a lan-

guage assumes that a child will be able to pick up a vocabulary item in a single try. This picture of vocabulary learning requires constant attention and training – as behaviorists have always insisted, children have to be encouraged and discouraged over several "trials." Suppose the child looked at Fido and, rather than associating "dog" with <u>dog</u>, associated it instead with <u>has a tail</u>, and begins to use "dog" to speak of horses and kangaroos. And there are indefinitely many other associations that one could imagine, which would require that the child be discouraged and redirected. Moreover, on the model supposed by the myth, children – even those in the same linguistic community – should learn different words at different times, and learn them at different rates. In reality, we find that children all acquire words at approximately the same rate. The idea that they are brought to approximately adult competence by the training efforts of those who have already acquired a language is a myth.

The myth does, however, have a small element of truth in it. When acquiring a vocabulary item, children have to associate a sound (which can be phonetically characterized) with a meaning (which can be described in terms of semantic and formal features), and while typically they make this association in a way that allows them to communicate with others in their speech communities, they need not, for any sound available in a natural language can be associated with any meaning. This unconstrained association of sound and meaning is what Chomsky calls "Saussurean arbitrariness," reflecting the obvious fact about human languages that sounds and meanings can be put together in various pairings. The same meaning represented in the concept <u>house</u> appears in English speakers associated with the sound "house," in French with the sound "maison," Spanish "casa," and German "Haus." So some sort of association has to be effected. However, the myth is wrong in almost every other respect. There is no training; the myth misconceives what gets associated with what; and the associated items are innately specified. In order to build into a lexicon the association desirable for a child's community, the child need only – often on a single occasion – associate a sound provided within his or her phonetic group with a meaning that he or she already has available. This one-off (or small number) association works only if both human linguistic sounds and the meanings themselves are innately specified. While Saussurean arbitrariness recognizes that, in the case of a single lexical item, the child must associate a sound with a meaning, recognizing this does not suggest that in "learning a word" in this

sense (the sound–meaning pairing in the child's speech community), the child must also somehow figure out what the sound is,
what the meaning, and what the association. He or she just associates two innately specified items, both – sound and meaning –
inside the head.

To embellish the case for an impoverished stimulus in the case
of language, consider how comparatively rare errors are in a child's
speech, for the child typically begins to produce grammatically
correct ("well-formed" is problematic, because philosophers give it
an inappropriate use; "non-crashing" is best) expressions immediately and with very few errors. And often when errors do appear,
they in fact support innateness, as most instances involve a
child applying general rules and making an 'error' only because
usage demands irregularity. The child says, "Jeremy bringed it yesterday." The parent says, "No, brought." The eager-to-please child
says, "Oh, Jeremy *bringed* it yesterday." In this case – the child's
"bringed" follows the phonological rule for English that one adds
"ed" to form a past tense verb – the child's expressions are more
regular than the adult's, and are incorrect only according to a speech
community (or, at least, to "preferred usage" within a speech community). The fact that he or she cannot be discouraged from applying the rule underscores the case for innateness and against
training. If the training myth applied, surely the eager-to-please
child's supposedly plastic mind would be more modifiable.

Following Plato, some of the rationalists in the seventeenth
through early nineteenth centuries also contributed to arguments
for innateness. Unlike Plato, whom Chomsky does not discuss in
detail, rationalists such as Descartes, Cordemoy, and Cudworth
play a prominent role in his writings. He discusses their work in
considerable detail, especially in *Cartesian Linguistics*, and often uses
quotations from their work in both his philosophical and relatively
informal linguistic writings to make his point, suggesting that it
is not necessary to improve upon what was already recognized
several centuries ago. He has explicitly said that his work revital-
izes this tradition, thereby suggesting that much intervening work
in linguistics has been misguided.

These earlier rationalists contributed to discussions of innateness
in two ways. First, some of them attempted to construct a universal grammar that could capture the mental processes that all
humans use when they produce linguistic expressions – a grammar
that could also, in principle, describe particular languages. This
project was carried out in useful and interesting detail largely by

the Port Royal grammarians and their intellectual progeny in France during the seventeenth and eighteenth centuries. Less detailed and formal, but interesting and suggestive, contributions were made to the project by the German linguist Wilhelm von Humboldt during the early nineteenth century. Chomsky's work has ties to both efforts. In *Cartesian Linguistics* Chomsky suggests some close parallels between the work of the Port Royal grammarians and his own work in transformational grammar at the time (1966). In some respects, however, the basic commitments of his recent Minimalist Program more closely echo Humboldt's provocative but informal suggestions.

For both Chomsky and the Port Royal grammarians, one of the most important matters to decide in constructing a universal grammar (or for the Port Royalists, a "philosophical grammar") is how to deal with the fact that while languages sound different from each other and display some differences in phrasal structure, they can nevertheless be thought to be variants of the same fundamental scheme. For the Port Royalists, and for Chomsky for a short period in his early work, one plausible answer was to introduce "levels" of representation in the grammar and suggest that at one level, which Chomsky called "Deep Structure," languages are in important respects the same. This is the level at which meaning is represented (suggesting, as Chomsky seems always to have held, that meanings are universal). At another level – Chomsky called it "Surface Structure" – languages differ. The basic idea is that languages are the same in meanings but differ in sounds and surface form, and that a grammar links one level to the other. A transformational grammar states the "transformational rules" that connect Deep to Surface structures. Another part of the grammar – which Chomsky called a "phrase structure grammar" – would show how to generate deep structure representations for individual sentences, resulting in an overall grammar for a particular language that puts together deep structures (meanings) and, through transformations linking these to surface structures (sounds), shows how universal elements get the particular phonetic and syntactic "shapes" (sounds, clausal structure, tense markings, case assignment markers, . . .) that they have in English as opposed to Miskito. The differing ways in which languages deal with case marking (nominative case or "subject," accusative case or "direct object," and oblique case (dative, genitive, ablative, . . .) so that a speaker of that language knows who or what in a sentence is said to be doing something (subject), and to which or what he or she or it is doing it (object) was one of the topics under discussion. Another was relative clause formation. Arnauld was among those who made contributions to a transformational grammar in the Port Royal grammar (1660) and in his *Logique* (1662). In the next century these and others issues were further explored by several other philosopher-grammarians, including Du Marsais (1729) and Beauzée (1767).

The attempt to construct a philosophical grammar made considerable progress, although Chomsky notes (*CL* 57–8) that it lacked "a theory of linguistic structure that is articulated with sufficient precision and is sufficiently rich to bear the burden of justification." Lack of sufficient precision is remedied in recent linguistics by making the theory of universal grammar mathematical and formal; this also makes it much more nearly descriptively adequate, for it provides the machinery needed to show how through recursive procedures a system can produce the boundless numbers of expressions or sentences that are available in a natural language. Richness is provided by detailed accounts of phonological (sound-related), formal (noun, verb, etc.), and semantic features, along with an account of how these enter the computational system. Adding these also helps provide for explanatory adequacy – which, in addition to descriptive adequacy, is crucial for justification. As Chomsky glosses the issue of explanatory adequacy in his early work, it is a matter of showing why "just these and not other descriptions are selected by the child acquiring the language or the linguist describing it, *on the basis of the data available to them*" (*CL* 58; emphasis added). (The more recent and improved approach to "solving Plato's problem" – as Chomsky now speaks of it – by appeal to parameters is mentioned below and discussed in the next chapter.) The emphasized phrase should be read "the impoverished data available." From the beginning, Chomsky saw that explanatory adequacy required a formal theory that could show how a child can acquire a rich and highly structured language in a short time, given a very thin data set.

If one had a successful Universal Grammar (UG) in hand, it would be very difficult for empiricist critics to deny that every child who acquires any of the 6,000 or so natural languages under poverty of stimulus conditions is able to do so only because this UG is innate. An innate UG easily makes sense of the short-time, same-time facts; it explains why there is uniformity in this respect across the human population. There have been some empiricist attempts to at least take these facts seriously and provide an alternative explanation. Hilary Putnam (1967) tried this, as well as Nelson

Goodman (1967), but both efforts miss the point. In order to explain uniformity, they assume that all languages must have branched from a single Ur-language, and they suggest that commonalities among languages be explained by common inheritance – through inculturation (in effect, training) by a community – from a single source. They fail, of course, to make any sense of how, with empiricist-understood training procedures, even one child could have acquired any one of these languages, not to mention the Ur-language they need to insist upon. And if they are generously but unreasonably allowed their hypothesis, their "single common origin" offers nothing to make sense of the actual, observed facts about how languages differ – that they differ in systematic ways in phonology and basic syntactic structure but not in meaning. Take the phrasal structure that every language exhibits. While it varies, it varies in only a very small number of configurations, and some of this small number of variations covary with other differences, which also appear in a small number of configurations. Since the early 1980s, Chomsky has argued that a UG equipped with para-meters (*LPK* 16, 25f) explains this easily. Each possible parametric variation in structure is set by a 'switch'. Some of these parameters are independent of others; in other cases, having set one, a few others may also have to be set. This model of a UG also makes it easy to see how a child could, at a very early age, readily acquire the clausal structure of one language as opposed to another that differs in clausal structure. A child who acquires Japanese as opposed to English need only set a single 'switch' to provide for the difference between a head-initial language (English, French, where the verb in a verb phrase precedes the direct object) and a head-final language (Japanese, where the verb in a verb phrase generally appears after the direct object). Empiricists who suggest a common origin do not deal with the fact that there are so few possible variations in clausal structure, or (of course) the fact that these vari-ations are as systematically interrelated as they sometimes are. In fact, it is difficult to conceive of how the empiricist could provide a plausible account of phrasal/clausal structure at all. A system that lacked it would be 'simpler' in several respects. It turns out, though, that many such 'simpler' systems are impossible to learn (cf. 1995: 15–16).

Nor can the empiricist make sense of evidence that children can acquire a language that satisfies principles of UG even if *no one* in his or her speech community produces expressions that satisfy UG principles. Very interesting cases are those presented by deaf children born to deaf parents who do not themselves have a signing language that fully satisfies UG. Such deaf adults are not rare: often, they were not exposed to signing when young, perhaps because they had partial hearing at the time, or because they were discouraged from signing, or because there was no signing community, and thus they lacked the necessary triggering experiences to acquire a full linguistic structure within the relevant and biologically limited time frame of human language acquisition. Nevertheless, as adults they often learn to sign from others who 'speak' a standard sign language – A(merican) S(ign) L(anguage), for example. What they learn is rarely fully fluent. Worse, it often fails to meet the principles of UG, even if it serves for communication: if the parents 'learn' ASL, they sign a mangled form of it. They use this communication system in the presence of their deaf children, of course, perhaps encouraging them to use it too. The fascinating outcome is that the children, with no more prompting than the impoverished and mangled stimuli their parents' *non-UG* signing provides, automatically and quickly develop a sign language that satisfies the principles of UG and does everything that any natural language can. In one reported case, a child produced a far more fluent ASL than his parents.[5] Obviously, nothing like training takes place here. The myth does not make sense: the parents (who do not have mastery of ASL) cannot be said to know what they are 'teaching'. They do not know what to correct or encourage. The only plausible assumption is that UG is innate, and that it takes very little to trigger the development of a natural language that conforms to it in a young child.

Reflecting on the case so far for innateness, it should be apparent that it is not just the abstract (structured) character of natural languages that suggests that they are innate. Their universality plays a crucial role. This is implicit in the observations themselves – *everyone* (uneducated slave-boy, Chomsky) acquires a natural language readily and at about the same time. Universality also plays a role when one argues for innateness by appealing to the richness of natural languages. Again, the rationalists of the seventeenth to early nineteenth century recognized this. They offered detailed discussions of individual concepts such as triangle, house, and give, each of which can be seen to specify the meaning of a particular word or lexical item. Their aim was to show that these concepts must come pre-specified in the mind, for there is no way to imagine learning them; nor can one attribute them to sensory faculties, which can at most be expected to provide an occasion for the mind to mobilize an idea that it already has available to it. The ideas provided by sensation are far too impoverished (colors, pitches, felt textures, bitterness, odors) to yield the complex, rich ideas or concepts triangle, house and give.

In fact, Descartes made sensation out to be *really* impoverished; it does not even provide colors and sounds. Geometric concepts such as triangle plus many of what might these days be called the sensory and affective qualities – colors, figures, sounds, and pains – are discussed in his work in connection with an account of vision and of what the mind must have available to it beforehand in order to discern geometric things with these properties. In Haldane and Ross's translation of Descartes' *Notes Directed against a Certain Program*, for example, Descartes speaks (442–3) of the "limitations of the senses" and wants to convince us that none of the "ideas of things, in the shape in which we envisage them by thought" can come directly from the senses. For, he says, "nothing reaches our mind from external objects through the organs of sense beyond certain corporeal movements." Yet "even these movements, and the figures that arise from them, are not conceived by us in the shape they assume in the organs of sense, but because they transmitted something which gave the mind occasion to form these ideas, by means of an innate faculty" (cf. *CL* 66–7). The motion of the organs is only the occasion for the idea to arise in a particular case; the idea itself must come from elsewhere – an innate source. Some of Descartes' discussion presupposes his concept of material objects and the application of his contact mechanics to a picture of the organs of sense, so must be taken with a grain of salt (cf. *PP* 1f). But the basic point remains valid: it is very difficult to explain where 'ideas' of figure and motion, color, and the rest come from, unless from the innately specified mind, by an innate faculty. A modern version of Descartes' argument might locate colors in certain kinds of neurophysiological events, but would point out that these events are in the head and are characteristic of members of a species that has the right kind of neurophysiological machinery to produce (generate) them. The basic Platonic argument that emphasizes the impoverished stimulus and the rich 'idea' would remain the same. Furthermore, Descartes observes, this kind of argument is even more obviously correct when it comes to "common notions" such as equality and abstract and "perfect" notions such as triangle. In no case is it conceivable that these notions or ideas have instances within the senses themselves. They must be brought by our minds to a perceptual situation, where they are then applied.

Ralph Cudworth (cf. *CL* 67f; 1997), onetime master of Christ's College, Cambridge, generalizes these moves to all concepts. His primary aim was to show that moral concepts such as <u>good</u> and <u>right</u> are innately determined. He saw that a good way to convince people that <u>good</u> and <u>just</u> are innate might be to first convince them that all sorts of ideas that they might have otherwise conceived to be learned from experience must also be innate. For, living in a time in which "Debauchery, Scepticism, and Infidelity . . . flourished," encouraged in this by "the [false] Doctrine of the Fatal Necessity of all Actions and Events" (as the preface to his 1731 posthumous *A Treatise Concerning Eternal and Immutable Morality* (hereafter *TEIM*) notes), Cudworth was well aware that convincing people of the innateness of <u>good</u> might be difficult. So he shows that many of the concepts for natural objects (<u>tree</u>, <u>horse</u>, <u>water</u>), artifacts (<u>house</u>, <u>table</u>, <u>watch</u>), and actions and states (<u>give</u>, <u>like</u>) must be innate, for they could not have been provided by the senses. The *Treatise* adopts a concept of sensation not unlike Descartes' impoverished and 'mechanical' one. He remarks that a thing outside the head offers some sort of causal relationship "nothing at all but Local Motion or Pressure" which provides the occasion for the "Awakening and Exciting of the Inward Active Powers of the Mind" (*TEIM* 99–100). These active powers do all the work in providing knowledge of the world. The concepts that are required to describe things perceived, such as <u>house</u>, <u>dog</u>, and <u>water</u>, cannot come from the senses alone; nor can they come from some sort of unspecified learning powers (a "strange Chymistry" (*TEIM* 147)) that just happens to mysteriously produce them. They must be innately specified in some way, for they all involve ideas that can come only from the intellect, because only the intellect "raises and excites within itself" not only "Figure, Colour, Magnitude and Motions," but "the Intelligible Ideas of Cause, Effect, Means, End, Priority and Posteriority, Equality and Inequality, Order and Proportion, Symmetry and Asymmetry, Aptitude and Inaptitude, Sign and Thing signified, Whole and Part, in a manner all the Logical and Relative Notions there are" (*TEIM* 154–5).

The surprise that the nativist counts upon to convince others of innateness depends not only on demonstrating to audiences the poverty of the stimulus, but also on emphasizing the richness and/ or abstractness (structured character) of the concept. Cudworth achieves this by asking if a beast with sensory capacities like ours could see what we see when it looked at a watch or a house. It could not, he suggests, not only because the machinery of sense available is inadequate, but because the idea or concept is much too rich and structured. He says:

> As for Example, an House or Palace is not only Stone, Brick, Mortar, Timber, Iron, Glass, heaped together; but the Very Essence and Formal *Reason* of it is made up of Relative or Schetical Notions, it being a certain Disposition of those several Materials into a Whole or Collection, consisting of several Parts, Rooms, Stairs, Passages, Doors, Chimneys, Windows, convenient for Habitation, and fit for the several Uses of Men; in which there is the Logick of Whole and Parts, Order, Proportion, Symmetry, Aptitude, Concinnity, all complicated with Wood, Stone, Iron and Glass, as it were informing and adorning the Rude and Confused Mass of Matter, and making it both beautiful and Serviceable. (*TEIM* 168)

Cudworth's plausible description of the surprisingly rich concept house can be supplemented with contemporary points about the "Logick" of the concept that help make sense of why when people speak of painting their houses, the first thing that comes to mind is that they are painting the outsides of their houses. In contemporary terms, it is because 'house' is a container word. Even more important, this description of this specific concept or "idea" should be supplemented with descriptions of other concepts, and an effort should be made to find common structure. When this is done, it turns out that this concept shares an explanatory structure with many other concepts that are expressed by nouns. The compelling result is that the various features that make up Cudworth's description of the concept house slot into categories that look a lot like Aristotle's four "causes" – answers to what something is made of, how it came to be, what it is for, and what its essence is. The features Cudworth lists provide these answers, for they say what things described by the concept house are made of ("Stone, Brick, Mortar, Timber, Iron, Glass") and what their function is, or what they are for ("convenient for Habitation, and fit for the several Uses of Men"). How they come about is simply assumed and can be taken to be implied by many of the features: houses are made by human beings, or are artifacts. Saying what their essence or formal definition is, is more difficult, as has been recognized since Aristotle's time. For our purposes, though, since this concept will be asked to play a role in a generative theory of natural languages, we can say that its formal definition (which will include information that determines how it produces compound meanings when combined with other concepts, as with small house) should be provided by the theory of how it does it. If Chomsky is right, the theory must slot this concept, along with thousands of others, into the lexicon of a formal generative grammar that describes a state of Universal Grammar and attempts to deal scientifically with the way in which a biologically based innate faculty in the human mind brings all the features and structure mentioned above to bear when placed with features of other lexical items. This anachronistic theoretical note about the lexicon, its features, and their computational roles aside, Chomsky can and does take over much of what Cudworth, Herbert, Descartes, and other rationalists had to say about various innately specified individual concepts.

While the case for the innateness of individual concepts seems strong in part because of their richness and complex structure, this very richness and complexity, as well as the fact that centuries of work have shown how difficult it is to produce a formal definition of a concept, suggest that it will not be easy to provide a formal theory of a natural language that describes these concepts and shows how they can be combined with others to produce the complex concepts that are the meanings of sentences. Nevertheless, there has been considerable progress in constructing descriptions of concepts within what is called "lexical semantics" (e.g., Pustejovsky 1995), in constructing formal syntactic theories that show how these individual concepts can be combined, and in showing how to conceive of the whole project.[6] Arguably, in addition to introducing formal syntactic theories and constantly improving them, showing how to conceive of the whole project may be Chomsky's greatest contribution. That is why the poverty of stimulus and creativity observations are so important. They not only support Chomsky's nativism, internalism, and constructivism, but help indicate what can and cannot be accomplished in building a theory of the mind.

The creative aspect of language use

Descartes should be credited with first highlighting the observations that Chomsky packages and calls "the creative aspect of language use." Not only did he make the observations and tell others about them, he set up the conditions that made the observations relevant and important. He introduced them in a context in which it was clear that they bore directly on what it is to be human – in a test for mind that he and others thought showed that human beings differ both from other organisms, such as parrots and apes, and from machines that have been constructed to try to simulate humans' normal language use. They differ because human language use is creative.

Descartes hypothesized that the difference between humans on the one hand and machines and other organisms on the other consists in the fact that humans have minds, while machines and other organisms do not. Humans can use language creatively only because their linguistic production is the result of the operation of a mind that only they have. The particular form of his explanation for why humans pass the test and machines and other animals do not turned out to be wrong – largely because of the way Descartes understood human minds and bodies. Furthermore, he let his misguided concept of the mind and its operations lead him to introduce a second test that is question begging, at best. The creativity test and the observations on which it is based seem to be correct, however, and remain valid today. While there have been many efforts in the intervening centuries to prove otherwise, it still looks as though nothing besides human beings, including computers, uses language in a way that is clearly *both* innovative and appropriate – that is stimulus-free, unbounded, and yet (recognizably) appropriate to circumstances. Efforts to show that there are, or could be, animals or machines that do, or might, pass the creativity test for mind – examples in recent years include the chimpanzee Nim Chimpsky and computers programmed to simulate human speech – have not come close.

If discovery implies uncovering something that was hidden and inaccessible before, then Descartes did not discover that human language use is creative (innovative and appropriate). But he was one of the first to recognize the importance of these observations. Until approximately his time, there was no serious threat to the idea that human beings are free agents with minds and natures very different from everything else in the world. Both the myth of special creation – that God created the world, then plants and animals, and then, separately and as the capstone to his efforts, human beings – and the lack of a serious challenge from the sciences, then in a very primitive state, supported it. By Descartes' time, however, divine assurances that humans are unique had begun to be taken less seriously, and a reasonably well-founded scientific framework had begun to develop. Descartes, a scientist-philosopher, contributed a great deal to this framework, both in physics and in physiology, extending his "mechanical philosophy" to explain much of how human beings work. Through what we would call "neurophysiology," he provided a way to describe the activities of human beings conceived of as mechanical devices. His scientific work thus helped to establish the mechanical philosophy that challenged the idea that human beings really are a 'thing apart.' He was, then, in an excellent position to recognize the importance of observations that seemed to show that humans are indeed different, and to do this in a way that anyone could recognize.

Descartes' discussion of 'the human difference' appears at the end of part V of his *Discourse on Method*. Much of what leads up to this discussion is devoted to explaining the details of the scientific work in mechanics, geometry, and physiology that he had done over several years. He thought that he had demonstrated – and, by the standards of the science of the day, he had – that the universe is a machine that obeys the principles of a contact mechanics. Intuitively, his model of a physical system was approximately what one would expect a nineteenth-century engineer to produce if asked to show how things work – rigid rods and fluids push and pull the things of the world. Things – that is, all things in the universe – work in the way that the mechanical devices that are built by human beings do, obeying all the principles of a contact mechanics, and apparently only these. The same, Descartes held, is true of the behavior of living organisms. He was aware of the role of receptors and nerves in perception, for example, and produced a detailed account of how sight and touch operated in terms of the impact of outside objects on receptors and on transmission of these impulses to the brain. The brain could be thought of as a mechanical device that "processes information," as we say today – perhaps along the lines of the mechanical calculators of not long ago, or Babbage's nineteenth-century calculating engine. It is just a complicated machine that mediates between sensory input and the movements of the organism, and it too obeys no laws but those of mechanics. If the mechanical philosophy is correct, and organisms are nothing but very complicated machines, all the behavior of organisms should be describable and predictable by appeal to mechanical categories and principles.

The mechanical philosophy cannot, however, deal with all the behavior exhibited by all organisms, for at least some human activities seem to be subject to a different principle, that of creativity. Ordinary use of language is the paradigm case. Unlike the artistic creativity that only some seem capable of, and unlike other forms of human activity that seem to be dependent upon particular talents, skills, or high intelligence, everyone is capable of linguistic creativity, and everyone exhibits it. It serves, then, as a good test for the kind of mind that *all* and *only* human beings have.

Descartes described three observations which he thought were relevant to this creativity, all of which anyone with common sense could make. (In outlining them, I adapt Descartes' language to the terminology that Chomsky uses.) First, there seems to be no strict correlation or one-to-one mapping between a person's circumstances (sitting at the breakfast table reading the paper, for example) and what issues from that person's mouth ("How many times did Mary remind us to be on time?" "I wonder what kind of tree to put in the corner," etc.) *Prima facie*, people's linguistic productions are not tied to circumstance; no one expects that, given a particular circumstance, anyone, or even a single individual, will always say the same thing. Chomsky calls this "stimulus freedom," meaning that what a person says is not tied to any particular stimulus or class of stimuli, or, in fact, to stimuli at all. Some 'theoretical' conclusions seem to follow from this observation: there is no reason to think that there is a causal relationship between environment and speech production. Furthermore, there is no reason to think that there is a causal theory that links circumstances and words. The conclusions are not needed to make the observations, however.

Second, the words that issue from a person's mouth, while all recognizably (say) English and usually understandable, come in any number of combinations of several varieties of construction with any of thousands of words. *Prima facie*, then, there is no reason to expect an upper bound on either the number or the multiplicity of combinations of understandable different words and structures that a person can produce. Call this "unboundedness." For Chomsky, this suggests that if we have both unlimited numbers and understandability, the generation of the sentences of languages proceeds by various generative principles, including recursive principles. This is a plausible theoretical explanation of the observation, but again, it is not needed to make the observation, and the observation seems to be one that anyone with common sense could make.

Third, while stimulus-free and, by implication, not tied to circumstance by any causal principles, and apparently unbounded in number, people's linguistic outputs are nevertheless typically recognizably *appropriate* to the circumstances in which they are produced. This observation notes that while what someone says may occasionally strike you as odd, it is rarely, if ever, loony. If the multiplicity of words in various combinations that people produce is not coherent and appropriate to circumstances at first pass, we try to make them so in any number of ways, by adjusting our inter-pretation of what is said, our understanding of the circumstances (perhaps we are dealing with a fictional context, for example), our understanding of the other's beliefs, and so on. Throughout, one presumes that people "say things for a reason"; it is only when we have exhausted our resources that we declare something truly out of bounds. This feature of the creative aspect of language use – (rec-ognizable) appropriateness where there is no reason to think that there is any form of causal correlation between what a person says and the circumstances in which he or she says them – proves to be the most impenetrable and intractable to theory: it is hard to know what to do with it. Perhaps we should just take it to be a result of human freedom and creativity – an explanation, of sorts, although clearly not needed to make the observation.

These three observations constitute Descartes' first test for mind. In his terms and focusing on machines, not animals, a machine would have to "use words, or put together other signs, as we do in order to declare our thoughts to others." Specifically, it would have to "produce different arrangements of words so as to give an appro-priately meaningful answer to whatever is said in its presence, as the dullest of men can do" (1637: 140). I take up this test below.

Descartes also introduced a second test for mind, one that Chomsky does not adopt. It is instructive to see why he does not. Descartes held that a machine, though it might "do some things as well as we do them, or perhaps even better, . . . would inevitably fail in others, which would reveal that [it was] acting not through understanding, but only from the disposition of [its] organs. For whereas reason is a universal instrument which can be used in all kinds of situations, these organs need some particular disposition for each particular action; hence it is for all practical purposes impossible for a machine to have enough different organs to make it act in all the contingencies of life in the way in which our reason makes us act" (1637: 140). Quite clearly, Descartes assumes that the human mind can do anything machines (and creatures with other kinds of cognitive capacities) can, and more that they cannot. And he adds that the human mind seems to be a "universal instrument"; it seems reasonable to gloss this as holding that reason can solve any problem.

He is wrong on both counts. First, the human mind cannot do things that some machines and some animals do. To take some trivial examples, sufficiently powerful computers can use brute-strength elimination of cases to solve the four-color topological mapping problem; the European starling can navigate visually and automatically by the stars at night; and it seems that pigeons – hardly the most intelligent of beasts – can (because their eyes and visual systems are not just "more powerful" but *different* from ours) detect finer-grained color gratings than we will ever be able to – that is, they can make finer discriminations between colored lines than we can.

Second, and more important, the human mind is not a 'universal instrument'. The idea that the mind can solve any problem does not demand that reason come up with easy or ready solutions to problems. If it demanded this, reason's scope would obviously be limited to a familiar part of the common sense world, at best, a world in which even a small child can usually navigate with confidence. Nor does it require that the reasoning procedures employed be transparent and readily formalized; if it did, reason in the form of science would be favored, for the sciences taken as theories of the world are in fact *very* much more articulated than common sense understanding, and the domains that sciences deal with are *much* simpler in structure and interrelationships than the common sense world. Assuming that reason includes both science and common sense, the claim requires that there be no problem for which the mind in science *or* common sense is inadequate. If so, (Chomsky points out) Descartes contradicts himself when he claims universality of scope. For, while he claims that reason is a universal instrument, he also claims to observe (I quote Chomsky in an entry on Descartes in the *Oxford Companion to the Mind*)

> that we may not "have intelligence enough" to comprehend the creative aspect of language use and other kinds of free choice and action, though "we are so conscious of the liberty and indifference which exist in us that there is nothing that we comprehend more clearly and perfectly," and "it would be absurd to doubt that of which we inwardly experience and perceive as existing within ourselves" just because it lies beyond our comprehension.

If this contradicts the universality claim (as it seems to), and if we can choose at most one of the two, surely the observation that free action is beyond the powers of reason is right, so that there is at least one problem with which reason cannot deal. (No doubt there are others, but this is the relevant one.) That reason cannot deal with freedom is shown by the fact that neither common sense (whether in the relatively systematic form found in the social sciences or not) nor science (in any of its developed forms) have made any progress in 'solving' it. So, even though Descartes' second test was wrong and we lack universality, this fact along with lack of progress in explaining freedom suggests strongly that humans are free – a result that Descartes took to be obvious, that Chomsky wants, and that the first test shows.

Why did Descartes come to the conclusion that the mind is a universal device? One reason might be that he firmly believed that reason could in principle deal with any problem in any domain; enthusiasm about the powers of the human mind was not uncommon in Enlightenment times, and it is still taken seriously by many: it is an article of faith among those who assume that science will somehow, some day, come to the one final theory of the world that explains and describes everything. Another possible reason for his view is hinted at above: the human mind, with its various faculties, deals readily with the common sense world. It operates, often effortlessly, in a diverse and only loosely related set of circumstances, proving to be a reliable device for helping us survive, and sometimes thrive, in the helter-skelter of ordinary life, for the common sense world is not the uniformly structured world of a serious science. Because it does well in the common sense domain, the mind can easily appear to be a reasonably good general-purpose device. It can, then, be easily forgotten that it is not just outdone but fails completely outside this domain except in those cases – also limited by our cognitive capacities and by no means natively enabled to the extent that common sense knowledge is – where science seems to be able to get a grip. This points, of course, to the crucial difference between Chomsky's biological form of rationalism and Descartes'. If the mind is biologically based, it is limited. But it is still creative and free. Like the Cartesians, we may be "incited and inclined" to do things by circumstance, but we are not caused to act.

The first test for mind does not suffer from enthusiasms and misconceptions; in fact, in the form of what is often called the "Turing test" applied to machines, and in the form of the tests applied to apes which experimenters attempt to train to 'speak' human natural languages, it is still the test of choice. Let us look at the machine case first. The term "Turing test" labels a procedure devised by Alan Turing, a British mathematician, who suggested that machines be compared to humans through a test that explored the extent to which a machine might convince humans that they are dealing with another human. Specifically, he suggested getting humans to judge whether they were 'conversing' with a human or a machine by communicating through terminals with both, although the person who makes the judgment is not told which terminal has a human on the other side and which a machine. The judge is allowed to ask any question of either A or B (machine or human) and, based upon the answers received, decide which is which. The test is, in effect, a way of checking whether a machine could 'use' a natural language in the ways in which human beings do and, by allowing questions on any topic, focuses on the issue of whether the respondent speaks in ways that are appropriate to (arbitrary) circumstances. Adapting the Turing test, the Loebner Prize offers $100,000 to the computer program that can convince a panel of judges that they are 'conversing' over a computer terminal with a human. The prize has never been given. To provide a test that a machine might pass, a variation was introduced: the creator of a computer program that could convince a panel that they were conversing with a human *on a particular topic* would receive $1,500. The creator of the machine program is allowed to choose the topic of conversation. To make the test even easier, no trick questions are allowed from the judges. Even with this set of restrictions, all judges chose humans as more humanlike than any machine. But a prize was given to the creator of a program that convinced half the panel that they were engaged in conversation with a human. The winning program had as its 'topic' whimsical conversation. This 'topic' in effect sets the standard of "appropriateness to context" very low, to a point where it can be met by a machine program that picks up on a part of the questioner's question ("What would you look for if you were wandering through the Black Forest?") and provides an answer ("I don't wander") that is appropriate as a 'whimsical' answer. This standard allows many more of a machine's responses to questions to appear to be appropriately meaningful than other topics might. The real test – Descartes' and Turing's – allows any topic (thereby, circumstance). That is a standard that has not been met, and probably will not be.

Appropriateness to situation constitutes the core of this test. Unlike the kinds of machines Descartes had in mind, it is easy enough to build and program computers that meet the stimulus freedom condition. All one has to do is build a randomizing device into the machine's system or program so that it produces words that have nothing to do with input or circumstance. Again unlike Descartes' machines, it is also easy to satisfy the unbounded condition, at least so long as this is interpreted simply as a matter of being able to produce an indeterminate number of responses with various combinations of words in certain structural configurations; for machines can be programmed to perform recursive procedures, so that they can produce structured sentences of indefinite length. But if the results of the Loebner competition are any indication, no computer does, or is likely to, meet the appropriateness part of the test in the unrestricted competition.

Might computers be given a program that would provide them with what the human language faculty and all the other faculties provide us with? This seems to be possible in principle for the formal and general aspects of the computations that the language faculty performs. Computers could be programmed with the algorithms that human brains follow when they produce sentences from selections of lexical items with their features. But it is not at all clear that they could be given the full set of other faculties – vision, audition, facial recognition, and others – with which the human is endowed, and which the person who speaks also uses to deal with the world, solve problems, and the like – that is, to exercise common sense understanding. Nor do computers have human sensory organs, or anything like a proprioceptive sense. Nevertheless, assume that they could be 'given' all this. Would such computers also have human interests, the interests that the lexical items of natural language seem virtually designed to deal with? A positive or a negative answer to this amounts to mere speculation. And, as Chomsky often points out, even Turing thought that there was no fact of the matter here – that the test, even if satisfied, provides at most some reason to decide to treat specific machines running specific programs as humanoid. This is a matter of practical decision, not a question of fact.

Descartes thought that the same tests could be applied to animals. The difference between animals and humans is not that it is only human beings who have the ability to produce what sounds like speech, for magpies and parrots can produce these sounds too. Furthermore, humans who lack speech organs construct sentences and converse by signing just as humans with speech organs do, so speech organs are not needed to use language. Nor is the difference between animals and humans something like intelligence; there are probably some apes that are more intelligent, on some plausible scale of general intelligence, than some people. Rather – paralleling the first test applied to machines – the difference is that "there are no men so dull-witted or stupid – and this includes even madmen – that they are incapable of arranging various words together and forming an utterance from them in order to make their thoughts understood." Not as sharply stated as in the case of machines, this test places observations of unboundedness and appropriateness together.

The first test and the observations on which it rests remain valid. In fact – unlike the machine case, where the Loebner competition shows that computers make the idea of whether machines can 'speak' like humans still an interesting issue – it is difficult to take seriously the idea that nonhumans have a natural language. No one has been able to train a creature in such a way that its 'linguistic' output comes close to what one finds in human language use. The problem, as Descartes pointed out, is not a matter of being unable to produce human sounds. Chimpanzees and gorillas have arms and faces and presumably could be trained in a form of signing. Failing that, they could be trained to press visually distinctive panels. But while apes have been trained over long periods to communicate with humans by means of both these methods, all such attempts have been failures. Whether by signing or by using visual symbols, no ape has produced anything that could count as human language use: the linguistic output of apes does not have the structure of human language, nor does it provide reason to think that apes can produce an unlimited number of 'sentences'; their linguistic output is not "unbounded." Nor does it display anything like the storytelling and musing, while remaining appropriate, of which even a small child is capable; it is not stimulus-free. And, too, often, what one gets is completely inappropriate to the circumstances. These trained apes *communicate* with humans and each other. They engage in routines that look a little like Wittgenstein's primitive "language games." But this is irrelevant. Communication is not *the*, or even *a*, defining characteristic of human language; ants communicate by the use of pheromones, whales by the use of interesting forms of sound, bees by a kind of dance. Yet no creature can acquire or use a human language, including apes – surely the most plausible candidates for creatures that might do so. Descartes seems to have been right: there is an essential difference between human beings as a group and other organisms, and this difference has something to do with language. His explanation, that this difference is the result of a separate and immaterial mind with universal powers expressed in language, was wrong, as was his mechanical philosophy; but the test and its results stand, because neither depends on his explanations or on his mechanical philosophy.

The central assumption of the model of the mind which Chomsky suggests is not that the mind is a universal device, "reason," but rather that it is a device made up of a collection of biologically based faculties that are put to use in various combinations at various times in dealing with the world, thereby offering us in science and common sense what we think of as reason. Interestingly, the language faculty and all the other faculties that make up the mind are "mental organs," embodying in each case a kind of 'instinct', for they operate automatically and blindly – well beyond our consciousness and accessible only to painstaking theory construction. Like all other organs in the body, each is limited in what it is and what it can do. Each may provide for a potential infinity of output states, but each item of this potentially infinite set must have a permissible combination of specific configurations, set by nature. Thus language, like the other mental organs that embody special and different kinds of instinct, provides us with an instinct that humans do not share with other animals. The difference between humans and other animals is not then – *pace* Descartes – that humans have reason and animals are purely instinctual, operating merely by "the disposition of their organs," but that humans have an organ, and therefore an 'instinct', that other animals do not have.

An enthusiast for reason might think of these biologically limited faculties as somehow undermining human potential. Interestingly, though, this kind of reaction is more characteristic – as Chomsky notes in his discussion of Harris and Herder early in *Cartesian Linguistics* – of the empiricist, who likes to think of the mind as provided with a reason that constructs hypotheses concerning any subject matter whatsoever and tests them. We have already seen what Chomsky's reaction to this attitude is: his view is that it is only because our mental organs or faculties *are* 'instincts' that develop within a short period after birth without appeal to a learning procedure that we have any of the benefits of being human beings at all. They provide us with the machinery that quickly enables us to communicate and get along in the world: without it, we would have to struggle through a long learning period and would be advantaged or disadvantaged by any number of circumstances and particular talents. Suppose the starling had to be taught to navigate by the stars at night; without instinct, we too would be in sad cognitive straits indeed. This is Chomsky's enablement by limitation thesis again: we have minds with limited faculties, but it is only because we have limited, biologically based faculties and capacities that we have access to a rich range of experiences and cognitive opportunities (*LPK* 151f). No doubt different cultures and different individuals can and do utilize these faculties and capacities in different ways, sometimes virtually ignoring some, such as the science-forming capacity, or mathematics. But we can use and develop what they provide in different ways and pursue our own cognitive paths as individuals only if we have these faculties and potential capacities at birth.

I do not mean to suggest that Descartes' view of the mind had no virtues at all. In the first place, it was not just a piece of empty speculation. Constructed against the backdrop of a mechanical philosophy, it was at the time a reasonable scientific hypothesis introduced to explain certain observations that called the mechanical explanation into question. These are observations that anyone can make, requiring no more machinery than that which common sense provides. They are obviously important facts that any serious theory of the mind must take into account. Furthermore, they continue to constitute a working test for mind, or, more accurately, a test for a human mind. Second, while by identifying the mind with a substance that thinks or reasons and the body with extended matter Descartes made a hash of both, he did at least initiate a scientific research program, carried out by later rationalists, that respected the fundamental observations that his hypothesis tried to speak to and that continued to show that human beings are indeed different and uniquely endowed with a cognitive faculty that everything else lacks. Third, his work on geometry and perception strongly supported nativist claims by arguing that concepts like <u>triangle</u> must be innate, for it would be impossible to form this 'idea' and organize perceptual experience in accordance with it unless it were already available to the operations of the mind. Descartes' arguments in this domain, like those of others in the Cartesian linguistics tradition, such as Cudworth and Humboldt, do not seem to depend on the defects of his view of mind and matter.

Constructivism and the biological rationalist

The rationalist constructivist argues that ideas or concepts are produced inside the head, and that, while their acquisition is perhaps triggered by 'inputs' of various sorts from the outside world (in the case of common sense concepts, at least), they are not determined by those things in the outside world that lead to triggerings. Yet these are the concepts that we humans use to characterize the things that we think populate the outside world. They include the event-concept <u>give</u>, the thing-concept <u>book</u>, the relation-concept <u>to</u>, and the situation-concept <u>Stuart gave his book to Alice</u>. We typically assume that these concepts characterize things – that the world has 'givings' and the relation 'to'. But if the concepts are not derived from these things and are located inside the head, why do we so easily say that what we see is Stuart giving his book to Alice? Somehow, these ideas have to be transported outside the head. Constructivism is the thesis that they are projected out there when we hold that they correctly describe. For Descartes, projection needs the aid of God to assure us that inner ideas correspond to what is out there. There are, however, alternative rationalist ways to construe projection.

The biological rationalist constructivist who, like Chomsky, holds that most of the ideas that play a role in our common sense knowledge are innately specified but that the majority of those in the sciences have to be invented, often with considerable difficulty, can both sharpen the issue and point to a different account of 'correspondence'. The biological rationalist who populates the mind with several mental organs that provide for two different forms of problem-solving capacities can also add that it would not be surprising if there were cases where concepts used in common sense seem to conflict with those used in the sciences. The common sense person sees the blue mail box; the scientist operating as scientist holds that nothing like the visual concept <u>blue</u> could be a property of a physical surface as understood by physics or chemistry. This emphasizes that the worlds of the sciences of physical surfaces (physics, chemistry, etc.) are discontinuous with and different from the common sense world. Constructivism helps make sense of how this could be: the way a world is (seen/conceived/thought to be) is in part a matter of the concepts that are used to describe it. In physics there is no concept <u>give</u>, or <u>to</u>, but we routinely think that our common sense world has givings and relations like <u>to</u> in it. In physics there are certain fundamental forces that are not the forces of natural language – the strong force of quantum physics is not the <u>force</u> of verbal "She forced the problem out of her mind" or nominal "She hit the cat with considerable force."

A remark in *Cartesian Linguistics* indicates that Chomsky thinks that it is part of rationalism to rely on constructivist projection and – for common sense concepts – on an attendant concept of triggering to make sense of how the human mind 'makes' a world. He notes:

The strong assumptions about innate mental structure made by rationalistic psychology and philosophy of mind eliminated the necessity for any sharp distinction between a theory of perception [for the common sense world, at least] and a theory of learning. In both cases, essentially the same processes are at work; a store of latent principles [innate concepts or ideas] is brought to the interpretation of the data of sense. There is, to be sure, a difference between the initial "activation" of latent structure and the use of it once it has become readily available for the interpretation (*more accurately the determination*) of experience" (*CL* 65; emphasis added).

We think of perception as providing us with knowledge of the current state of our immediate surroundings. We open our eyes and see Stuart giving his book to Alice. The mental mechanisms that allow us to accomplish this cognitive feat are not yet clear. They must provide for both triggering of concepts and their use or application to immediate surroundings. It is not even obvious how triggering, or what Chomsky speaks of as "activation," takes place. Fodor (1982) once spoke of it as "brute causal," but except for emphasizing that it is not something carried out by the 'rational' procedure of hypothesis formation and testing, that is not much help. Let it suffice that it takes place; work by Jacques Mehler and colleagues on extremely early activation of phonological 'concepts' helps show that it must. The important consideration for our purposes is its implications for the rationalist view of mind and perception.

It helps to keep in mind both that the common sense concepts involved in triggering are often linguistic ones (give, book, and to) that are not available to other organisms and that they do not include the concepts of science. No dog can open its eyes and see the complicated event of Stuart (an agent with an intention) giving (an action with giver, receiver, and thing given) his book (the item given and an artifact that contains information and is produced with the intention of informing/entertaining/ . . .) to Alice (the agent "target" of the giving); and machines are far from being able to "recognize" anything like this. The dog sees something, of course, but not this event. But the small child sees the event we do, typically before he or she can even talk. Moreover, he or she manages to accomplish similar feats over a wide range of other cases, with any number of other events, processes, and states and in ways that, though they require further development and sophistication in use, approximate adult capacities. The child does not do this, however, with the concepts found in the sciences. That is because scientific concepts are not triggered by things "out there," as those used in common sense are. The concepts in <u>Big Bird forced Cookie Monster to sit down</u> are easily acquired and applied in perception; those involved in field equations dealing with electromagnetic forces are not – not even by the typical adult – and they rarely figure, if at all, in perception.

The fact that some concepts are easily acquired and applied shows that there is something about the concepts triggered and used in perceiving the things of the common sense world that makes them apt for these accomplishments. Perhaps that is what Chomsky is suggesting in "Language and Nature" when he speaks of the concepts (perspectives) provided by the language faculty as "crucially involving human interests and concerns even in the simplest cases" (1995: 20). It is very likely what Cudworth was after when he spoke of experience "inviting" concepts that "anticipate" the experience (*TEIM* 135, 129). I return to this issue in chapter 6, after the discussion of Chomsky's theory of language has provided a better grip on what he thinks these perspectives and their biological roles are. It is enough for the moment to appreciate that it does not seem to be an accident that inner and innate concepts are so readily acquired and applied in perception and other dealings with 'our' world of common sense understanding. Perhaps it has something to do with our evolved biology. But, whatever the explanation, the character of our common sense world depends heavily on innate linguistic concepts which provide us with much of our access to the everyday world (cf. Chomsky 1997).

Helpful insights are found in Chomsky's discussion of how "individuation" of the things of the common sense world "turns on such factors as design, intended and characteristic use, institutional role," (1997:14), origin, material makeup, e.g. – features characteristic of Chomsky's and Cudworth's innately specified thing-concepts, such as <u>house</u> or <u>water</u>. Adopting a nativist version of Hobbes's, Locke's, and Hume's views that the individuation of things is the work of the mind, Chomsky seems to think that the things we perceive and deal with in everyday affairs are 'cut up' to suit the (biologically based) interests our innate concepts so obviously serve. The mechanism of individuation – the way concepts are 'applied' – is unclear, although Cudworth's interesting suggestion that one look to a generative system in the mind "anticipating" things is discussed later. For the moment, conceive of mind as making things 'out there' by thinking of biologically generated concepts in the head as ways of perceiving/thinking of things (1997: 15–16, n21; *CL* 50). When used or 'applied', the 'knowledge' these 'ideas' contain *configures* experience, 'making' the relevant things and events.

Although this discussion of how concepts provided by the language faculty help 'make' the common sense world focuses on their role in perception, the basic constructivist point about the place of concepts in cognitive activities applies to the worlds of science too. The things of the worlds of science are 'made' by descriptions thought to be correct. The concepts used in the sciences are not innate and triggered, but manufactured. Nevertheless, in both common sense and science, there is no direct access. All our access to 'things' is mediated by inner concepts, whether common sense and innate or scientific and made (although with some aid from innate factors). In this sense, our minds make our worlds.

What, however, can the biological rationalist say about our confidence – almost instinctual in the case of common sense and wary in the case of science – that the world (or worlds) contains entities corresponding to our concepts? Eliminating Descartes' God, practical success for the common sense world and descriptive and explanatory success for scientific worlds are our only guarantees that inner concepts 'correspond' to things 'out there'. Gesturing towards evolution (*not* selection, Chomsky is careful to add) makes sense only for anthropocentric common sense concepts. With created scientific concepts, Chomsky speaks of the fact that they can sometimes be both descriptively and explanatorily adequate as a bit of a "miracle."[7] Whether instinctual or wary, though, success (or adequacy) is sufficient for us to think that our concepts are true of the common sense world and the scientific worlds.

It should be clear that Chomsky the biological rationalist adopts and adapts traditional rationalist constructivist views, just as he adopts and adapts rationalist nativist and internalist views. His constructivism, like that of traditional rationalists, depends heavily on a picture of mind that is drawn to speak to the poverty and creativity observations. The twists that biological rationalist constructivism makes in tradition lie in the effort to locate the difference between our two problem-solving capacities in our biological endowment and in eliminating any appeals to divinity to provide assurance that things 'out there' correspond to the concepts we think we truly apply.

4

Languages and the Science of Language

Chomsky labels the issue of scientifically accounting for the poverty observations "Plato's problem," and accounting for the creativity observations "Descartes' problem" – or rather, a part of it. So far as the science of language is concerned, the first really *is* a problem; an explanatorily adequate theory of language must be able to explain the poverty observations. To the extent that a science of language is explanatorily adequate in this sense, it solves Plato's problem. Constructing a Universal Grammar (UG) is crucial to providing for explanatory adequacy; we look at what is involved below. Descartes' problem is another matter. If it is thought of as the issue of making sense of what is involved in speech production and perception, some parts of it pose problems for the sciences. There has been progress in the science of speech perception, and at least some in that of speech production (by the larynx, mouth, etc.). In effect, there has been progress in dealing scientifically with some of the other systems in the head with which the language faculty interacts. But the aspect of speech production represented in the creativity observations – appropriateness of language use in particular – seems to be beyond the capacity of science. If so, this important part of Descartes' problem is not really a problem: it is – and is likely to remain – a mystery.[1]

In this chapter I discuss why Chomsky's science of language is a science and, in that vein, how it responds to the poverty and creativity observations. The discussion is basically nontechnical. Although it is necessary to introduce at least some technical terms, I focus not on their technical roles, but on their function in demarcating linguistics from other studies involving language, dividing up the field of linguistics, dividing up languages, and distinguishing good theories of language from bad. A more technical discussion of how Chomsky's theories actually work appears in the next chapter.

Some terms of the science of language

Several of the terms introduced here are fairly recent ("interface"), some quite recent ("Bare Output Condition"), but even those that date back to the earliest of Chomsky's grammars are currently used. The outline of the development of Chomsky's theories of language that appears in the next chapter helps indicate when some later ones were introduced, and why.

Everyone knows, or thinks they know, that languages are made up of words and sentences. There is something correct in this, but serious theorizing about language requires a major reworking of everyday understandings of sentence and word. It also requires introducing a grammar to link words and sentences, as well as a clear understanding of the task of the linguist-scientist who is committed to constructing a theory of sentence, word, and the grammar that links selections of words to sentences. Let us start with a working grasp of how the linguist conceives of words. (Technical terms are italicized as they are introduced.) From one point of view, words are the subject matter of "morphology" – the study of word stems, inflection, and how words are put together (such as "affixing" 'ed' to 'want' to form the past tense 'wanted'). While an important matter, Chomsky's work also illuminates another conception of word. According to it, words are mental objects. Think of a person as having something like a mental dictionary. The entries in this mental dictionary constitute a person's "lexicon," which includes various "lexical items." Unlike the words of dictionaries like the *Oxford*, which do not really define words so much (Chomsky holds) as provide those who have sounds and meanings (innately) specified in their minds with "superficial details of the kind provided by experience" (*PP* 24) (such as which meaning is linked to which sound and how the word is often used), the lexical items of the linguist are (ideally) defined in terms of the innately specified features that make them up. That is, they are defined in terms of "phonological," "formal," and "semantic features."[2] The phonological features are those that, after mental computations, lead to the production of a sound, represented in the "phonetic" features at the "phonetic interface" (PHON). The formal features (N(oun), V(erb), A(djective), P(re(post)position)) and semantic features (± ABSTRACT, **aperture**, etc.: there is no settled vocabulary yet) – particularly the latter – lead, after mental computations, to the production of a specific meaning, represented in a configuration of features at the "semantic interface" (SEM).

The mental computations that produce sounds and meanings from the features of lexical items are described by a theory of a language that is called a "grammar of a language." Theories, as we have seen, involve formalization. In Chomsky's case, a theory of *a* language must be related to a theory of language called "Universal Grammar." There are various forms of grammar: traditional grammars are often little more than descriptions of a few oddities of specific languages. But to be a part of a formal science and to capture natural languages, a grammar must be "generative," that is, it must rely on various stated and formalized principles or rules or procedures that include at least some with recursive or iterative capacity. These allow a grammar to provide an abstract and formal characterization of how, from a finite stock of lexical items with their phonological, formal, and semantic features, a potential infinity of sentences or "expressions" can be produced or "derived."[3] ("Expression" is the (current) theoretical substitute for the ordinary notion of a sentence; earlier, Chomsky used "sentence" and gave it a technical sense.) Grammars that are capable of generating an infinite set of sentences/expressions do not, obviously, represent a particular person's linguistic "performance," for no person or group of people can produce an infinite set of expressions. They represent people's linguistic "competence" (*ATS* 4–9) or their linguistic "knowledge" (a technical term that does not require awareness of what one knows or that one be able to justify what one knows (*KL* 225); sometimes, to avoid the suggestion that it involves either of these, Chomsky speaks of "cognizing" a language). A theory of UG represents what a child knows before acquiring a language – a great deal of highly detailed and structured information, as we will see. In recent work Chomsky has spoken of all particular "natural" languages (French, Tlingit, etc.) as being instances of UG that can (almost) be 'deduced' from UG. A related notion is that of a "core" grammar, which is an idealized instance of UG (*LGB* 7f). In work since the beginning of the 1980s, Chomsky holds that every actual and possible natural language is a state of UG with certain "parameters" set; in this sense, UG contains all possible natural languages, where each is conceived as the result of a different setting of a set of 'switches' (parameters) available in UG. In addition, Chomsky defines an "I-language," which amounts to something like an "idiolect," or specific person's language (or languages): one can think of an I-language as a natural language found in a particular person's language faculty at a particular stage of development. It contains a specific list of lexical items, each of which pairs a specific meaning(-specifying set of features) to a specific sound(-specifying set of features). (Different meanings can be paired with the same sound; this is called "ambiguity.") A grammar of a particular I-language is, then, a theory of a (particular person's) language faculty at a particular time.

Expressions, as we have seen, are sound–meaning pairs: they are the closest theoretical analog to the idea that a sentence is 'a sound with a meaning'. Sounds and meanings appear at two separate "interfaces," where the language faculty interacts with other systems in the head. Recapitulating chapter 2 a bit, Chomsky calls a theoretical representation of a sound a "PF" (phonetic form) or a "PHON" (phonetic representation interface); meanings are "LFs" (logical forms) or "SEMs" (semantic representation interfaces). An expression, then, is a ⟨PHON, SEM⟩ (or ⟨PF, LF⟩) pair. Each PHON, each SEM, and (therefore) each expression is fully defined by a list of phonetic, formal, and semantic features. The features found within a particular PHON interact with sound production (larynx control, etc.) and reception (audition) systems by providing 'instructions' to these systems; SEMs interact with conceptual and intentional systems. It is not exactly clear what conceptual and intentional systems are, although Chomsky thinks that recent work has begun to reveal this; sound production and reception systems are better understood. In carrying out the central task of linguistic theory, though, the linguist does not have to be too concerned with these systems on the other side of PHON and SEM: as Chomsky understands it, the central task of the linguist is to construct a theory of how expressions are produced. (This parallels the scientist of vision's task of showing how visual spaces are produced.) The task is carried out by constructing a theory of the language faculty's initial state (UG) and showing how its developed states (I-languages) are readily acquired on the basis of primary linguistic data – that is, by solving Plato's problem. The other systems need be seen only as imposing certain constraints on computations of expressions, constraints Chomsky calls "Bare Output Conditions." There are further conditions on how the theory of a language faculty at a particular time and a theory of UG must proceed if they are to do their job well, or "adequately." Some conditions are general, applying to all scientific theories. Others are specific to linguistic theories, especially the condition of explanatory adequacy – explaining how *any* child could acquire *any* natural language under poverty of stimulus conditions.

Locating Chomsky's theoretical approach to language: syntax, semantics, and pragmatics

Many linguists, philosophers, and cognitive scientists classify the tasks of constructing a theory of language in terms of a three-way distinction between syntax, semantics, and pragmatics.[4] Something like this classification of theoretical approaches to language has been around since the American philosopher C.S. Peirce in the nineteenth century, but it was probably Charles Morris who introduced the distinction in its modern form in his 1938 *Foundations of the Theory of Signs*. He suggested that one think of approaches to language in terms of the kinds of domain a theory or account of language is committed to dealing with. These domains can be thought of as nested, so that an approach with a broader domain includes a narrower. Syntax deals with the most nested and narrowest domain – the intrinsic properties of signs and how they relate to one another. Thus, syntax might treat a specific verb as one that has two obligatory "argument positions":[5] any sentence in which this verb appears must provide two nouns, usually with one serving as subject noun and the other as object noun. "Wash" is such a verb, for it must appear with a personal noun and a thing-noun: "John washed the dishes." Syntax might also deal with the structure of a particular verb phrase (VP) by saying not just what it is composed of (e.g., the verb "walk" and the prepositional phrase (PP) "under the roof," which is itself composed of a preposition (P), a determiner (D), and a noun (N)), but how it came to be composed in this way, by showing how its various parts (nouns, verbs, prepositions, determiners) get put together – that is, how its various elements come to stand in various syntactic relations to each other. As these examples indicate, syntactic relations include phrasal structure relationships (the positions of verbs relative to other elements in verb phrases) and the like. A syntactic theory might speak to the issue of what kinds of syntactic entities, such as nouns, fill argument positions. And a generative syntactic theory might speak to how, where, and which syntactic elements participate in the production of a sentence – how to move elements around (what kinds of transformations they can undergo, for example), the kinds of initial and final configurations that they assume, and so on. But while a syntactic theory can get quite complicated and introduce a number of elements and rules of combination, in the final analysis it has a single homogeneous subject matter – linguistic objects alone, without consideration of *who* produced a sentence, *what uses* a sentence happens to be put to, or *what relationships* might exist between linguistic objects and things in the world. Consider this syntactic rule: S → NP + VP. This is known as a "phrase structure rewrite rule," and it says (speaking very informally) that sentences can be formed by joining a noun phrase and a verb phrase. No persons are mentioned, or uses to which persons might put a sentence, or relationships between a sentence's NP and things in the world. We will see that Chomsky's theories of language deal with syntax in this sense alone, even when they speak – as they always do – to issues of sound and meaning.

An example of a semantic relationship is the statement that the proper noun "Bill Clinton" refers to Bill Clinton. Semantics widens the domain with which the linguist deals by – Morris claimed – extending it to things in the world. A word, semantically speaking, has both a syntactic description and – according to this standard conception of semantics – a specification of the thing or things in the world to which the word *refers*. Those who "do semantics" as understood in this way also tend to call on the concept of *truth*, no doubt because it seems inextricably involved with the concept of reference: a word refers to a particular item, it might be said, in case it is true of that thing, or correctly describes or characterizes it. That was Bertrand Russell's position on the matter, at least in 1905; he used the term "denote," and said that except in the special case of proper nouns, which cannot help but denote the things they name, other expressions (such as "the present king of France") denote only if there is something of which the expression is true (if there is a present king of France). But others have found reference and truth insufficient for semantics. Frege pointed out that "the morning star" and "the evening star" refer to, and are true of, the same thing, and remarked that there is an obvious difference between them: they seem to have different meanings. Surely, then, a semantic account ought to introduce devices to speak of the different meanings these phrases have, even if they are supposed to have the same referent. To do this, Frege introduced the concept of the *sense* of a word. For present purposes, the sense of a word can be thought of as whatever a word has (in some sense of "has") that counts as its meaning and that plays a role in determining that the word refers to whatever it is supposed to refer to (Venus, in the case of "the morning star" and "the evening star"). But, while Frege insisted on giving words senses, it was never clear exactly what a theory of senses should look like. He thought that it should *not* be a psychological theory, because he believed that this would make it depend on the varying psychological states of individuals. Thinking of senses as somehow dependent on individual psychological states makes them private, and he did not want that. If senses are private, it is impossible to account for how people manage to communicate with one another or come to agree on the truth of various phrases; for if the senses of each person's words depend on the individual psychological states of that person, it is hard to see how words could have the same meanings for different people.[6] Generally, Frege did not want persons to play any role in semantics – in sense, truth, or reference. Frege's followers – Donald Davidson, for example – have tended to agree: semantics puts at risk its hope of becoming a science (of being a serious theory) if it must cope with individual variation.[7]

Nor did Frege – or anyone else, for that matter – think of sense as an intrinsic feature of a word, in the way that being a noun might be thought to be an intrinsic feature of a word – something the word has to have to be the lexical item it is. This is of some significance, because it is exactly what Chomsky proposes: he moves something like Frege's senses, in the form of SEMs, into syntax, so that meaning becomes part of a serious science, and the rest of semantics – reference and truth – becomes pragmatics. But before sketching Chomsky's iconoclastic view of the matter, we must first find out what pragmatics amounts to.

Pragmatics broadens the study of language still further. It adds speakers with their activities and projects to syntax (words) and semantics (word–world relations). Here is an example of a pragmatic claim: Harriet used the words "Get out of the tree" in speaking to her children, and she thought at the time that they were in danger and insisted that they get out of the tree. To think of a word pragmatically is to think of it as used by a speaker to effect various ends. Inevitably, a pragmatic account of the use of a word gets very complicated indeed. It must involve the word's intrinsic syntactic features, which is easy enough. But one must also take into account who the speaker is, what intentions and desires he or she has, what kind of job he or she is hoping to accomplish by using the word, under what circumstances he or she uses the word, and so on. It becomes very difficult to keep all this in mind, much less under control, in constructing a reasonably comprehensive but also simple theory that generalizes beyond a single case, such as Harriet's. This suggests that it might be impossible to construct a pragmatic *theory* of a word at all. Some of those who construct syntactic theories of words and languages think of pragmatics as a swamp that should be avoided by those with hopes for a theory. Those who enter it are treated with admiration mixed with a bit of puzzlement: that's not for me, and I can't understand why anyone would do it, but if you come up with something theoretically interesting, let me know.

If the study of syntax is seen as a responsible, respectable exercise, and the study of pragmatics sometimes as a bit daring, perhaps rash (interesting observations, no doubt, but where's the science?), what of attitudes towards semantics? These days, the term "semantic theory" has been more or less appropriated by those who try to deal with natural languages by restricting themselves to syntax plus the machinery Frege introduced. They realize that there is some danger in being seen to associate too closely with those who do pragmatics and deal with users of language, so they insist that theirs is a field of study that deals with senses and word–world relationships in isolation from individual speakers. Like Frege, they are very careful to point out that they are *not* dealing with the variable psychological states of speakers.[8] So, for example, if they feel they have to introduce terms like the "sense" of a word or its "meaning," or if they wish to speak of a word's "referent" theoretically, they assure us that these notions can be identified in a way that does not vary from speaker to speaker. If they could not be, their use in a theory would be undermined, becoming little more than a set of remarks about how individuals, and perhaps some groups, use language, sometimes. The result, they fear, would be no theory at all.[9]

What, then, of Chomsky's position? We have seen enough already in what he says about linguistic behavior or language use to know that he has serious doubts about the prospects of pragmatics thought of as a *science of language use*: the domain of language use is the domain of "ordinary linguistic creativity." To the extent that pragmatics includes people who use language, it includes free agents whose actions cannot be dealt with by any theory that humans are capable of understanding. He is an eminently respectable and responsible syntactician, not only virtually creating the field but setting it in the direction it is still going. Like others 'doing syntax', he takes the target of his theoretical efforts to be the intrinsic properties or features of words (lexical items, sentences, phrases, etc.). To be sure, he holds that syntax is a biological, and even in some sense a psychological, enterprise. But syntax does not speak of people as *agents* who *use* language: it deals only with the automatically functioning computational systems in people's heads under the rubrics of UG, natural language, and I-language. It treats people as biological organisms with a special 'organ' that contains biologically based innate knowledge and that functions in ways that can be dealt with by a computational theory of the workings of this organ. As a result of innateness, syntax deals with what is uniform among all speakers (UG) and groups of speakers (natural language). Even when dealing with individual speakers, it treats their I-languages as states of UG. The study of syntax is essentially nativist and internalist: the domain of intrinsic features is fixed by nature, but their use by speakers is not.

So far, Chomsky's attitudes toward syntax and pragmatics parallel those of some others. The interesting issue is what he says about the theoretical prospects of semantics thought of as independent of pragmatics – about its prospects as a serious theory of word–world relationships and of senses. His basic view on this matter seems to be that one cannot speak of word–world relationships (1993; 1995: 30–51; *PP* 46f; 1997) without speaking of people as agents who use words and sentences to deal with the world, or for other purposes. You cannot make sense of whether an expression is appropriate to the circumstances in which a person (of which there is no science) uses it and the way in which the person understands (of which there is no science) these circumstances (ditto), unless you know something about what the person is trying to effect (ditto), so that you can see what reasons (ditto) he or she might have for using that term in this case. Thus, reference, thought of as essentially involving speakers as agents and mind-independent entities, can and should be absorbed into pragmatics, where it can be dealt with on its own terms, even if these terms do not suit the aims of serious theory.

Unlike some others, Chomsky never treats the domain of pragmatics as a swamp, but sees it as the domain of free and creative activity. This domain is certainly not to be despised, even if it is beyond the reach of serious science and available only to insightful description. It is even to be celebrated, as the Romantics insisted. Moreover, he thinks that some work done by those who work in pragmatics – relatively informal work such as Grice's on implicature, Austin's on speech acts, and Wilson and Sperber's work on relevance, plus more formal work (e.g., Soames) on presupposition projection – is of interest to the scientist. Perhaps one can even expect that certain restricted parts of the study of pragmatics could become science by being absorbed into syntax, as Chomsky proposes for meanings.

If truth and reference are placed in pragmatics, what of Frege's suggestion that in 'doing semantics' the sense of a word somehow plays a role in determining the word's referent – without, however, allowing senses to covertly bring in speakers understood as psychologically unique entities or as agents? Remember that while Frege was adamant that senses are not 'private', he was never able to say precisely what status they had. As a result, he – and other would-be serious semanticians who followed him – came to devote what, from Chomsky's point of view, amount to useless efforts to save the notion of sense from empty abstraction on the one hand or individual psychology on the other. Chomsky offers a suggestion that seems radical to a Fregean. Just as he suggests moving reference from semantics to pragmatics, so he suggests moving something like what Frege would have called the sense of a word from semantics into syntax. That is, he suggests including within the syntactic (intrinsic, internal, individual, intensional) description of a lexical item the formal, finely textured 'semantic' features that make it the specific lexical item it is. Such features include specification of the theta-roles of various words, as well as such features as + HUMAN, part of the specification of the concept person, ± CONCRETE, part of the specification of village, and – if Cudworth is right – HABITABLE BY HUMANS, part of the specification of house. (Village gets ± CONCRETE because it is a general feature of towns, cities, hamlets, etc., that they can be thought of as locations (hence concrete) *or* as political abstract entities (hence, not concrete), and sometimes as both.) The feature-specifying terms I use here are crude, but that reflects the fact that lexicology is still in a relatively primitive state. They are enough, though, to point in what Chomsky takes to be the right direction, for it is not difficult to think of them as specifying (and in some sense defining) the meaning of a lexical item. Specifically, they help specify and determine (in computation) a SEM, which is the 'meaning' interface part of an expression (⟨PHON, SEM⟩ pair). As SEMs, meanings are the closest analogs to Fregean senses in Chomsky's theory of language, in which they are syntactically produced and defined entities. They by no means determine referents; reference to mind-independent entities is a pragmatic relationship and involves people using language. But meanings or *concepts* (or *intrinsic contents*) might be said to guide their own use or interpretation by people in perception (see the end of chapter 3), judgment, and action. This topic is taken up in chapter 6.

While this makes meanings biological and in some sense psychological, it by no means makes them private in a way that is intractable to serious theory of an internalist, nativist sort. For, first, meanings are not themselves fixed by, or defined by, how they happen to be used by one or more persons – or even by the "linguistic community." They are defined by appeal to a set of innately specified features, including those that fix all the possible combinations of formal and semantic features available in all natural languages. This is the result of assigning meanings to syntax – of locating them in a system that can produce an infinite set of perspectives, but only in certain configurations. This makes them far from unique to a particular speaker, so Frege's worries disappear. But second, ironically, we know that they are not private in a way that undermines theory, because we know that they are psychological entities in a way different from anything Frege's conception of psychology ever envisioned. The features in terms of which the meanings of words are defined are introduced by an explicitly psychological-mental theory that shows how features clustered together in the ways that the theory determines define concepts (intrinsic meanings that constitute perspectives). According to the theory – a theory of UG – they are not private, because the features and the possible configurations are – parametric variations in formal features between natural languages aside – shared across the whole of the human population. While the specific selection of them that happens to be available in a particular person's working lexicon may differ from that available in another person's, the features themselves, and to an extent their permissible configurations, are largely innately fixed and so can be assumed to be available in principle to all humans in common. Meanings become scientific entities.

Chomsky introduces independent reasons for thinking of features such as ± CONCRETE and the concepts they help define as syntactic. Like N and NP, they are specifically linguistic,[10] intrinsic features of words that are internal to the mind/brain and are intensionally defined – that is, defined in terms of the theory that deals with them. They are, then, just as syntactic as formal, phonological, phonetic, or morphological features. They are not only the kinds of features with which linguists deal, but linguistic features of the lexical item that have an effect on the linguistic computations that go on within the head.

The result of all this is that not only have reference and truth been placed in pragmatics but meaning has been moved out of semantics into syntax. Semantics as a separate, autonomous domain disappears, absorbed into a pragmatics that is no longer merely a swamp and into a much-enriched, far more exciting syntax. Nothing but the illusion of a separate science is lost; most of what is scientifically significant in the findings of those who have been 'doing semantics' can be absorbed into syntax, broadly conceived. One can even introduce a concept of reference that is stipulated to hold between perspectives and certain theoretical entities that might be called "semantic values" (*LGB* 324; 1993), where these values are taken to be, as perspectives are, inside the head (although the point of doing this would have to be made clear; see chapter 6 and its comparison with phonetic values). And there are advantages to this absorption. Meanings cease to be the mysterious entities that philosophers and others have puzzled over for centuries and become the subject matters of a science that seems to be making considerable progress. And a syntax enriched with meanings (linguistic perspectives) is much more interesting than pushing nouns and verbs around to yield certain formal syntactic configurations. It becomes clear, too, why most purely syntactic arguments seem to have a semantic air: syntax has been driven all along by issues of meaning because syntactic processing aims to produce meanings (SEMs). And an enriched syntax becomes sufficiently powerful to provide a set of cognitive perspectives that people can use to cope with their world and to engage in free and creative activity.

Science, 'science', and common sense: I-language, E-language, and differences between languages

Intuitively, if a person knows how to distinguish one language from another, he or she must have some notion of what a single language is. Philosophers call the notions in terms of which things are distinguished from one another "principles of individuation." (Think informally of a notion of *x* as amounting to "how *x* is understood.")

There is no uniform way to individuate things; or, to put it another way, different kinds of things differ from each other in a number of ways. For instance, wines are divided up in terms of varieties of grape (Barbera, Zinfandel, etc.), regions of production (California, Australia/Burgundy, Alsace), methods of production (still, charmant, etc.), method of delivery (bulk, bottled), type of use (table, dinner), taste (sweet, dry), origin (vineyard, marque), source (grape, apple, etc.), and so on, but not in terms of indivisible whole units. The closest analog to an indivisible unit is a *quantity* of wine. Because wines themselves are not divided by quantitative units, philosophers call "wine" a "mass noun": while there are all sorts of ways to count wines, they are all different ways to state how masses with different properties are distinguished from one another, for any number of purposes. (There can, incidentally, be mass terms which allow of grain; "sand" is one, for people speak of individual grains of sand. But "wine" does not allow even this.) Humans, by contrast with both wine and sand, are not masses and are not distinguished in the same way. Distinct humans are not distinct quantities of some mass, Human: no one siphons off a quantity of Human into a container. Each human is an individual unit. Thus, when one counts people, one does not count different varieties or methods of production, but individual people. To recognize this fact, philosophers call "human" a "count noun."

The individuation of languages follows neither the mass noun nor the count noun pattern; there is no mass, Language, which is siphoned off into individual speakers, and there is no individual and indecomposable unit, Language English. There is no parallel to sand either. While one might think that languages are made up of words, languages do not come in heaps, and only certain words can be combined with others. Languages have structure; they are *systems*.

We will look at how common sense understanding tends to divide up languages in a moment; let us start with theoretical approaches. Chomsky points out that people with scientific pretensions have attempted two basically different ways of dividing up languages. One way attempts to treat languages as patterns of human action or behavior; this is what he calls the 'E-language' approach (*KL* 19f), for external language, or language considered as an external phenomenon. The other way he calls 'I-language' (*KL* 21f), for "internal, individual, and intensional." To conceive of languages as I-languages is to think of them as mental entities (internal), possibly unique to each individual person (individual), and requiring that a particular I-language be defined in terms of the best theory of the system of language (intensional). For Chomsky, this is a theory of UG.

The E-language way of dividing languages focuses on linguistic behavior and tends to rely heavily on common sense understandings of language and linguistic structure and elements. Characteristically, those who adopt an E-language approach give the mind/brain little or no role to play; if there is mention of mind/brain, it is primarily as a mediator between inputs and linguistic behavioral outputs. Most social scientists have an E-language approach in mind when they specify what a language is – a pattern of behavior engaged in by communities or groups of individuals. E-language individuation is also what many philosophers of language adopt: their concern for language use, whether it appears in their discussions of truth, correctness, and reference or in what kinds of 'games' people play with languages, leads them to focus on issues of communication, belief, and the role of the community in 'sustaining' a language. E-languages are also what the American structuralist school of linguistics headed by Bloomfield thought languages to be: they held that a language is (is to be identified by) some totality of utterances, by which they meant speech events thought of as linguistic behavior. Because they thought that language is merely a form of behavior or a publicly observable event produced by a speaker, they limited the task of the linguist to providing a kind of taxonomy of linguistic behavior. This led them to focus on how languages appear – on phonetics (the study of linguistic sounds) and morphology (the study of word formation and inflection) – and to avoid formal syntactic structure and meanings, which are difficult to deal with by taxonomic techniques. Not coincidentally, their focus also led them to avoid anything like a generative theory of linguistic phenomena.[11]

As this sketch indicates, Chomsky introduced the concepts of E-language and I-language to distinguish two different (purported) *theoretical* approaches to language – one that focused on linguistic behavior and hoped to explain it causally, another that suggested that one could not hope to explain linguistic behavior and sought instead to construct theories of the rich and highly specific operations in the head that make linguistic behavior possible. But it is important to keep in mind that Chomsky's point in introducing this distinction was, and is, not to indicate that there really are two different but viable theoretical approaches, but rather to point out that there is no coherent theoretical conception of E-language available to the natural sciences. It is not just that over the centuries no E-language approach has actually succeeded in coming up with something that is austere, focused on a defined subject matter, simple, and explanatorily and descriptively adequate. It is rather that there should be no expectation that any will. The basic point is an extension of the creativity observations: once you deal with language in a way that goes outside the head, you are in the domain of language use – in the domain of representing the world, the community's role, correctness and appropriateness of use. You are not dealing with anything that can be identified (for theory) as a language at all.

I- and E-language represent very different approaches, but the common sense understanding of language seems to contain elements of both. For example, if you ask someone you encounter how many languages she knows and you get the answer "two," it is unlikely that she took this to be a matter of remarking that her linguistic behavior displays two different patterns; for knowing a language is not usually seen, even by the randomly encountered person, as *just* a matter of displaying certain kinds of behavior. It is likely that her views are better represented by saying that she thinks that she has two different systems of knowledge in her head that represent two different forms of competence (cf. *KL* 269).

On the other hand, there seems to be both a sociopolitical and a normative-teleological dimension to the common sense notion of language that tends toward the E-language conception (*KL* 15–16). The sociopolitical aspect is reflected in the tendency to name languages after the countries in which they are spoken – French in France, Chinese in China. It is also tightly related to the connection that many people seem to think exists between language, culture, and (especially in the last two centuries) nations and 'peoples'. It is difficult to make sense of this connection unless it is somehow built into the common sense concept. Perhaps the temptation to attribute languages to political entities is a reflection of the fact that nouns (including "language," apparently) raise and – by virtue of their apparently Aristotelian explanatory structures – invite one to answer questions about the origin or source of the things these nouns are used to refer to. If languages are seen as artifacts, or as produced by human beings, and if nouns demand answers to questions about origin, then, perhaps because no one person, factory, or business seems to be the author or creator of a language, it is attributed to a community or group of people living in proximity to one another – a polity of some sort. The fact that language is innate and that the behavior of a community of speakers serves only to trigger its development, can come to seem misguided. Intuitions are led by sociopolitical considerations, and it becomes difficult for a serious theory of language to dislodge them.[12]

Chomsky speaks of a normative-teleological dimension to the common sense understanding of language. A normative understanding of language would be one that took language to be a form of correct behavior of some sort. A teleological understanding could well be related to this, but amounts primarily to the idea that languages can be thought of as completed wholes that individuals strive to grasp. The normative dimension of language is reflected in the emphasis in schooling and etiquette on rules of correct pronunciation, proper usage, and polite forms of speech, and in the emphasis in law, politics, and philosophy on rhetoric and argument strategy. It is assumed that there is a correct way of saying things, and individuals are asked to conform to it. The teleological aspect is reflected in discussions of language learning, and it is this aspect of the normative-teleological dimension of common sense understanding that Chomsky focuses on – no doubt because it bears so directly on his concern with language acquisition.[13] When one speaks of native German or Yoruba speakers "learning English," it seems plausible to speak of their partial understanding of English, or of their being on the way towards learning English, as if there were a whole or completed entity called "English" that constituted the *telos*, or goal, of the project. Perhaps because this supposed complete entity, English, is not a readily available 'thing' that the person of common sense can point to – it is not a mass or an individual – it is often construed by philosophers as an abstract object, or as perhaps lodged in the speech habits and linguistic practices of a community.

Both the sociopolitical and the normative-teleological dimensions of the commonsense notion of language invite us to focus on similarities or differences in linguistic behavior, political entities, cultures, abstract entities, and linguistic communities – on how individuals use language. These dimensions thus encourage the E-language view of how to individuate languages. If the only respect in which the commonsense view of language suggests the I-language approach lies in the tendency to acknowledge that people know languages, and sometime several languages, it is no surprise that uses of the common sense concept <u>language</u> and the intuitions that follow it veer towards thinking that language is a form of behavior or action. This last conjecture is mine, not Chomsky's;

he does not speculate about whether ordinary usage is skewed towards the E-language approach.[14] Such a skew would, however, make partial sense of the grip that E-language conceptions of language appear to have on many of those attempting a theoretical approach to language. Furthermore, it makes sense of the extraordinary (but even on a superficial analysis puzzling) grip on the imagination that the supposed language–culture–nation (or community) connection seems to have, not to mention the naive acceptance of the linguist as a cataloger of rules of linguistic etiquette who can be called upon to settle issues of schooling and rhetoric.

Unfortunately, the behavior-based views of language differences that underlie E-language approaches are useless for serious theoretical purposes. No one wants to reject observations of behavior, of course: close, insightful descriptions of linguistic behavior and the contexts in which it appears can serve as evidence about the language organ in the head and how it functions. But making linguistic behavior the subject matter of serious science is to attempt to make a stable natural object out of what are, in fact, highly variable, interest-dependent, context-sensitive, creative efforts of people. The best that an E-language approach can hope for is not natural objects but fairly stable patterns of behavior. But these tend to arise only when people are constrained by a specific task, the need to cooperate, or regimentation – where people speaking a language are asked to have their language use serve a social, project, corporation, or ritual function. To get a grip on these functions, those who attempt an E-language approach must look to culture, communities, social practices, and the like. But that only makes things worse. The supposed subject matter expands even further, and it is difficult to see how to exclude *anything*.

Chomsky's view of UG provides another way to make the point that E-language approaches offer little or nothing of theoretical interest, a way that focuses on the issue of the principles of individuation for languages. Notice that there is no suggestion in the discussion above that E-language approaches take a single form or that they have a single aim. Nor is there a suggestion that they are totally uninteresting scientifically. They do include observations that are useful to the theoretician. They include not just various conjectures but the careful empirical work of Bloomfield, Harris, and others (particularly on Amerindian languages) and a considerable amount of insightful work on discourse (e.g., Sperber and Wilson 1986). And they can be motivated by an effort to produce precise descriptions and categories, as well as by behaviorist wishful thinking. So there can be much of value in the results of various E-language approaches, including scientific value. But if Chomsky's overall picture of language is right, they cannot hope to provide a serious, principled way of distinguishing one language from another or of counting languages. Dealing with linguistic behavior and its description as they do, they depend upon intention and desire, task and project. A quick glance at Wittgenstein's favored way of distinguishing languages from one another indicates this. He spoke of language as a collection of games in which linguistic sounds figure, and he explained how one can distinguish one language game from another. For Wittgenstein, language games include not only the rules of the game (largely normative, and presumably held to be lodged in the linguistic community that 'teaches' the young to speak and maintains the 'standards' by maintaining various practices), but the speakers, the individual acts of speaking, the actions into which these acts of speaking are woven, and the world in which the whole exercise takes place. Very little, if anything, is excluded. How, then, is one language game distinguished from another? It turns out (Wittgenstein 1953) that they differ from one another by virtue of the intentions of those involved in the game. In effect, they differ by virtue of the fact that each different game amounts to a different task or represents a different practice in which language figures. If so, there are no hard-and-fast distinctions to be found, and, as with all human actions, one should not expect a canonical and agreed-upon classification that places each practice in its distinct place. There are no natural objects, and there is no science.

For a serious, principled way to distinguish languages from one another, one needs a method of individuation that is based on a science that goes beyond description and categorization of uses of language to provide a theory of natural language as a whole. Chomsky has stated this claim in various ways throughout his career, by emphasizing that his approach is empirical, realist, and (most recently) naturalistic[15] and by aligning linguistics with biology – a trend emphasized recently in his Minimalist Program, where a theory of language must recognize Bare Output Conditions that are set by the other biological systems in the human mind. But the basic theme is the same throughout: a serious theory of any language must be formally simple (systematic) and descriptively and explanatorily adequate.

The point of insisting on naturalism and biology in efforts to produce a principled way of distinguishing languages is to emphasize the difference between Chomsky's approach and that of E-language theorists, who want to make language a social phenomenon and treat the study of language as a form of social science. Typically, we have seen, they treat the mind as plastic and malleable, as the product of external influence. Chomsky wants to insist that language is fixed in its nature, even though it can be used in all sorts of ways, often creatively. And he wants to insist that the study of language is like any other natural science. It is the investigation of a fixed natural phenomenon – in this case, a biological phenomenon. If it is, one must – as with other natural sciences – expect convergence among those who study a domain. If there is no agreement, and there appears to be no prospect of reaching one, the rational person abandons the effort. Obviously, the domain about which one is making a decision and the way that agreement is reached are crucial. To see what convergence amounts to in scientific judgment, consider the contrasting, but still rational, ways of reaching agreement in legislation and legal decision. (No doubt holding a machine gun to a person's head might yield agreement, but that is pathological and irrelevant.) There could be a dispute about whether a wine is really a Merlot, or whether bubbly white wines produced outside the Champagne region are champagnes. (In fact, the second dispute actually took place and was settled in court: they are not.) Deciding such issues is not a matter of settling a dispute among scientists about the best way to describe and explain a natural phenomenon. One does not carry out experiments and make predictions that may or may not be borne out. In the wine case the issue is not empirical, and the dispute is not about the natural divisions between things but over permission to use marketable terminology on a label. This is a practical (moral in a general sense, or action-related), legal-political dispute about valuable property. The same is true of languages individuated sociopolitically and in Wittgenstein's task-oriented way. Sociopolitical, normative-teleological, and Wittgensteinian distinctions between languages may not always lead to decisions about legal permission and prohibition, but they turn on practical issues involving human tasks, rights, desires, and intentions. And if disputes about whether one language is the same as another ever get beyond philosophers' ruminations about differences between games and become matters that individuals and polities take seriously, short of the machine gun, one has to – as in the wine case – appeal to legal, legislative, and arbitration-based solutions. Should Spanish be an official language of the United States? Is Ebonics a form of English? Does it need to be taught? Does the Glaswegian really speak English? Involving matters of power, authority, and privilege, as these latter disputes do, they can be highly charged and difficult to settle rationally. But where they are settled, agreement is not reached by scientific investigation. Agreement is not the product of compelling, growing evidence that a theory of a domain is descriptively and explanatorily adequate to its domain. Such agreement is required in the natural sciences – which is where Chomsky tries to show linguistics should be placed. This is reaching agreement in a way that parallels how it came to be realized that phlogiston is not a proper explanation of combustion, but oxidation is. Chomsky argues that this sort of agreement is required to determine the correct account of the language organ that every biologically normal human being has. Only a theory with such support allows languages to be counted in the natural way.

The natural way to count languages: UG, natural language, and I-language

Now we can take up in earnest how Chomsky's science of language counts languages. The naturalistic approach to language represented by work that has appeared since the early 1980s in Chomsky's principles and parameters (P&P) framework allows for several ways to count languages, all of which are based on the nativist and internalist principles that have always informed his approaches to linguistic theory. Two of these ways of counting look a little bit like some of the sociopolitically based E-language ways indicated above, for they end up picking out related (perhaps overlapping) classes of speakers. But the means of individuation are very different, so that while there may be some overlap in who counts as speaking language L, the principles of individuation – and the motivations and justifications for them – are very different.

At one level, every human being who speaks a natural language has the same language, a (state of) Universal Grammar (UG). There are broad differences, noted earlier, between Japanese and English in terms of both sounds and structure: each employs a different cluster of sounds drawn from the stock of humanly possible linguistic sounds, and English is structurally a head-initial language in which the "head" of a phrase, such as a verbal head (e.g., "carry") of a verb phrase, appears before the object of the verb (e.g., "carry a skiff"), and Japanese is a head-final language in which the verb in a verb phrase appears after its object ("a skiff carry"). But both the sounds that are available for use in these languages and the broad structural differences are *included* in UG. The structural options are represented as two possible positions of a head-initial/final 'switch' (parameter) that the child sets very early when he or she acquires a language. (There is ample evidence that there is such a switch/parameter, and that it is set very early – certainly before the child actually begins to utter anything out loud.) There are other head-final languages too, such as Miskito, which is spoken in parts of eastern Nicaragua and Honduras; but these differ from Japanese by virtue of other switch settings (structure) and by differences in sounds. It takes very few switches or parameters to cover all the broad structural differences between known natural languages. By one count, there are about 6,000 natural languages, so conceived. If one assumed that there were 14 switches in UG, that each had no more than two possible positions, and that their settings were independent of one another, one could have $2^{14} = 16,384$ structurally different languages. That is a comfortable margin above 6,000, although it should be kept in mind that it is the number not of actual languages but of possible languages that UG needs to define, and that might be considerably higher. The specifics are still unsettled: the claim that there are some 6,000 structurally different languages is certainly subject to change, as is the decision about just how many parameters there are in UG, how they interrelate and/or covary, and whether at least some of them have default settings (preferable for purposes of language acquisition, because then the child has only to set those switches that need changing) or are all initially unset. The aim here is not to try to settle these issues, but to indicate Chomsky's way of expressing the point that there could well be a large number of structurally distinct humanly possible natural languages contained within a single overarching system. Determining the total number depends on settling the issue of how many parameters there are. This determination must be tied to the question of how many structurally different languages are found by the linguist working in the field, for any parameter-based decision about the number of possible human languages had better not conflict with the facts, so far as they can be determined: clear cases of structurally distinct languages that do not fill slots in a matrix of theoretically possible languages would indicate that the theory of UG is wrong. Furthermore, decisions must depend on providing reasonably easy strategies for a child to (unconsciously) set switches. If it is assumed that switches are set early and virtually automatically, given minimal experience, it had better be possible to conceive of a way for the child to automatically set switches one way as opposed to another. Otherwise, while the overall formal proposal might be pretty, it has no empirical warrant.

The results of naturalistic decisions might overlap the sociopolitical terminology of French, English, Malagasy, and the like, but they are not bound to. There is good reason, for example, to think that there are at least two Spanishes, representing distinct settings of a parameter switch, since some who call themselves Spanish-speakers systematically disagree over whether a particular structurally based construction is grammatical (*LPK* 16–24). So there are at least two structurally different natural languages spoken among those who call themselves Spanish-speakers. The fact that speakers who fall into two structurally different groups nevertheless typically manage to communicate with each other and not be misunderstood and the fact that they live in proximity to each other are important considerations for those who think of languages in sociopolitical and normative terms, but irrelevant for the purposes of naturalistic theoretical individuation.

With a well-founded theoretical classification of languages backed up by a good theory of UG, however, it is easy to see why sociopolitical classifications of languages might end up classifying similar classes of people as "speakers of L" – end up, for example, classifying overlapping sets of people as speaking Warlpiri. Children in a community whose members speak a structurally classified language naturally set their parametric switches in the ways that others in that community have set them. Switches are set early, and virtually automatically, on the basis of a child's early experiences, so of course children born to those who speak Warlpiri become Warlpiri-speakers: the speech to which the child is exposed is set one way, and the child reflexively sets his or her parameters that way. In addition, the child typically 'chooses' to associate sounds and meanings in individual lexical items in ways that allow him or her to communicate with others. The result is that the child speaks Warlpiri in a way that makes it look as if he or she is conforming to the speech habits of the community in which he or she is born. But we now know that this is not the correct explanation of what happens.

There is phonological-phonetic, or linguistic sound parameterization as well as structural parameterization. For instance, while young native speakers of Japanese or German develop their Japanese-sounding or German-sounding accents virtually automatically at a very early age, it is difficult for a Japanese-speaker who later learns German to sound to a native German-speaker like another native German-speaker, no matter how much effort is made. It is as if once a child has set a particular set of sound-switches, after a certain age other options become either unavailable (switches cannot be reset, or they become very much more difficult to reset) or one has to resort to other acquisition strategies, including perhaps associative learning and bypassing – at least in part – the phonological component of UG. The result is a little like what one finds in much more radical form in the development of the visual system in the cat or other animals (*LPK* 172): unless the right kind of experience is provided to the kitten within a critical time period soon after birth, development does not proceed (no switches are set), and the cat either never manages to see at all or develops such defective vision in certain (specifiable) respects that it is incapable of carrying out normal activities that rely on fully developed vision. Similarly, infants seem to need certain kinds of experience at certain times in order to develop recognizable phonetic or structural forms of UG. Those who fail to get it – such as Genie, whose story is told in the book of that name – never fully recover the capacity, no matter how much 'training' they get. In the case of phonological-phonetic switches, there is good reason to think that these are set at a very early age: infants seem to 'choose' a set of sounds from those available within natural languages within days of birth (Mehler and Christophe 1994; Christophe et al. 1994). Assuming parameterization of some sort, phonological-phonetic structural differences also yield ways to count languages. Interestingly, the phonological-phonetic count of languages might come closer to the sociopolitical individuation that the individual relying on common sense understanding provides when he or she lists French, English, Malagasy, etc. as different languages. Both variants of Spanish I mentioned above, for example, *sound* like Spanish. On the other hand, there are places in Holland where spoken Dutch sounds more like German than Dutch elsewhere in Holland, and there is little doubt that Swiss German sounds unlike German variants in other areas. Chomsky's point is that, as in the syntactic structural case, the proper reaction to these observations is not that the theory has to match the common sense sociopolitical form of individuation or the related efforts of devotees of language games. The theory's phonological individuation provides a principled form of individuation, whereas E-language approaches rely on various political and social considerations that make naturalistic individuation impossible.

The careful reader will have noticed that the discussion has focused on syntactic structure and on phonological-phonetic features of language – on formal structure and sound. This seems to leave out – or to deal very inadequately with – meanings. While meanings are also represented within Chomsky's theory of UG's machinery, they are not included in this discussion of differences between languages, because there seems to be little reason to think that meanings differ from one language to another. Obviously meanings get paired with different sounds, and perhaps different structures, in different languages: they are differently "lexicalized." But that is irrelevant – what Chomsky calls "Saussurean arbitrariness." These are merely associations, and the naturalist need not deal with them. The only interesting fact about them is that, in the case of lexical items, such associations are often made on a single occasion – indicating that both sound and meaning must be innate.

We have seen that specific natural languages are instances of UG with parameters set. What, then, of I-languages? These employ all the resources of UG and natural languages, but are more specific still. An I-language is an instance of a natural language (hence, parameters are set) specified in terms of a particular selection of lexical items at a certain time. It can also be seen as a "state" of UG – UG as developed in an individual at a time. People's lexicons grow over time and change, although all the features that define lexical items are provided by UG. Note that if a person has two pronunciations of a word – perhaps she uses one in formal contexts, another in informal contexts – she has two I-languages. Naturalistic individuation can get this fine, and it is important that it be able to. But it often need not.

Notice, finally, that there can, and no doubt will, be tremendous differences in the ways in which individuals use their languages. This applies also to what are sometimes called "language skills." Harriet may well be an accomplished author and orator, and Harry may be considered a complete loss by his writing instructor. But these differences are irrelevant to naturalistic individuation of language. Harriet and Harry need the same inner computational system to succeed or not succeed at being 'skillful' with language.

I have discussed the parameters presented in the P&P framework; what about its *principles*? Principles help define UG and are exceptionless: they represent linguistic universals of all natural languages (and I-languages). To illustrate briefly, the "causative construction" seems to be uniform across all languages. Causative constructions have a characteristic signature: a causal verb is followed by a clausal (sentential) embedded event-indicating element, and the meaning of the full sentence (main clause and embedded element together) is that someone causes the event indicated by the embedded element. The following examples are taken from *LPK* 13f. In Spanish, one can say "Juan hizo [arreglar el carro a María]": Juan made Maria fix the car. In English, one might say "Juan had Maria fix the car." In both English and Spanish – and all other natural languages – the principle applies. This English and Spanish pair also illustrates a parametric difference between the two languages. In the embedded event clause in English, the subject of the clause is in its usual position, in front of the verb. In Spanish, however (as in Italian), the subject of the embedded event clause ("María") appears in an adjoined prepositional phrase ("a María"). The parametric difference seen here is not limited to causative constructions. It is a more general difference that appears, in causative constructions, as a difference in how the subject of the embedded event clause is 'marked'. Further examples of principles appear in the next chapter. In the P&P framework, they appear in several 'theories' – sub-components of UG; I illustrate two of the principles of one of these, known as binding theory.

Adequacy in linguistic theory and progress in linguistics

Scientific theories are (largely) made. They are artifacts. While our innately enabled science-forming capacity provides the opportunity, to a large degree we create the sciences that yield what we hope are objective (nonanthropocentric) understandings of various domains. A closely related point is that the standards of good science are those we impose. Calling a theory adequate, good, or excellent, like calling an automobile adequate, good, or excellent, presupposes that one has some notion of what makes a theory or an automobile good. In the case of autos, the answer is given in terms of human purposes, interests, and needs. The same can be said of good scientific theories. Scientific theories, like autos (and unlike natural languages), are artifacts put together by human beings to serve human purposes. But there is a crucial difference. Autos no doubt have to be made in a way that is supported by the facts of nature; otherwise they would fall apart. But no one would list "correctly describing and explaining the facts of nature" as among the functions of automobiles. Scientific theories, though, have as at least part of their explicit function an effort to describe and explain the way things are. While this is correctly seen as the aim to be objective, it does not make the aim any less human or the product any less an artifact.

Among the facts that a good naturalistic theory of language must deal with are not just the detailed facts of specific languages, but the poverty and creativity facts. This is important, because both – particularly the poverty ones – play a crucial role in defining what counts as an adequate linguistic theory. A linguistic theory, like any theory, must meet general conditions on a good theory: it must be simple and systematic (austere in the sense of ch. 1). An attempt to state what counts as a good theory for a *particular* domain, however, is an attempt to state adequacy conditions for that theory. Typically, theoreticians in natural sciences demand, and perhaps try to state, conditions of both descriptive and explanatory adequacy. The more central notion of these two for Chomsky's linguistic work has always been explanatory adequacy. It carries the major burden of stating what a good theory of language is and of distinguishing Chomsky's approach to language from E-language approaches. A descriptively adequate theory, to the extent that it can be disentangled from an explanatorily adequate theory of language, amounts to the demand that for each natural language a grammar be provided that generates that language. Notice the assumed distinction between a linguistic theory (theory of language) and a grammar for a particular language. A hypothesized grammar for a particular language can be called a theory of *that* language and is descriptively adequate to that language if it generates all and only the sentences of that language. A grammar/theory of English generates all and only the sentences of English. A theory of language – Chomsky's aim – is another animal altogether; it provides grammars for *all* natural languages. A "linguistic theory is descriptively adequate if it makes a descriptively adequate grammar available for each natural language" (*ATS* 24). A good linguistic theory is a theory of UG.

Chomsky's use of the term "description" in connection with theories of a language and of language in general calls for some clarification. For one thing, "description" must not be limited to the use of ordinary descriptive terms. Describing languages in a science of language is a matter of using the theoretical vocabulary provided by that science. The linguist does not rely on the common understanding of "word" and "sentence" (unless speaking informally, or unless new, defined concepts are introduced to replace the common sense ones), but on "schwa," "VP," "lexical item," "expression," and so on. Nor is the linguist tied to some philosopher's idea of what a proper or canonical description is. Linguists describe natural language sounds and meanings – not pitches and not the sensory 'concepts' of color and taste. Nor is the linguist limited to describing a finite set of sentences: that would limit the linguist to performance, not competence. A grammar or theory of language describes not the sum of sentences produced by Harry and Harriet and all their fellows, but – by using a generative theory – a potentially infinite set of expressions. That is why when Chomsky says what a descriptively adequate theory is, he points out that it is one that generates an infinite set of expressions with their structural descriptions. The theoretical *description* is unavoidably generative and is provided by a grammar/theory of *a* language and theories of language. A description of a language is not a list of sentences, but a theory; a description of language is a theory of UG.

For Chomsky, explanatory adequacy is primary. Moreover, only linguistic theories, not specific grammars, are explanatorily adequate in Chomsky's sense. This is because only they speak to Plato's problem – how *any* child can acquire *any* language. An important early statement of explanatory adequacy went:

> [To] the extent that a linguistic theory succeeds in selecting a descriptively adequate grammar on the basis of primary linguistic data, we can say that it meets the condition of *explanatory adequacy*. That is, to this extent, it offers an explanation for the intuition of the native speaker on the basis of an empirical hypothesis concerning the innate predisposition of the child to develop a certain kind of theory to deal with the evidence presented to him. Any such hypothesis can be falsified (all too easily, in actual fact) by showing that it fails to provide a descriptively adequate grammar for primary linguistic data from some other language. (*ATS* 25–6)

The linguistic theory must be true and – the crucial words are – "succeed in selecting a descriptively adequate grammar." Unfortunately, this important 1965 statement is one of Chomsky's more obscure. To remedy this and indicate how to progress in dealing with explanatory adequacy, I will restate the point in terms of the P&P framework's way of individuating languages and then go back to the idiom of the 1960s.

Answering Plato's problem within the P&P framework is producing a true theory of UG that states all the principles of all natural languages plus all the parametric differences between them *and* that provides for an easy way to understand how a child unconsciously selects one language over another, given what Chomsky calls "primary linguistic data" (perception of a fairly small set of sentences in a relatively homogeneous speech community). The P&P framework speaks to how a child selects a grammar by construing parameters as 'switches' that are set automatically in a way not unlike that whereby a kitten's visual system that receives the relevant input sets the 'switches' that provide the capacity to (say) see horizontal lines. In the linguistic case, it is not difficult to imagine – *assuming that a child has available in tacit knowledge the relevant concepts* (phrase, NP, N, etc.) – that on hearing a few sentences from a head-initial language, he or she would reflexively set his or her initial/final switch for "head-initial." And so on for the other parameters (in some order, perhaps). Given that parameters determine a natural language, the child soon acquires a natural language. That oversimplifies, of course. The child also has to acquire lexical items, and this cannot be done independently of setting parametric switches. But on the assumption that the relevant concepts and possible 'choices' are innate – and the poverty of stimulus observations make this highly plausible – the capacity to recognize instances in which they are realized or instantiated can be presupposed. Remember that *all* the principles and parameters of natural languages can be thought to be at hand; they are all included in UG. So the P&P framework with the strategy of switch setting makes it very easy indeed to understand how any child could acquire any natural language. Coming up with a true theory of UG is, of course, extremely difficult. But it is not difficult to see how UG as understood in the P&P framework shows a way to solve Plato's problem.

In the 1960s, however, Chomsky did not have a theory of UG with principles and parameters (and lots of evidence that there must be something like them). In speaking to the question of how a child selects a grammar, he put the issue in terms of "simplicity." Philosophers have noted that two theories that both seem to describe the same phenomena might differ in terms of how *simple* they are and proposed (reasonably) that the simpler theory is better – and so more adequate – than the more complex. It does not much matter that it is difficult to state what simplicity is beyond gesturing in the direction of minimal theoretical devices and elegant law statements. People seem to agree on which theory is simpler than another, and it looked as though simplicity offered a theory-independent way to measure one theory's superiority to another, assuming that both are descriptively adequate to the phenomena they describe. Perhaps, then, simplicity explains how a child chooses a grammar for some linguistic data: a grammar is, after all, a theory that generates all and only the sentences of a language, and a child has to choose between grammars or – in current terminology – I-languages.

One problem with this move is that the general, theory-external notion of simplicity to which it appeals really only makes sense of how the theoretician (linguist) constructing a theory of language might select one over another. No *child* can be expected to construct a theory of a language as the linguist does, much less appeal to simplicity in this theory-general sense to choose between theories. The child's choice is unconscious, virtually automatic – a variety of triggering. So, while this theory-independent notion of simplicity helps both the physicist and the linguist choose between theories, it seems to be hopeless for the child's reflexive, automatic choice between theories (grammars) for linguistic data. If Chomsky is to appeal to a concept of simplicity at all, it had better be a different one. Recognizing this, he introduced what he called a theory-*internal* notion of simplicity.

The goal of internal simplicity, as of the later idea of parameter setting, was to provide a way to make sense of how a child's mind could, given minimal data, automatically 'select' a grammar/theory for a particular language. This goal was expressed in *Current Issues in Linguistic Theory*, a small book that appeared earlier than *ATS*. There Chomsky says that in choosing a grammar to fit some data, the child's mind must rely on "an innate specification of certain heuristic procedures and certain built-in constraints on the character of the task to be performed" (*CILT* 26). The heuristic and built-in constraints together constitute the "language acquisition device" (LAD); Chomsky also calls them the "initial state" (i.e., UG). A heuristic is a learning aid or procedure; an innate one works for all languages and proceeds automatically; a good one presumably offers a ready, biologically possible way to 'choose', as explained below. The "built-in constraints on the character of the task to be performed" play crucial supporting roles. One of these constraints is found in linguistic universals that are innate and present in all languages. (The principles of the P&P framework are examples.) If they are inherent in all languages, the heuristic does not 'select' them. This reduces the number of choices needed. Universals also make the construction of hypotheses possible: because of universals, data come to the heuristic already structured. (The alternative is massive empiricist bootstrapping.) Another constraint is found in Chomsky's demonstration that only certain forms of grammar suit natural language. The point is illustrated in chapter 5: finite state grammars, for example, just do not suit natural languages, while transformational ones do. This fact suggests that the child's heuristic device can entertain only certain kinds of grammatical hypotheses. Both constraints, then, narrow the field of hypotheses the heuristic needs to construct and evaluate, making it easier to understand how this early view of the LAD could speak to Plato's problem. Assuming that hypotheses are available, Chomsky suggested thinking of the heuristic operating by 'evaluating' them, where this involves 'choosing' shorter hypothesis statements over longer ones. For a given set of data, a grammar that is expressed in a theory with shorter theoretical statements than another theory (grammar) is more highly valued (simpler) in this sense (*LSLT* 117–18; *ATS* 42f); the evaluation device selects a grammar by choosing the more highly valued ones. (An example of a short theoretical statement that replaces several others while capturing a wide range of data is found in chapter 5 in Chomsky's elegantly compressed phrase structure rule for English (cf. *ATS* 43).) In effect, this heuristic embodies Chomsky's old internal simplicity measure: 'choose' brevity. This evaluation procedure might look arcane, for brevity of theoretical statement might not seem to have anything to do with the internal engineering of a biological LAD. It actually does, however: short theoretical statements capture the "natural classes" and "significant generalizations" of natural languages. They capture a child's predisposition to seek simplifying regularity (*ATS* 44) in the data confronted.

The P&P framework's biologically set 'switches' – those parts of the LAD or UG that unconsciously and automatically select natural languages, given data – represent a later effort to understand the biological heuristic in a child's mind. But there is a crucial difference between the earlier effort to understand the LAD and its operations and the later P&P version. The earlier version compared grammars, relying on length of statement to do so. To the extent that parameters are set independently (i.e., without need for comparison), the P&P framework offers something quite close to a *discovery* procedure (Chomsky, personal communication, December 31, 1998). On this assumption, the P&P framework provides a way to solve Plato's problem without appeal to evaluation procedures, suggesting a rather clean break between the pre- and post-P&P periods. It also signals an opportunity to shift attention from solving Plato's problem to other explanatory tasks. The Minimalist Program in particular seems to raise new questions about explanation that were beyond the scope of earlier theories of language. It seems to be pointing to an understanding of the function and design of the language faculty, and so to an understanding of what the best engineering for it would be. If it succeeds, linguistics progresses not only by solving Plato's problem but in other ways. I return to these themes in the next chapter.

Notice that not only do the P&P framework's parameters represent progress in capturing the heuristic, but the overall structure and principles of the framework represent progress in clarifying "built-in constraints." In *ATS*, Chomsky said: "we are very far from being able to present a system of formal and substantive linguistic universals that will be sufficiently rich and detailed to account for the facts of language learning" (*ATS* 46). If the P&P form of grammar and its various principles (universals) are on the right track, this melancholy assessment is no longer apt.

5

How to Make an Expression

My aim here is not to introduce Chomsky's linguistics to neophytes. That would take a lot of space, demanding that the reader perform many exercises (the linguistic analog of experimentation) and requiring a focus that is out of place in this discussion of Chomsky's intellectual project. For a very helpful introduction to Chomsky's early work, see John Lyon's classic *Noam Chomsky* (1970). For a focused and clear introduction to Chomsky's recent P&P framework, there is Cook and Newsom's (1996) *Chomsky's Universal Grammar* (the recent edition points to minimalist developments). Chomsky's own semi-popular linguistic and philosophical work is accessible to many, particularly his earlier *Reflections on Language* (1975) and the more recent *Language and Problems of Knowledge: The Managua Lectures* (1988). His exposition is not necessarily simpler or easier to understand than that of some of his expositors – often it is neither – but no one else ties his linguistic theories and their development as directly to his internalist, nativist, and constructivist rationalist philosophical views – and their foundations in the poverty and creativity observations – as well as he does.

What I hope to do instead is provide just enough of Chomsky's linguistic work to make it apparent how much progress he – in cooperation and dispute with many others – has made over the last 40 years in addressing the poverty and creativity observations. This chapter focuses on the first (Plato's problem), but because all Chomsky's theories of language have been internalist and generative, by default they speak to the stimulus freedom and unboundedness aspects of the creativity observations. To emphasize the progress, I focus only on the earliest and the latest periods of Chomsky's work. The early period began with *LSLT* and *SyS* in the mid-1950s and extended to 1965, when *ATS* offered an influential conception of grammar, the Standard Theory. The latest is the P&P period, which began in the early 1980s and has continued since, although with several modifications and improvements in its latest stage, the Minimalist Program (from the early 1990s on). The intervening years saw development of the Extended Standard Theory. No one thing characterized each period, and there is no single respect in which they differed. Certainly, though, the P&P period represents real progress in solving Plato's problem and speaking to other explanatory issues – even greater in its minimalist form – and it is possible to pick themes that illustrate this.

First, though, a technical term, a useful *aide-mémoire*, and a caveat. The technical term is "base component." In the Standard Theory of *ATS* it was assumed that there is a transformational component of a grammar whose job it is to move items around. The base component provided the items to move around. It was thought to consist of a phrase structure component (on which below) and a lexicon; intuitively, the base component generated basic sentence-like formal entities on which transformations operated. The term "base component" remained even when the phrase structure component later began to erode.

The purpose of the *aide-mémoire* is to provide a simple picture of the different ways in which the computational system of the language faculty is construed in 1965's *ATS* and in the 1982 and later P&P framework. Capital letters F and Y provide the pictures. Starting with *ATS*'s Standard Theory model, the trunk of the F from the bottom to the first branch pictures the base component plus obligatory transformations – those that must be applied to arrive at something like a recognizable basic sentence. The derivation of a sentence 'begins' with this trunk. The node at the base of the first branch is the (in)famous Deep Structure; the branch is the semantic system that 'interprets' Deep Structure. The rest of the trunk to the top node pictures the optional part of the transformational component; the top node is Surface Structure. The branch from Surface Structure is the phonological-phonetic interpretational system. Basically, Deep Structure is a meaning-representation produced by the base and a few obligatory transformations, and it is linked by optional transformations to Surface Structure, a sound-representation.[1] Derivation in the P&P framework takes the form of a Y beginning at the bottom with D-structure (a successor to Deep

Structure) or DS and proceeding to the node from which two branches grow. The node is S-structure (another successor term) or SS, and the tops of the branches are PF (PHON) and LF (SEM). In minimalism – at risk of sounding enigmatic – DS and SS disappear, leaving only sound (PHON) and meaning (SEM). But the derivational picture still provides a reasonable *aide-mémoire*.

The caveat concerns the terms "representation of meaning" and "representation of sound." For many philosophers and a considerable number of linguists, "representation of x" suggests or implies that there is something – a meaning or a sound – that the representation re-presents. For Chomsky, "representation of x" amounts only to "theoretical term of category x": a representation of meaning is a *kind* of representation, and "of x" says what kind. To avoid misunderstanding, it is often better to use the terms I used above: "meaning-representation" (in recent work, a representation written with semantic features) and "sound-representation" (one with phonetic features). Notice that a meaning-representation *is* a (theory-defined) meaning; it need not refer to or be *of* a meaning.

Why transformational grammar?

Very early in his career Chomsky argued that some grammars – specifically, finite state and phrase structure grammars – are inadequate to natural languages, and that, at a minimum, an adequate grammar would have to involve transformations. Since our aim is to see why and how his latest grammars improve on his earliest transformational efforts, we should first see on what grounds he rejected finite state and phrase structure grammars in favor of transformational ones. Keep in mind in what follows that, for linguists, sentences are theoretical entities. Remember too that a sentence of a natural language cannot be defined apart from theoretically specifying the language it is a sentence in. It is not enough for theoretical purposes to say that S is a sentence of English, period. Not only does that invite political and social E-language considerations, but a natural language is an infinite set that can be captured theoretically only by describing it with a unique generative grammar. Furthermore, a grammar cannot be shown to be unique unless it is itself generated in a true and explanatorily adequate theory of UG. In effect, any attempt to offer a theoretical characterization of a sentence automatically raises issues of descriptive and explanatory adequacy. Chomsky rejects finite state grammars because they are not even minimally descriptively adequate. A pure phrase structure grammar might conceivably be made minimally descriptively adequate, but it cannot provide for explanatory adequacy.

Because a grammar for a natural language must generate a potential infinity of sentences, and because the number of elements (e.g., lexical items) available within natural languages is finite, any grammar must rely on *recursive* procedures. Recursion – production of a sequence of elements by a finite procedure that operates on one or more preceding elements – introduces the possibility of repetition, allowing for sentences of indefinitely great length. It is a powerful device: the infinite set of natural numbers, for example, can be generated by a simple recursive procedure that starts with 1, adds 1 to it to get 2, and then 1 to 2 to get 3, etc. Recursion in natural languages can be mere repetition of an element: the adverb "very" can be iterated any number of times: "very simple example," "very very very very very . . . simple example." Natural language recursion, however, often involves phrases. "The dog that bit the man who left the car that lost its wheels that . . . is under the table." It can also very soon tax our performance systems: "That that that that Wanda likes Harry is striking is worrisome is terrible is monstrous." Keep in mind, of course, that what is at issue here is what the computational system of the language faculty can in principle 'do', not what the person who has this faculty (and limited memory, limited time, difficulty with some kinds of embedding, etc.) can actually process, as in the "That that that that . . ." case.

If a grammar for a natural language must provide recursion, consider the merits of what is, from one point of view, a very simple recursive grammar – a finite state one. Finite state grammars are very likely to appeal to those who have a naive engineer's view of what a language is, and Chomsky's argument against these grammars in *SyS* was designed for just such people. *SyS* is a set of lecture notes for an undergraduate course Chomsky gave at MIT in the 1950s that he hoped would wean a group of young engineers and mathematicians away from their conviction that the newly minted mathematics of information and computational systems would, with a bit of ingenuity, be able to treat the sentences of natural languages as sequences of words constructed by a simple Markovian computational system (cf. *SyS* 20).[2] A finite state grammar is a Markovian system: after choosing a particular word, one then chooses another to follow it on the basis of the stated probabilities of that element (word) being followed by one or a specified set of others; with the second chosen, a third is chosen by appeal to another such rule, and so on. For example, "the" is likely to be followed by any of these elements: {book, bookmark, wombat, . . .}. These are hopeless grammars for natural languages and do not work even for formal symbol systems such as a predicate calculus, which has nested dependencies (quantifiers that bind embedded variables, for example), so that formulae cannot be constructed by appeal to simple left-to-right rules. Long-range dependencies between words also ruin any chance of such grammars working for natural languages. "Someone who Harry had mentioned to George won the lottery Tuesday walked the dog last night" is an example; "someone" is read as the subject of "walked the dog," so constructing or reading the sentence from left to right without representing this distant connection is impossible. Perhaps rules could be introduced to generate such strings. But any rules would also produce indefinitely large numbers of sentences that are ungrammatical. Finite state grammars provide no criterion for what gets counted as a sentence of English (or any other natural language) and what does not. They are not even marginally descriptively adequate. And as for explanatory adequacy, it is hard to imagine what a finite state theory of all languages (a finite state UG) would even look like.

Pure phrase structure grammars are better candidates for natural languages, but still far from adequate. As the name suggests, a phrase structure grammar recognizes grammatical categories of constituents and generates strings of elements that have *grammatical structure*. Unlike finite state grammars as understood by Chomsky's undergraduates,[3] a phrase structure grammar recognizes categories of elements (N, V, . . .) and offers ways to relate them in phrasal and clausal structures (NP, S, etc.). Chomsky's phrase structure grammars consist of a set of *rewrite rules*. Rewrite rules take as input formal category symbols such as S and, as output of the operation "rewrite as," other formal category symbols such as NP and VP. A context-free phrase structure grammar does not specify in what environments a rewrite rule applies, while a context-dependent one does. Chomsky's early phrase structure grammars are context-dependent. For simplicity of presentation, though, I limit this exposition to a few context-free rewrite rules. One rewrite rule says that the symbol S can be rewritten as the symbol NP plus the symbol VP: S $\rightarrow$ NP + VP. NP and VP can in turn be rewritten. To capture a VP such as "left Harry's book" we need a symbol V (for verb "left") plus a symbol NP (for "Harry's book"). We need, then, a rewrite rule like this: VP $\rightarrow$ V + NP. After continued successive application of categorial (S, NP, . . .) symbol rewrite rules, one eventually reaches single lexical category symbols like N (for noun) and V. At this point in *SyS* Chomsky introduces rewrite rules that say which lexical items can be inserted. There might, for example, be a rule V → {*wash, rinse,* . . .}, which says that V can be rewritten by substituting any of a specified group of verbs. He has a more complicated procedure in *ATS* which rewrites lexical category symbols as sets of lexical features.

A particularly important set of rewrite rules for English captures verbal auxiliary structure, which is crucial for the assignment of tense, modality, and the distribution of the auxiliaries "have" and "be"; without this set of rules, one could not have anything like a recognizable English sentence. (Notice that every sentence in English is tensed.) Chomsky's two rules in *SyS* (p. 39) are models of simplicity:

Verb → Aux + V

Aux → C(M) (have+en) (be+ing) (be+en)

with M = modal and C, for present purposes, identified with tense. Modals ("must," "can," . . .) include "will," so that one can get the effect of the future tense, even if the only morphophonemic (which is what Chomsky then called the component that yields phonemes, or 'sounds') tense markings in English are the past ("-ed," as in "walked") and the present, which is 'unmarked' (without "-ed," as in "walk"). Parentheses around a symbol indicate that it is optional; thus, only C is obligatory. C's role in subject–verb agreement and the rules that provide for progressive verbs, introduce word boundaries, and do the other work necessary to make a string interpretable by the morphophonemic part of a grammar can be ignored. But we need to move beyond the rewrite rules of a phrase structure grammar to add at least one transformation, which is needed to have affixes 'hop' across word stems so that we get an English string. The hopping rule is: "Let *Af* stand for any of the affixes *past, S, Ø, en, ing.* Let *v* stand for an *M* or *V*, or *have* or *be* (i.e., for any non-affix in the phrase *Verb*). Then:

$$Af + v \rightarrow v + Af\#,$$

where # is interpreted as word boundary" (*SyS* 39). In other words, to make "walked," we need to have past "ed" jump over "walk" and attach itself, after which there is a word boundary. Transformations, as this example illustrates, take *structural descriptions* and subject them to a *structural change*, so introducing *movement* of elements. (The passive transformation rule as it appears in *SyS*, to provide another example, takes the structured string NP–Aux–V–NP ("Beavers build dams," with Aux here amounting to the present tense alone) and transforms it according to the passive rule X_1–X_2–X_3–$X_4 \rightarrow X_4$–X_2+be+en-X_3-by X_1 ("Dams are built by beavers," or more accurately, before relevant other transformations apply: "Dams PRES be+en build by beavers").) The two phrase structure rules V $\rightarrow$ Aux + V and Aux $\rightarrow$ C(M) (have+en) (be+ing) (be+en) plus the affix-hopping transformational rule and appropriate lexical rules provide any English auxiliary sequence, such as any of these:

Harry washed the car.
Harry will wash the car.
Harry will have washed the car.
Harry will have been washing the car.
Harry has washed the car.
Harry has been washing the car.
etc.

However, the fact that we cannot attach affixes in the right way without transformations hints at trouble if one asks a pure phrase structure grammar to deal with English or other natural languages.

Phrase structure grammars make it easier to see how a system could produce a large number of constructions. But a pure phrase structure grammar must produce strings in a regimented way: its rules cannot move the elements in a string, once they have been produced. That is why an affix transformation was needed. Rewrite rules to deal with affixes could be provided, but only at the cost of losing the simplicity of the basic auxiliary rewrite rules and substituting several rules to deal with each class of cases. Lost too, surely, would be any hope of learnability: the more rules one must learn, the harder it is to learn a language. To be descriptively adequate, a pure phrase structure grammar would have to include all the rules required to produce various passive constructions for different tenses and modals, different kinds of relative clause constructions, and the large number of other forms that the sentences of English can take. It would have to be extraordinarily complicated and unwieldy, requiring many additional 'rules', many of which would have to be not just specific to English, but ad hoc to differences in particular constructions, lexical items, etc. A phrase structure grammar cannot, therefore, be explanatorily adequate for English. The plethora of rules needed for English, and similarly for all other natural languages, would make it impossible to conceive of how a child could acquire anything like such a grammar under the conditions the poverty observations indicate. So, Chomsky argued, any grammar adequate to English and other natural languages must at least include transformations. They greatly reduce the number of rules needed to construct a grammar of a natural language.

Before proceeding, an important matter concerning transformations: near the beginning of his career, Chomsky, following his teacher Zellig Harris (who used them for different purposes), adopted the term "transformation." When introduced, transformations were defined over structural descriptions and mandated structural changes, virtually presupposing a phrase structure grammar (plus lexical insertion, both together constituting a base component (*ATS* 84f)) to provide the elements and structures to be transformed.

In later usage, transformations are not tied to this picture, which is characteristic of *SyS* and *ATS* (the latter representing the Standard Theory). Increasingly, "transformation" came simply to characterize any transition in the derivation of a sentence where an element changes position. Derivations of sentences in late minimalism – which has abandoned a base component, the infamous Deep Structure, its successor D-structure, and S-structure too – still has transformations in this sense. In fact, for this usage, it is difficult to conceive of a grammar that is not transformational. All grammars, Chomsky reminds us, must deal with what he has called the "displacement property" (*MP* 50, 222, 324f): all grammars must account for how some sentential elements come to be displaced from the positions where they are naturally interpreted – that is, from proximity to elements with which they need to be linked semantically. "Wh" words are paradigm cases. The sentence "Who did Harry and Harriet hope might work for them?" must be understood in a way that requires that the person "who" is used to refer to be understood as the referent of the subject of the embedded element "*x* work for Harry and Harriet," despite the fact that what is seen or heard (the expression's phonetic or graphic appearance) puts "who" far away from "work." A grammar must show both how "who" came to be displaced from its natural place, and how and why we automatically link it to its "natural" place. Any grammar must capture this movement and provide for its recovery. Thus, any grammar will involve transformations in this second usage.

The early transformational grammars did not last long. Without going into details, while they offered a tremendous improvement in descriptive and explanatory adequacy over phrase structure grammars, they did not offer much in the way of linguistic universals and thus required that too much of a language be learned. Some universals were discovered then and survive still. An example is the principle of the cycle: transformations apply to "minimal" clauses/phrases in phrase markers, then to those sentences/clauses that contain them, and so on. This very strong empirical claim about how processing takes place in all natural languages turns out to be correct on all the evidence so far, thus making an important contribution to a theory of UG and to the "theory-internal" concept of simplicity that captures how children acquire languages readily and automatically. It survives in changing forms in Chomsky's later theories of language. But these earlier grammars were not very successful at ridding themselves of a great many language-specific rules. The early English passive rule mentioned above is an example: it is specific to the way in which affixing occurs in English, and, worse, it bears little structural resemblance to the way in which some other languages work. So, while there were excellent reasons to choose a transformational (*ATS* usage) theory of language over a finite state or phrase structure one, it was also clear that better theories could be developed. Explanatory adequacy particularly was still far away.

How the P&P framework makes a sentence

The details of the post-*ATS* and pre-P&P period (from about 1965 to 1980), with its many adjustments and the development of the Extended Standard Theory, are fascinating and reward study, but there is not space enough to discuss them in this book. One way of looking at them is that it became increasingly obvious that a clean break from earlier efforts was necessary; another is to see the details as a constant accumulation of changes moving in the direction of P&P, the signs of which were, in hindsight, apparent in earlier work. These two apparently very different perspectives can both be supported. But the clean break perspective is better as far as making progress with solving Plato's problem is concerned. The last chapter showed why in an informal way the old picture of acquisition as involving an "evaluation metric" effectively disappeared when parameters came along. Here we see another reason: the P&P framework dispensed "entirely with rule systems for particular languages and particular constructions" (*MP* 52). I discuss one of Chomsky's more technical ways of describing the progress later. First, we need to get clear about how the P&P system works.

Binding theory

The P&P framework clusters many of its language-universal principles together in "theories" that deal with various interconnected language-universal phenomena. Case theory, for example, speaks to how the cases of nouns (nominative, accusative, and oblique (which includes Latin's dative, genitive, ablative, etc.)) are assigned and marked. I focus instead on another of these – binding theory. (My discussion is drawn from the relatively informal *LPK*, but I simplify the already simplified discussion there.) Binding theory deals with several important issues, among which are how a person who hears a sentence knows which pronouns are bound by nouns (when bound, a pronoun must refer to whatever the noun is used to refer to), which nouns they are bound by, and which pronouns are 'free' (can be used to refer to anything/anyone, without regard to what other nouns and pronouns in the sentence are used to refer to). Binding theory answers these questions without supposing that a child 'learns' the answers to them by appeal to generalizations of specific cases, such as "the pronoun and the noun in that sentence Harry muttered are both used by him to refer to the same thing." Facts about reference are very complicated and include knowing what a person is referring to, which requires knowledge of context and speaker intention. It would be far better, given Plato's problem, if binding were dealt with in syntax through universal principles, so that it becomes part of our innate language acquisition mechanism and a part of the structure of language itself, operative whenever we hear a sentence, but independent of knowledge of context and intention. Binding theory shows that this is the case.

Binding theory is defined over units of language called "phrases." The concept of a phrase for natural languages amounts to the idea that there is a cluster of words that have a certain kind of structure.[4] Specifically, phrases have a *head* and a *complement*. Examples of heads of phrases are nouns (Ns) and verbs (Vs). If the head of a phrase is a noun, it is a noun phrase (NP); if the head of a phrase is a verb, it is a verb phrase (VP). Heads can appear before or after their complements, so the general form of phrases allows order to be free; parametric differences in languages set the order in one way (head-initial) or the other (head-final). With this in mind, we can represent the general form of a phrase as $XP = X - YP$. As Chomsky says (*LPK* 69): "we understand this formula to mean that for each choice of X (V, N, A[djective], P[re(post)position]) there is a phrase XP (VP, NP, AP, PP) with the lexical category X as its head and the phrase YP as its complement." In the verb phrase (VP) "left her under the tree," the verb "left" is the head, and the complement includes a pronoun and a prepositional phrase "under the tree" with prepositional head "under" and noun phrase (really, determiner phrase) "the tree" that includes a determiner "the." What is the status of "her?" Binding theory provides a partial answer to this. It is crucial to the answer that the pronoun appears within a phrase, for phrases help define (*minimal*) *domains* (*LPK* 51). The (minimal) domain of a word is the smallest phrase in which it appears. In the case of "Él ama a Juan" (He loves Juan), the domain of the pronoun "Él" / "He" is the entire sentence. The pronoun is not in the VP; the next smallest phrase is, then, the whole clause, a sentence. In "John thinks he is intelligent," the smallest domain containing "he" is the clause "he is intelligent."

Binding theory includes three principles. Two deal with forms of pronominal binding phenomena; the third deals with what are called "r-expressions" ((quasi)referring[5] expressions). I ignore the last and discuss only the two principles. One binding relationship is between nouns (and other pronouns) and pronouns like "her" above. (Do not confuse this with the possessive pronoun "her," which binding theory does not deal with.) Another is the binding relationship between nouns (and other pronouns) and a special class of cases that are traditionally called "reflexive pronouns" which include – in the case of a language like Spanish, which has terms such as "*se*" that precede a verb – *clitics*. Reflexives and the relevant kinds of clitics are called "anaphors."[6] Spanish clitic construction "se afeitar" translates into English as "shave himself," a reflexive construction. An example of a reflexive sentence in English is "Harriet washed herself," where "herself" is the anaphor. Anaphoric pronouns must be bound by some other element in the sentence. You cannot interpret "Harriet washed herself" in such a way that "herself" refers to anyone other than what "Harriet" refers to. It cannot refer to Jane, for example. The same applies to all natural languages. Binding theory must capture this fact in its principles. It must also capture the fact that in "She wanted to leave before her dogs came back" there is a "she" that can be used to refer to any woman (or female dog or hippopotamus, for that matter), while the "her" in this sentence can refer either to the person (or dog or hippopotamus) referred to by the subject "she" or to some other female creature. Similar points apply to all other sentences in English, and to all other natural languages. A pronoun that can be used to refer to anything without regard to what other nouns or pronouns in a sentence are used to refer to is *free*.

I discuss two principles of binding theory:

1 An anaphor must be bound within the minimal domain of a subject. (*LPK* 77)
2 A pronoun must be free in the minimal domain of a subject. (*LPK* 78)

(The third principle is that r-expressions are free; there are exceptions (cf. *KL* 80), but none of this is discussed here.) According to the second principle, a pronoun must be free in a phrase/clause containing a subject. That makes sense for "She left him": "she" is the subject pronoun; both it and the pronoun "him" are in the minimal domain of a subject; and both are free. Switching examples, if we are to find out whether or not "her" in "Harriet washed her under the tree" is bound or free, we cannot restrict ourselves to the phrase that contains "her" – the VP "washed her under the tree" – but must look for a minimal domain that contains the element and also contains a subject. The minimal domain of "her" that contains a subject is in this case the whole sentence. Clearly, "her" is free; it *cannot* be bound by "Harriet." So, on the basis of this further bit of evidence, principle 2 again seems plausible. Consider now "Harriet washed herself under the tree." Here, "herself" is an anaphoric pronoun, so questions about binding are dealt with by principle 1. According to the principle, "herself" must be bound within the minimal domain of a subject (here, "Harriet"). And it is, by "Harriet." So this principle has some evidence in its favor. "Herself" need not be bound by the subject itself; it might be bound by an object term. But let us restrict ourselves to cases where the reflexive pronoun is bound by the subject NP. Consider: "Whom did Harry have shave himself?" ("whom" is a "wh" word, mentioned before as causing trouble for finite state grammars (and other grammars too)). Who is "himself?" It does not look as if it is Harry, even though "Harry" is a subject of a sentential clause and is the closest noun, on surface appearances at least, to "himself." If surface closeness to a reflexive element were all there were to defining a minimal domain of a subject, "Harry" would be the subject of a minimal domain containing "himself," and Harry, according to the principle, would have to be "himself." So, if the principle is to be saved, there must be another subject somewhere that serves to bind "himself." Chomsky's hypothesis (supported by other aspects of the theory of syntax and by massive evidence) is that "himself" is bound to a hidden element that refers to whoever the interrogative pronoun "whom" is used to refer to (cf. *LPK* 84). To see how it is tied, it helps to put the sentence in the quantificational phraseology that logicians favor. In that phraseology, the sentence amounts to something like this: "Who is the person x such that Harry had x shave x?" On this way of looking at it, the interrogative pronoun is actually a *quantifier* binding a *variable* x that operates over a clause of the form "x shave x." If that is the case, we must think of the sentence "Whom did Harry have shave himself" as containing, although hidden in what appears to the ear alone, what Chomsky calls a "trace" element that serves as the subject that defines the minimal domain of a subject for the reflexive element "himself." When hearing something that is said, or producing a sound, the mind "sees" a trace which has the role of a bound variable within logic, and it is this variable that constitutes the subject that defines the minimal domain of a subject containing "himself." To say much more, we would have to begin to delve into trace theory and into the third principle of binding theory, but we have seen enough to establish the point for present purposes. The basic idea is that traces are left when elements are moved from their original positions during a derivation of an expression from another form and that these traces are apparent to the mind. This preserves principle 1 of binding theory (and supports trace theory and its principles too). Binding – at least on this limited evidence – is internal to the language faculty (syntactic) and universal across all languages. This result presupposes, though, that one can provide an independent account of what a phrase is, for binding is stated over phrases. Let us turn, then, to the question of how the P&P approach deals with phrases.

X-bar theory

As we saw, the *ATS* Standard Theory had too many language-particular transformational rules to solve Plato's problem. Its base component – phrase structure plus lexicon component – had the same problem. The P&P framework (*LGB* on) spoke to the surfeit of transformational rules by introducing a single transformational rule – "move-α" (something like "move anything anywhere"). It spoke to the lack of uniformity in the base by adopting and adapting X-bar theory, which had been developing in the intervening Extended Standard Theory framework for some time.[7] X-bar theory, essentially, finds the same structure in all languages (parametric variations such as head-initial/head-final aside) and in phrases of all sorts, whether noun phrases, verb phrases, etc. The definition in the last section of a phrase having a head and a complement ($XP = X - YP$) incorporates this point: it makes no difference what category a head is (noun, verb, etc.), it heads a phrase of that category (NP, VP, etc.) that can take a complement consisting of a phrase of some category or another. The question is, where does this structure come from? In *LGB* (p. 29) Chomsky suggested it be seen as *projected* from a lexical item of a particular category,[8] where projection takes the features of a lexical item with it to higher levels of processing. The discussion below will give some idea of what is involved, but it is important to recognize that the *LGB* adaptation of X-bar theory and the concept of projection are incomplete solutions when seen from the viewpoint of very recent developments in the Minimalist Program. The structure that X-bar theory finds in all phrases and the mechanism of projection call out for explanation in terms of more fundamental theoretical devices – and that is what Chomsky's recent minimalism attempts. In doing so, it gets rid of this lingering residue of a base component in grammar. To be clear about where this discussion of the earlier, pre-minimalist effort is going, this is the progression: binding theory needs phrases; phrases need X-bar theory and projection; X-bar theory and projection, and thus the "base component," can be absorbed into something else.

The discussion that follows is close to the *LGB* exposition (cf. *MP* 51–3) but draws from Cook and Newsom's (1996) well-developed exposition. The term "X-bar" can be confusing. "X" is easy enough; it is a placeholder – a kind of variable – for *categories*. Categories include N, V, A, P, and, as we will see, I(nflectional), D(eterminer), and C(omplementizer). The first four are *lexical* categories; the last three are *functional* categories. (Functional categories are disputed for reasons that are beyond the scope of this book.) The notion of 'bar' confuses the uninitiated, particularly as the convention that started the terminology is now defunct. It comes from a time when levels found in phrase structure were designated by putting no, one, or two bars above a category label; for a noun, one would have N, $\bar{\text{N}}$, or $\bar{\bar{\text{N}}}$. To adapt the convention to easier typing and typography, though, zero-level category indicators are as before, N, A, V, P, (or N^0, etc.), single bar is now N', V' (or N^1, V^1, . . .), and double bar, N", V" (or N^2, V^2, . . .). As having a uniform variable for different kinds of category suggests, all categories – N, V, D, etc. – project the three bar levels and their associated phrasal structures in the same way. In effect, X-bar theory claims that the basic phrasal structure of all categories of lexical items in natural languages is the same. Each category of lexical item projects in the same way and carries with it its demands on the kinds of item that can be placed in a full phrase structure with it. The schema for phrase structure in the discussion of binding theory, 'XP = X – YP', with '–' unordered to allow *heads* (N, V, . . .) to precede or follow *complement* YPs is captured by projection and X-bar theory. Let us see how.

I offer only a few illustrations limited to English, a head-initial language; readers can vary lexical items and choose other languages. A noun phrase, as the phrasal structure schema claims, consists of a noun head N and a complement, where a complement is a (complete) phrase of some sort. The phrase "horse under cover" has a noun head N ("horse") and a PP complement, "under cover," which itself has a preposition head P ("under") and an NP complement that has an N head and null (or no) complement. It is diagrammed as in (1).

(1)

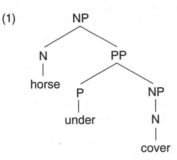

The idea is straightforward: choose a lexical item of any of the four categories, and it projects the same basic structure as any other category of item – a head of that category and a phrasal complement, both "under" and dominated by an *X*P (NP, VP, or N", V"). In addition, the lexical item makes other demands on the structure, dependent on its particular features (which are projected along with the item to "higher" levels in the structure of a sentence). The verb "build," for example, is happy with a D(eterminer) P(hrase) complement ("build the bicycle"), but "lurk" seems to exclude one: "lurk the building" is odd, at the very least. The noun "cover" – as above – does not require an explicit complement, so can go null; it could, however, have a PP complement ("under cover in the barn"), which itself has a determiner phrase complement. Intuitively, if all the words in a sentence are satisfied with their complements and any other items involved in projection of a category, all is well: we are on the way to projecting a grammatical sentence/expression which – assuming it does not overload our performance systems – we can speak/hear and understand.

The structure indicated in (1) is not enough, however. So far, we have an illustration of only two bar levels, one for XP (NP, VP, . . .) and one for heads X (N, V, . . .) and their complements. We have no place to attach *specifiers* for phrasal structure, among which are *determiners* (Ds), which include "the" and "a:" "the horse" is a deter-miner phrase that includes a specifier D ("the") that 'specifies' the NP head with null complement "horse." D cannot be a complement for this NP; nor can it be the head N ("horse"); it also seems to be off on the left side of N in English, a head-initial language. To slot in specifiers, we need to insert another position and another level into phrasal structure. Another motivation is that we need to insert a second level between head X and XP to deal with the different status of the complements of some verbs that appear to take two phrasal complements. Different complements can have different degrees of "connection" to the verb: the verb "watch" in the phrase "watched Harry on Friday," for example, insists on a much tighter connection with "Harry" than with the PP "on Friday," which we could, for example, drop. This tighter connection is represented by making the NP structure for N "Harry" a *sister* of the V "watch" and placing the PP "on Friday" in a structurally detached position away from the sisters. Sister elements are immediately dominated by the same element; they are, then, at the same *bar level*. The sisterhood of the V "watch" and the NP structure for "Harry" is rep-resented by placing another bar level, V', between the lexical cate-gory head level, here the V level, and the VP (V"), and having both V "watch" and NP "Harry" dominated by V'. The 'detached' char-acter of the PP "on Friday" is represented by making it a sister of V' (not V), where both are dominated by the VP (V") – see (2).

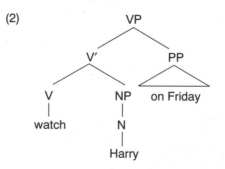

(2)

In effect, X-bar theory requires that each lexical item project three bar levels, X (which in effect says what category of lexical item it is), X′ (which is less intuitively clear, but is needed for the reasons indicated above), and X″ (which is the obviously needed level VP, NP, PP, etc.). Notice, too, that the information specific to the lexical item (represented in its features) is carried along to higher bar levels, where it can play a role in determining with which other lexical items and their projected structures it can be placed to make an expression grammatical.

Now for specifiers: where are they to be put? If phrasal complements are sisters to N, V, etc. and are dominated by an X′ level, specifiers are at the same bar level as V′. Thus, X″ levels (NPs, VPs, etc.) may have a specifier alongside their X′s (N′, V′, etc.). On one plausible account, Ds or determiners are specifiers of NPs, so that for the DP "the wombat," we have (3).

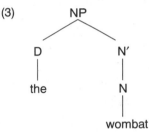

A special category of phrase called an "inflectional phrase," or IP, takes a special I′ that dominates and makes sisters of an abstract element, called "I," in specifier position whose features represent the requirements for subject–verb agreement and tense for a sentence and – as sister to I – a VP for its complement. This complement is the VP which represents the rest of the sentence and contains the sentence's subject in its NP specifier position. This leaves an odd-looking structure with a null specifier and a bunch of features under I see (4).

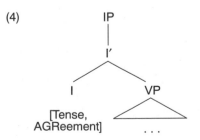

Something much closer to the familiar sentence structure we hear and see is provided by movement (the displacement property mentioned before). Intuitively, one can think of the VP's specifier NP 'moving into' the position provided by the currently empty specifier position for IP, and think of the VP's V head moving (leaving a trace) by a transformation into ('raised to') the I position, where tense and agreement are assigned to the verb. This ends up looking more like sentences we are familiar with. For "Harry sees Fido" (but without tense and number agreement) we have (5).

(5)

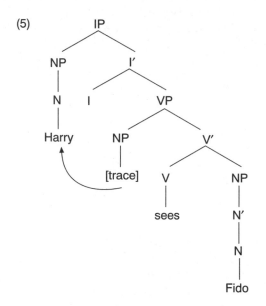

An IP, or inflectional phrase, with the abstract element I in specifier position is, then, a before-movement approximation to the ordinary notion of a sentence.

Two more details need to be dealt with: adjuncts and complementizer phrases. X' levels can take *adjuncts*. Adjuncts include adverbs (for V's), relative clauses (for N's), and "wh" constructions for V' ("wondered whether he would be able to survive"). Relative clauses such as "that Harry decided to leave" and "wh" constructions constitute a special class of phrases called "complementizer phrases," or CPs; a CP is a bit like a sentence with subject, predicate, and (often) tensed verb, but is embedded within another sentence: "The woman *who lost at darts today* won the match yesterday."

A CP has a complementizer C at level X (complementizers include "who," "that," "which," and "whether"), and its single-bar C' governs the sisters C and an IP. The categories C and I are called "functional categories." This is not the occasion to go into the complicated and disputed territory of functional categories and functional phrases. They do, however, play a crucial role in movement, as the earlier brief discussion of IPs suggests, and thus play a crucial role in making a sentence represented in X-bar theory into something that looks like the sentences we are familiar with. In the Minimalist Program they help meet the bare output conditions that the language faculty's operations must satisfy in order to speak to other systems. As for adjuncts, part of their importance lies in their role in natural language productivity. Part of creativity (specifically, part of unboundedness) lies in the fact that adjuncts can iterate, allowing sentences of unlimited length that nevertheless all meet the universal demands of X-bar theory, suitably parameterized with respect to order for specific natural languages. In English they iterate to the right of a phrasal head (N, P, . . .) by supplying another X' and making the adjunct the sister of the head's original X'. An N' iterates as shown in (6).

(6)

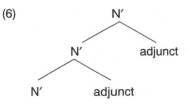

Much more could be said, but we have seen enough to appreciate that projection and X-bar theory yield powerful generalizations over all languages, providing support for Chomsky's solution of Plato's problem. But what is projection, and where did the structure – sometimes a bit arcane, as with X' – come from? It would be preferable if we could get rid of unexplained primitives by showing that projection and the structure of X-bar theory are merely epiphenomena, the way things look to the theoretician who hasn't quite got to the heart of the matter. Specifically, it would be preferable if projection were the result of extremely primitive operations on lexical items, biologically motivated if motivation is necessary, and if the structure found in X-bar theory were located entirely within lexical items themselves, not adventitiously imposed on them. That is what the very latest version of Chomsky's Minimalist Program is meant to accomplish.

One basic assumption of the Minimalist Program is that structure introduced into the computation of an expression (a ⟨PHON, SEM⟩ pair) must be "constituted of elements already present in the lexical items" (*MP* 228); bar levels, not being among the features of a lexical item itself, cannot be introduced later in a computation. The motivation behind this assumption is clear: a true minimalist will want to eliminate anything as complex and unexplained as X-bar theory, especially if it is read not merely as a description of phenomena, but as structural conditions imposed from outside on permissible grammatical structures. We need something better grounded and simpler that does the same work. Granted, projection and X-bar theory quite nicely describe various levels within the grammars of all languages and provide a convenient and plausible framework for dealing with movement; so we must somehow get its positions, levels, and – more important – such relations as head to complement, without leaving what philosophers of science call a "dangler."

So how do we get the appearance of bar levels described by X-bar theory? I can only hint at how it works. Assume first that any plausible grammar is going to have to provide for two levels, even if not levels as construed in X-bar syntax. One is a lexical, or X, level, and the other can be called an X^{max} level. Lexical items themselves do duty for the X level; X^{max} is defined in terms of operations in the system and is an analog for XP. The reason for instituting these two levels is that (in terms of X-bar theory) only XPs and Xs (now just lexical items) move to appear at interface levels. X'-level items do not, hinting that there might be a reason for the unintuitive character of this bar level. Because the interface levels are where the computational system meets the biological and externally imposed constraints that movement is an effort to satisfy, one can think of these levels as biologically motivated.

As suggested above, Chomsky's minimalism is an ongoing project that has been becoming more minimalist as time goes on. In its early stages at the beginning of the 1990s, there was no real effort to actually replace X-bar theory. The attempt to do so is recent – in chapter 4 of *MP* and Chomsky's lectures, particularly his fall syntax lectures at MIT in 1995 and 1996. (He did not lecture in 1997.) A discussion of some of the most recent work is in "Minimalist Inquiries" (1998). The key to this recent effort, in line with the assumption referred to in the last paragraph, is that one begins the computation that leads to an expression with a set of fully specified lexical items that in a sense *contain in themselves* all the combinatorial and structural properties found in X-bar theory plus projection. Think of lexical items as sets of features, and the elementary and ineliminable process that leads them to eventually express (to other systems) their combinatorial and structural properties at PHON or SEM as Merge. Merge places pairs of lexical items – sets of lexical features – together, and, like chemical substances, they either combine or fail to combine. If an attempt to combine fails because their intrinsic properties rule it out, the effort ceases. When they do combine, one of the two lexical items (just a set of features, actually, but for convenience I speak of lexical items) becomes the "label" of the combination and (in effect) the head. Using set notation to reflect the fact that we are dealing with sets of features and set inclusion, assume the following selection of lexical items: {the, river, Wanda, watch}, with "watch" having among its features [verbal] (i.e., V), "river" including [concrete] and [nominal] (i.e., N), "the" [determiner]. Imagine that Merge takes the "the" and "river;" the result is {the, {the, river}}, with "the" as label.[9] {River, {river, the}} is obviously ruled out by the lexical items' features: one of "the"s features is [determiner], and nouns do not determine determiners. So features control which lexical item is the label of the merged pair. Note that the result is, in effect, a DP, with "the" as head and "river" as complement, as shown in (7).

(7)

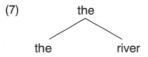

With this successful combination in place, Merge can then take another lexical item and attempt to merge it with the first successfully combined one (which is simply another, more complex lexical item, or "object"). Say it attempts to combine it with "watch." The combination works: a new label is chosen. With the choice between the old label ("the") and "watch," the choice is obvious: it is "watch." The result is {watch, {watch, {the, {the, river}}}} – in effect, "watch" makes itself into the "head" of a 'VP', "watch the river." ("Watch" could hardly be the 'complement' of a 'DP'.) Then Merge might also try to put together the label "watch" with the remaining lexical item, "Wanda." Here, the old label becomes the label of the combination; in effect, "Wanda" becomes the 'subject' term in the VP, while "watch" 'projects'. We get the effect of heads, levels, and dominance with sets of features and labels of merged items. We also get the effect of projection: lexical items are nothing but their features, and while features may be eliminated, none are added. Generally, as Chomsky puts it, "the syntactic objects we are considering are of the following types:

a.   lexical items
b. $K = \{\gamma, \{\alpha, \beta\}\}$, where α, β are objects and γ is the label of K

Objects of type [a] are complexes of features listed in the lexicon. The recursive step is [b]" (*MP* 243). Projection is not a matter of putting lexical items with their features into a fixed schema that all phrases must conform to but merely of merging and labeling the combinations, with the label assigned depending on the features of the items. Positions such as specifier are 'created' by functional features of lexical items. The two crucial 'levels' involved in movement, lexical items (Chomsky also speaks of them as X^{min}s) and 'XPs', or X^{max}s, are ways to describe merged lexical items. What were X' positions in X-bar theory occur where a label is repeated in a derivation. This is illustrated by the example above. Keeping in mind that "Wanda" will eventually Move out of the VP and that tense and verb agreement (functional matters both) have to be dealt with by further processing, the diagrammatic representation of what we have so far is as shown in (8).

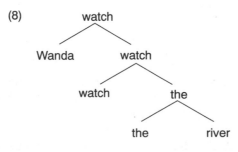

The top label "watch" is at the X^{max} position; the lower "watch" gives the effect of a X' level. What was the rather odd-looking intermediate level of X' becomes a no-longer X^{max} (or no-longer XP) that has lost any chance of appearing at the interface. Paraphrasing an observation of Sam Epstein's, Chomsky remarks that this result is "quite natural, these objects being 'fossils' that were maximal (hence visible at an interface) at an earlier stage of derivation, targeted by the operation that renders them invisible" (*MP* 382, n. 24). So one can squeeze all that one needs of X-bar theory out of lexical features and Merge (plus Move, which I have not discussed) and receive as a bonus a natural explanation of why the X-bar levels X, X', and X" have such different effects at SEM. It is difficult to be more emphatic about the centrality of the lexicon with its features, the simplicity that this program imputes to the language faculty's operations, and way it demystifies unmotivated structure introduced by earlier theories of language to make sense of the language faculty's operations.

The discussion of lexical (X^{min}) movement and 'XP' (X^{max}) movement (and the difference between them) is arguably the centerpiece of the Minimalist Program. While the issues are beyond the scope of this book, I should point out that the Minimalist Program locates all the functional features involved in movement in the lexicon and provides in interfaces a plausible answer to the crucial question, why move? Items move to suit bare output conditions at PHON/PF and SEM/LF, and lexical items seem to be 'programmed' to suit a biological engineering end. They move to make the outputs of the language faculty visible to other systems, and, as Chomsky emphasizes, the functional features involved seem to provide a near-'perfect' solution to the design problem that these other systems pose for the language faculty.

Simplicity again and optimality

I can say something about the design problem and its solution in the Minimalist Program by returning to the discussion of simplicity and the adequacy of a theory of language at the end of the last chapter. Doing so also provides a fine opportunity to discuss further the progress of linguistic theories (theories of language, or VGs).

Recall that we ended up with two notions of simplicity, a theory-internal one that amounts to something like "whatever a theory that captures UG and provides a way to 'choose' (and so solves Plato's problem) says" and a theory-general one as useful for the physicist as the linguist – and for the Standard Theory theorist as for the Minimalist. The theory-internal notion is articulated on the basis of empirical investigation; the theory-independent one seems to be a priori, perhaps an aspect of the science-forming capacity.[10] It leads the physicist to insist on simple formulae for physical constants (cf. *PP* 30). And in the guise of "conceptual naturalness," it is what Chomsky has in mind in a recent statement of a desideratum for his minimalist approach: a linguistic theory must meet "general considerations of conceptual naturalness that have some independent plausibility, namely, simplicity, economy, symmetry, nonredundancy, and the like" (*MP* 2). Certainly the Minimalist theorist strives to meet these general conditions, and largely succeeds. Redundant elements have disappeared. The operations by which the language faculty work are few and conceptually simple. Expressions are just sets of features, (ideally) all present in lexical items. All operations are 'local' and involve no look-ahead – that is, no need to make an operation depend on what is to come in a derivation.

Chomsky now tends to put matters in terms not of two senses of simplicity, but of two senses of *optimality*. He explains the first sense this way:

> It appears that the computations of language have to be optimal, in a certain well-defined sense. Suppose we think of the process of constructing an expression as selection of words from the mental lexicon, combining them, and performing certain operations on the structures so formed, continuing until an expression is constructed with a sound and a meaning. It seems that some such processes are blocked, even if legitimate at each step, because others are more optimal. If so, a linguistic expression is not just a symbolic object constructed by the computational system, but rather an object constructed in an optimal fashion. (*PP* 28–9)

Here the idea seems to be that optimal computations are more economical in a derivational, computational sense: shorter moves of elements rather than longer and local decisions about which way to proceed so as to avoid any need to run through a few extra steps in the computation. In his very recent work (1998), Chomsky has been trying to show that this economical form of optimality is so strong that it provides evidence in favor of his derivational approach to grammar. Of the other notion of optimality he says:

> Recent work also suggests that languages may be optimal in a different sense ... Suppose we have some account of the properties P of the systems with which language interacts at the interface. We can now ask a question that is not precise, but is not vacuous either: How good a solution is language to the conditions P? If a divine architect [more recently,

and more advisedly, "super-engineer"] were faced with the problem of designing something to satisfy these conditions, would actual human language be one of the candidates, or close to it? Recent work suggests that language is surprisingly 'perfect' in this sense, satisfying in a near-optimal way some rather general conditions imposed at the interface. Insofar as that is true, language seems unlike other objects of the biological world, which are typically a rather messy solution to some class of problems, given the physical constraints and the materials that history and accident have made available. (*PP* 29–30)

Chomsky seems to treat optimality in this sense as something like arriving at a solution to a design problem, and – in the form of getting grammars to meet bare output conditions – he has devoted considerable effort in his recent work to trying to assess the extent to which the language faculty is optimal in this sense.

How do these versions of optimality relate to the earlier versions of simplicity? Chomsky suggests answers in *MP*. After pointing out that the P&P program offers "a different cast to the question of how simplicity considerations enter into the theory of grammar," adding that one must clearly distinguish the concept of simplicity that "enters into rational inquiry generally" and that theory-internal form that selects among I-languages, he says:

> Nevertheless, rather similar ideas have resurfaced, this time in the form of economy considerations that select among derivations, barring those that are not optimal in a theory-internal sense. The external notion of simplicity remains unchanged: operative as always, even if only imprecisely.
>
> At this point still further questions arise, namely, those of the Minimalist Program. How "perfect" is language? One expects "imperfections" in morphological-formal features of the lexicon and aspects of language induced by [bare output] conditions at the A–P [sound] interface, at least. The essential question is whether, or to what extent, these components of the language faculty are the repository of departures from virtual conceptual necessity, so that the computational system C is otherwise not only unique [modular] but in some interesting sense optimal. (*MP* 8–9)

In other words, the external, a priori notion of simplicity continues to operate in all scientific inquiry in ways that remain obscure, and there is a remnant of the old internal version of simplicity in theory-specified economy conditions on effective computation. (Effective computation avoids computational bloat: it avoids look-ahead, look-back, and non-local comparisons of solutions.) The remnant of the old notion of internal simplicity lingers to the extent that there is comparison between derivations. Very recent work (1998) suggests that it can be eliminated.

The design notion of optimality speaks to new questions. It speaks in a theory-internal way to how the language faculty solves the problem of dealing with the biological constraints set by the other systems with which it must interact. As Chomsky notes, biological systems are not known for producing elegant solutions to such engineering problems (*PP* 30). The language faculty, however, seems to be quite an elegant solution to the problem of making sounds and meanings 'visible' at the PHON and SEM interfaces.

The relationship between explanatory and descriptive adequacy also changes. The early transformational approach provided a plethora of different rule systems for different languages, and hopes for explanatory adequacy were limited to finding a "permitted format" (as Chomsky says) for them. It looked as though descriptive and explanatory adequacy were in opposition. In the later work it is apparent that UG is uniform, while allowing a finite set of natural languages and very large numbers of I-languages (states of UG), *and* we can even deal with the issue of how well the language faculty performs its function of producing 'visible' expressions. All this encourages Chomsky to think that the P&P program and its minimalist variant in particular have changed the issues. Minimalism raises a "new leading problem that replaces the old: to show that restricting the resources of linguistic theory [to what the minimalist project provides does not hurt and even] preserves (and we hope, even enhances) descriptive adequacy while explanation deepens" (*MP* 317). Perhaps austerity – a version of simplicity – actually leads to improved descriptive adequacy.

6

Meanings and Their Use

Perspectives

If linguistic meanings in the head are to be useful to us in dealing with the world, there had better be a lot of them, so that they can serve for varying things and circumstances; they had better be accessible to our diverse cognitive devices (vision, etc.); and they had better be the sorts of things that serve our interests. Since they are SEMs, there is no danger of their running out: the language faculty is computationally capable of producing them in infinite numbers. As interfaces that give instructions to, or interact with, other systems in the head, they are accessible. And since they are put together from sets of features lodged in lexical items that are virtually 'designed' to serve the interests of creatures like ourselves, they serve our interests. Chomsky compresses these various aspects of linguistic meanings as SEMs into a single term when he calls them "perspectives." In "Language and Nature" he remarks that perhaps "the weakest plausible assumption about the LF [SEM] interface is that the semantic properties of the expression focus attention on selected aspects of the world as it is taken to be by other cognitive systems, and provide intricate and highly specialized perspectives from which to view them, crucially involving human interests and concerns even in the simplest cases" (1995: 20). So in making sentences or (Chomsky's preferred term) expressions that are ⟨PHON, SEM⟩ pairs, the language faculty makes perspectives, or – using Chomsky's acronym for 'semantic interfaces' – SEMs/LFs.

The idea that the language faculty makes cognitive perspectives that are of particular interest to humans continues a theme that goes back to *LSLT* and *SyS* and to the idea that one might appeal to a 'use theory' to deal with how humans use language to refer to and characterize things in the world – how they *interpret* language.[1] Even in the mid-1950s, then, Chomsky thought language provides 'tools' that people can use in various ways and situations to talk of things and themselves – perhaps to regale others with the antics of Mary's pet otter or to complain about the general lack of service now that the local shops are closed. There was a period when he thought it possible that interpretation of language took place 'underneath', at Deep Structure. I discuss that period briefly in the next section. It did not last long, and now, as for the most part before, he holds that in interpretation an 'output' of the language faculty, now called "SEM," instructs or interacts with "conceptual and intentional systems," and its and their contributions to cognition enable people to deal with the world. That complex of interchanges and human action is *interpretation*. It is not, and may never be, clear what interpretation is. It is clear that it involves interaction with other systems in the head ("focus attention on selected aspects of the world as it is taken to be by other cognitive systems") and that it involves free activity (including reference to things in the world). Chomsky suggests that the only grip science is likely to get on it concerns relations to "other systems" in the head, not reference to things outside the head. Nevertheless, he provides enough in his persistent view of language as a tool (captured now in the notion of a perspective), in his model of mind, and in his approval of Cudworth's attempt to show how inner ideas do indeed bear on a world outside, for us to see that his biological rationalist position leads to the idea that, in interpreting meanings (perspectives) by using them to refer and characterize, the human mind shapes and in some sense *makes* the world. His version of Goodman's world-making is discussed at the end of the chapter.

The initial and central task for this chapter is clarifying in an informal way what Chomsky takes linguistic perspectives to be. We know from the last chapter what SEMs are for the linguist – sets of formal and semantic features – and have an idea of how they are produced in endless numbers by a generative system. But this theoretical grasp only hints at SEMs' cognitive potential – particularly as understood in the Minimalist Program's view of them (on which I focus).

Deep Structure

For Chomsky, linguistic meanings are those syntactically defined elements produced in a derivation that 'feed' interpretation, understanding by this whatever is involved in relating the language faculty to "conceptual and intentional systems" and (perhaps) the world. Currently, meanings are SEMs that "give instruction to" these other systems and are found at the output of the computational process. For a while, at the time he wrote *ATS*, Chomsky adopted the idea that meanings are found 'underneath', at Deep Structure. This does not fit well with his view before and after *ATS* that meanings are tools, produced by an innate, unconscious computation, that appear at or near the end of their derivations and bear marks of their derivational history in the configuration of features found there. The persistent view puts meanings at the 'surface', where they have been configured by the language faculty's derivational process to make them into useful tools. It is instructive, however, to look briefly at some of the reasons why it might have seemed plausible to place them 'underneath'.

There were, of course, theoretical motivations at the time of *ATS* for introducing Deep Structure. Given commitment to a base (at the time phrase structure grammar plus lexical insertion) that feeds a transformational component, and moved by the idea that nouns and pronouns have to be assigned their roles as agent of action and as object ("theta-roles") before they are displaced from their "natural" positions by transformations,[2] in 1965 it seemed plausible to postulate a level of representation that preceded the transformational, where at least some meaning-relevant matters are settled. Katz and Fodor, picking up on this idea, in effect suggested that Deep Structure be the locus of semantic interpretation. This hypothesis commits one to the idea that Deep Structures are meanings, that in going from Deep to Surface Structure, transformations preserve meaning, and much more besides. In part because of the incautious nature of the commitment,[3] Chomsky was uncomfortable with this hypothesis, even in *ATS*. He pointed out (pp. 224–5, n. 9) that Surface Structure also seemed to play an important role in semantic interpretation. And he thought that "the grammatical relations expressed in the abstract deep structure are, in many cases, just those that determine the meaning of the sentence" (p. 162) – "many," not "all." Nevertheless, he thought there was sufficient evidence in favor of the hypothesis to adopt it. He said: "To the extent that relevant evidence is available today, it seems not unlikely that it is true" (p. 117).

I do not discuss the theoretical motivations further; they are irrelevant in Chomsky's Minimalist Program and only mildly relevant between 1965 and the 1990s as he continued to hold to a conception of a base component and to a successor of Deep Structure, D-structure. Arguably, they alone were never enough to tip the scales. There were other motivations, one of which Chomsky seems to have taken seriously. It is found in studies of language at least as old as the Port Royal grammarians. To appreciate it, forget what you have been told about UG, principles, parameters, and the irrelevance of Saussurean arbitrariness, and observe that languages differ orthographically and phonetically in ways that are apparent to everyone. While the alphabet (A, B, C, . . .) used might sometimes be the same, sounds and sound–meaning pairings can differ radically from one language to another, even from one person to another. On many people's pronunciations, "red," "rot," and "rouge" do not even have the same initial r-sound. But if languages differ as radically as this alone makes it appear, it is difficult to make sense of how there can be mutual comprehension. An appealing answer to how there can be sufficient uniformity to allow understanding, yet great differences in how languages appear, is that languages differ at the 'surface' but are uniform at another, deeper level that has something to do with meaning and thought. The Port Royal grammarians were driven by this sort of consideration. Lancelot and Arnauld acknowledged 'surface' differences in the sounds that appeared, but postulated a hidden, uniform level for meaning and introduced transformation-like rules to link the two. Chomsky acknowledged the parallel between his thinking and the Port Royalists' when he adopted Deep Structure as the locus of interpretation, saying that "base Phrase-markers may be regarded as the elementary content elements from which the semantic interpretations of actual sentences are constructed," continuing: "To say that formal properties of the base will provide the framework for the characterization of universal categories is to assume that much of the structure of the base is common to all languages. This is a way of stating a traditional view, whose origins can . . . be traced back at least to the *Grammaire générale et raisonnée* (Lancelot et al., 1660)" (*ATS* 117).

Another motivation amounts to the idea that what one finds in Deep Structures, as they were understood in the mid-1960s, are sentence-like entities that seem much easier to interpret than

"Surface Structures." They are not yet complicated by optional transformations such as passive. They seem to provide relatively simple formal objects that look like logical formulae and that might easily be mapped onto things and situations in the world. So it was tempting to think that at Deep Structure one could find much more nearly straightforward 'correspondences' between word and world. They seemed to offer a relatively easy way to secure interpretations.

Some of what Chomsky wrote might be taken to suggest that he was moved by this consideration too. There is, for example, the "elementary content" remark quoted above, although it is not clear that this is how to understand it. There is also a note in *SyS*: "Goodman has argued – to my mind, quite convincingly – that the notion of meaning of words can at least in part be reduced to that of reference of expressions containing these words. . . . Goodman's approach amounts to reformulating a part of the theory of meaning in the much clearer terms of the theory of reference" (p. 103, n. 10). This might look like commitment to the idea that clarity about meanings comes when we have mappings from word to world – to 'correspondences'. But then Chomsky continues: "just as much of our [previous] discussion can be understood as suggesting a reformulation of parts of the theory of meaning that deal with so-called 'structural meaning' in terms of the completely nonsemantic theory of grammatical structure." Structural meaning is what Chomsky now calls "meaning" (formally, SEM) – even in 1957, a "completely nonsemantical" notion. Given this, he was saying only that reference seems to give a grip on language use – Wittgenstein's sense of "meaning," which Chomsky now places in pragmatics. This does not imply that the linguistic entities (representations within the language faculty) used in reference are simple, or that they wear referents on their sleeves. Given that *SyS* was written during a period when Chomsky thought that the end products of a derivation constituted the tools used in interpretation, that these were *not* simple, and that they did not somehow refer by them selves, the second motivation played no role in *SyS*, at least. *SyS* (and *LSLT* with its "T-markers") suits only Chomsky's persistent view.[4]

Whether Chomsky was moved by this consideration in 1965 or not, though, it – plus perhaps the Port Royal one, and possibly others – proved compelling to other people. If Chomsky soon changed his mind about deep structure and returned to developing his persistent view, others did not. The idea that deep structure or perhaps something even more abstract is the apt place for semantic interpretation caught the imagination of many, including several linguists and philosophers with Fregean likings for the idea that sense (meaning) determines reference. Chomsky soon became embroiled in controversy with several linguists who could neither give up the idea that semantic interpretation applies at deep structure nor overcome their resentment that Chomsky had done so. The generative semanticists – including some of Chomsky's students, such as John Robert Ross – soon generalized their complaint to the claim that Chomsky did not leave enough room in his grammars for semantics or meaning. It was not always clear, however, what the controversy was about.[5]

Perspectives and the Minimalist Program

The Minimalist Program adapts the Y-shaped picture of a derivation characteristic of the P&P approach. Whereas the P&P program 'began' a derivation at the bottom of the Y (at D-structure) and went to the branch point (S-structure) where phonological-phonetic processing splits off from semantic, minimalism 'begins' with merely a selection of lexical items and Merges their features and, where required, Moves items around until Spell-Out, the point where phonological features are stripped off of the lexical items found at that stage and sent on a separate pathway to produce a phonetic representation, PF (PHON). Processing on the main path with Merge and Move continues to a semantic representation, LF (SEM). Minimalism gets rid of D-structure and S-structure, but gets their effect without P&P's machinery: a specification of lexical items (called "Numeration/Select" (N/S)) initiates a derivation, and Spell-Out initiates an apparently separate phonological/phonetic path (cf. *MP* 228, 381, n. 10). Crucially, all the materials needed for a derivation that succeeds (does not crash), including anything that leads to parametric differences between languages, must be available in features of lexical items: this is projection with a vengeance. Moreover, structure and computational machinery such as P&P's 'theories' (case theory, binding theory, etc.) and (we saw) even X-bar theory in late minimalism, come to be treated as epiphenomena of the language faculty's effort to produce in PHON and SEM representations that are legible to other systems in the head. The only levels of representation remaining are PHON and SEM, for obvious reasons: sound and meaning are ineliminable on any conception of language, or are "conceptually necessary." In minimalism, semantic interpretation *must* take place at SEM: no other representation is available.

This description of the overall architecture does not bring out a special contribution that minimalism makes to the study of meaning. In his most recent minimalist work Chomsky has suggested renaming one of the two operations performed in the language faculty, changing from "Move" to "Attract." The technical reason is straightforward: SEM is at the end of a computational derivation, and there are no 'earlier' positions at which the 'success' of a derivation (whether it crashes or not) can be determined. The nontechnical gloss is more interesting. In effect, the process of derivation is directed towards PHON and SEM in the sense that derivations have to speak to the biological conditions imposed there by "bare output conditions." These in effect say to the language faculty, "If you want to interact with other systems in the head and be used by them, you have to do such and such." So the preferred word is "Attract": when features move in a process of derivation, it is because they must do so to be "visible" to other systems. The imagery of attraction is volatile, and one must be cautious, but it helps to think of SEM as allowing only certain configurations and to think of lexical features as migrating into those configurations so that they can 'do something' there – they play a cognitive role in interpretation. This might seem a surprising way for a mathematically inclined formal linguist to put matters, but it is difficult to see how else to make the point: the features are attracted to their respective interfaces because it is there that they become "legible," "visible," or interpretable by other systems. Note the connection between these considerations and the fact that SEMs can serve as perspectives. If they are perspectives, they play a cognitive role. But they can do this only if they can 'communicate' with other systems in the head.

This story about attraction is related to the Minimalist Program's effort to isolate in a few lexical features the crucial differences between languages that have been the focus of study in generative syntactic theories from the earliest days – the differences that parameters represent in the P&P framework. Chomsky's hypothesis – and the focus of much of his recent syntactic work – is that the syntactic processing of different languages differs *solely* with respect to differences in *inflectional* formal features (those subject–verb agreement, case assignment, and tense issues I avoided in the last chapter). These are also, according to the hypothesis, the formal features that get parameterized, yielding different natural languages.

If the inflectional feature hypothesis turns out to be correct, one can think of attraction as operating on lexical items, which are parameterized by virtue of their functional features in different but biological engineering-wise viable ways, in order to 'make things usable' (interpretable). Natural language inflectional systems "displace" terms to solve the engineering problem of providing for interpretation. If so, except for Saussurean arbitrariness and perhaps a few phonological parameters, languages differ essentially only in the ways they represent tense, agreement, case marking, and the like.

The shape of the lexicon

Chomsky is not known for detailed contributions to lexicology, or for the study of individual lexical items, but his Minimalist Program sets an agenda for linguistics that not only assigns the lexicon a crucial role but requires that the lexical items it lists have a particular shape. They must include phonological, formal, and semantic features that specify (given UG) how they contribute to linguistic processing. The formal features indicate, for instance, that something is an N, not a V, with all the obvious consequences – that the N will be assigned a case (nominative, accusative, or oblique), for example. Formal features include the inflectional features that specify what 'moves' will be made when this item is inserted in a linguistic computational derivation of an expression. Some semantic features are simply carried through a derivation, but others probably play a role in it. For instance, the language faculty reacts very differently to a "bank" that is a noun as opposed to a verb and, where a verb, to a "bank" that takes an agent-subject (a doer of a deed) and an object ("Mary banked the fire") as opposed to one with different semantic features that takes no object but can take a PP: "The plane banked to the left." Whether a lexical item is compatible with other lexical items (feature sets), whether singular or plural, how it is voiced, whether it takes two arguments or three, whether one of its arguments is an agent, whether all are obligatory – these and other matters depend essentially on lexical features, sometimes the semantic ones. The full set of features of a set of lexical items selected at the beginning of a derivation determines whether a derivation crashes or gets to the interfaces.

Chomsky thinks of the lexicologist as providing the *exceptions* to UG in a set of theoretically defined features (*MP* 235–7). A lexical specification provides, then, anything "that does not follow from general principles" (*MP* 235). That an N gets a case assignment follows from principles of UG; that an N is third person and pairs the phonological features that produce the sound "shark" with the semantic features <u>shark</u> (such as ANIMATE) does not. The lexical specification for "book" provides a phonological feature specification, and it also either lists, or entails, that it has the categorial lexical feature noun [nominal] or N (*MP* 236). Generally, a lexical feature specification says which phonological features are paired with which formal and semantic features, thereby specifying in the lexicon the correlation that appears in a non-crashing derivation as a sound paired with a meaning. Given Saussurean arbitrariness and the differences among people's phonological feature sets, a maximally precise list of lexical items is limited to the specific features and associations available in a particular person's working vocabulary at a particular time (specifying, then, an I-language). Such a list can easily change over time. But there are ways to idealize over time and population. One can speak of the English word "book" and produce a feature set for it and for other words that have their functional and phonological parameters set for English; one can also, perhaps, produce a set of associations for an idealized English at a particular time. The illustrations that follow presuppose idealization, but remember that – especially with non-stereotypical words such as "yawl" and "ketch" – in addition to large phonological variations one can find total lack of either lexical item in an I-lexicon, assignment of the same formal and semantic features ("dunno, they're two-masted sailboats, right?"), and other variations.

If a lexical specification leaves a lot of work to UG, what happens to the richness of the lexicon that I emphasized in chapter 3's discussion of Cudworth's <u>house</u>? It remains, though with some possible qualifications mentioned below. Notice, though, that if Chomsky's lexical feature specifications consisting of exceptions to UG seem thin, it is only because they pale when compared to what is available after processing at SEM. Obvious examples, studied from the earliest days of generative grammar, show this: the ambiguities of "The chicken is ready to eat" and "Flying planes can be dangerous" certainly do not appear in lexical feature specifications. They appear only when lexical features are Merged with others to produce complex configurations of features at SEM.

Chomsky thinks that the lexical features that play a role in computation should be *fully* specified so that a lexical item's role in derivation is fully determined. It might be tempting to adopt a different strategy, letting later computation add features or further specify some underspecified ones. For instance, one might suggest placing a thin specification for the V "wash" (presumably, it would specify that it requires an agent and an object) in the lexicon, letting the issue of whether to make it past or present depend on later computational 'decisions'. This, however, complicates the computational process by giving it more to do – not a desirable outcome on minimalist assumptions. A better solution is to list all the possible options for the lexical item and Select among them before computation even begins (*MP* 237–9). This would require that the lexicon list the options available for a lexical item – unless these options are already predictable from UG, as is the fact that "wash" will get *some* tense features. But Chomsky thinks that the best strategy is to have Numeration place fully specified lexical items at the beginning of computation.[6] On this or the last strategy, though, N/S provides a fully specified set of lexical items over which computation proceeds. On either strategy, computation is very straightforward indeed, and it is fully determined whether a computation with a particular set of features crashes or reaches the interfaces.

Note that while a computation might be fully determined, there will be choices left up to the interpreting speaker and/or the other systems to which SEMs 'speak'. Uses are not predetermined. Moreover, some lexical features allow for changes in emphasis and focus. The features of book, for example, allow that this single lexical item, in its various possible configurations (accusative, nominative, singular, plural), can be 'read' as referring to either a physical object or an abstract container of information, or both. In effect, they have a "take it any of these ways" feature, perhaps representable as [physobj·info] (which can be read *very* informally as physical-object-and-container-of-information-although-can-be-considered-under-only-one-aspect-as-in: "shred the book"). This alternation is also among the features of newspaper, journal, magazine, thesis, article, . . . Arguably, in fact, all nouns have something like the feature [± abstract]. Chomsky remarks that "book" "can be used to refer to something that is simultaneously abstract and concrete, as in the expression "the book that I'm writing will weigh 5 pounds." That is a property of a broad range of nominal expressions, perhaps all" (*MP* 236). Because of it, one can speak of moving a flooded London to another location, which requires that London be conceived of as both a concrete entity (flooded as it is) that cannot in fact be moved, although, conceived as abstract, it can. No choice is made as computation begins; [± abstract] (in some form) is a feature that migrates to SEM along with the lexical item, oblivious to various Merges and Moves (although words with which it co-occurs might serve to skew interpretations in one direction rather than another). At SEM it provides a very useful special form of ambiguity that seems to be characteristic of natural languages. Chomsky suggests that the fact that something like [± abstract] may be among the features provided by UG for all nominals is "one of the reasons why standard theories of reference are not applicable to natural language" (*MP* 236). The point can be extended: SEM/LF need not meet the strict *logical* demand of a consistency that would rule out something being considered both abstract and concrete at the same time. Logics – or at least, logicians – tend to dislike incompatible-looking features like these; natural languages seem to thrive on them. This indicates clearly that LF is not the logician's "logical form."

There are still many undecided issues concerning the lexicon, even if the introduction of the Minimalist Program and its clear view of what a lexicon must do to contribute to the language faculty may lead to further progress in developing better lexical theories. I mention three of these issues. One concerns how to conceive of the relationship between formal and semantic features. Some features are clearly formal, such as [verbal]. Others are, or seem to be, clearly semantic, such as [± abstract] and [artifact]. Both are, of course, broadly syntactic in the sense that they deal with an internal, innate, and intensionally defined domain; but that is not the point. The problem is that it might well be that some formal features could be eliminated in favor of semantic ones, or, just possibly, vice versa. Perhaps a fuzzy distinction between formal and semantic is not so surprising: both appear at SEM. Significantly, the distinction between phonological-phonetic features and the others remains clear. As we have seen, sound and meaning have only the arbitrary connection found in association in a lexical item's feature set.

A second set of issues concerns how certain forms of semantic co-generation, or "polysemy," are to be represented and placed in a computational system. Using some of Pustejovsky's (1995) examples, a fast driver is very different from a fast game, a fast decision, or a fast book. Explaining how to represent fast's feature set in such a way that in a computation it can yield (or perhaps pick out) such different aspects of what counts as fast – depending on the word it 'modifies' – turns out to be a very difficult task. (Pustejovsky's effort is among the best I know.) Is this to be understood as part of the computational process, or as something else – perhaps a pragmatic effect?

A related issue is raised by the representation of semantic features. While there is no danger that Chomsky's semantic features are specified by appeal to relations to anything outside the head, how specific should semantic feature specifications be? The concept house clearly has to have some indication of function, but should it be so specific as to include something like Cudworth's [fit for human habitation]? Would [fit for habitation] do, so that house would cover 'ant house' too? What about [habitation], period? Would it be enough to point in the direction of a *set* of features that appear to be relevant to specifying a function and leave the specific choice of features open? If so, how would the 'pointing' be done, and where would the choice be made – by the person, 'before' computation begins, or automatically within the computational process?

Despite these issues, the general picture is clear. Lexical items, which are essentially sets of features, enter the computational system (the language faculty), which produces boundless numbers of expressions, each of which includes a linguistic perspective (SEM). This view of meaning ignores relationships to things in the world. While the meaning of a lexical item might be related by a speaker to something in the world – by, for example, using a sentence with its meaning to speak about that thing – the fact that it is so related on an occasion of use is irrelevant to its meaning. If "Gertrude left before her dogs could get into the garbage" is used on an occasion by a person to refer to Gertrude, her retrievers, and the accumulation behind Jane's house, that is a matter for pragmatics, not for a theory of meaning. Meanings are naturalistic objects, not artifacts.

Naturalized meanings

Chomsky is by no means the only one who has wanted to naturalize meanings. His teacher Nelson Goodman did too, in a way that fails, but not because it is completely misconceived. In fact, Goodman had the idea of making meanings into syntactic entities, which is what Chomsky does. His effort failed because he had a crude idea of what syntax is, was completely unwilling to even consider the nativist assumptions of Chomsky's far more successful variation on his strategy, and in the final analysis fell back into the Wittgensteinian quagmire of socialized, plastic linguistic meanings. Others of an externalist, anti-nativist, and generally empiricist bent have taken an even less promising route, trying to base a 'naturalistic' account of meaning on something like truth and reference. Chomsky's naturalization of meaning is distinct from other efforts.

Given what we already know about SEMs, we can avoid some possible misunderstandings about meanings and the naturalistic science of meaning. For one thing, a theory of linguistic meaning does not pretend to be a "complete theory of meaning," whatever that might be. Meaning – perhaps it is better to say several notions of meaning – has been disputed by philosophers for millennia without much to show for it. This unproductive history suggests that those who want to construct a serious theory of meaning need to look for a better grounding than various philosophers' intuitions about what is important and interesting and should be prepared to meet standard conditions on the adequacy of scientific theories. Chomsky's formally specified SEMs meet this condition. That does *not* indicate, however, that what his theory offers should be thought of as, or even considered as, a substitute for everyday common sense use of the words "mean" ("What did George mean by *that*?") or "meaning" ("What is the meaning of 'wombat'?"). These uses will continue as before, largely untouched. Meanings understood as SEMs might, however, diminish some of the philosophical disputation by uncovering some of the more blatant misconceptions on which various 'theories' of linguistic meaning have been based.

One misconception about meanings can be traced to the locution "meaning of a word," which makes it tempting to think that meanings are somehow lodged in words. There is a way in which this is not completely misguided, but only if "word," "meaning," and "of" are read technically, in the way they are in Chomsky's theory. There, "word" is better understood as SEM, or perhaps "a lexical item's formal and semantic features at SEM"; "meaning" is just a specification of the features involved; and "of" is understood only as "is a member of the set of features at SEM." This yields a well-defined theoretical conception of "meaning of a word." If it is abandoned in favor of intuition, one is likely to get something like this: a word is a sound that issues from a person's mouth, and its meaning is the use to which that sound is put in an (intentional) communicative act. This is actually quite a popular view among philosophers, although it might not be stated in quite this way. No doubt it gets support from remarks like "Mary didn't mean it when she said that," and the like. But, as we have seen, questions of use that involve speakers' intentions provide a very poor basis for a science.

It is connected with a second misconception: that meanings are not just resident in words but can be transported from one person to another. When I speak and am understood, surely that is because the meaning of my words was 'conveyed' from my mouth to another's ears? The difficulties with this view are obvious. No doubt it is important to recognize the involvement of audition or vision in the transmission of signals from one person to another. But one must recognize that what goes from one person's mouth to another person's ears in the form of an event that could be called a "signal" is just a set of compressions and decompressions in the air between them.[7] Not even a sound 'goes across', much less a linguistic sound or a linguistic meaning. Ordinary sounds like buzzings, linguistic sounds described by phonetics, and linguistic meanings are in people's heads, and only there. They are not to be found between people, whether in transit or not. Incidentally (a connected point) meanings are not to be found in some abstract realm of Being either. Why bother? – they can be dealt with naturalistically. Undermining the idea that meanings must also be found in some abstract realm can be surprisingly difficult, though; many philosophers, from Plato on, are very fond of it. The argument against the next misconception may help.

The two misconceptions already considered are relatively easy to expose once one has a theory of linguistic meaning that locates them firmly in the head. A third does not seem to be. It is the idea that meanings are in fact mental, so in the head, but are not located in the language faculty. They are concepts – whatever these are – and, while they enjoy a close relationship with language because linguistic entities *express* these concepts, language is really just a blind computational mechanism, not a creator of endless numbers of perspectives.

A full-fledged attack on this misconception would have to be far-ranging, but Chomsky offers a brief and compelling argument that might be enough to avoid long philosophical discussions. It consists of appropriating a surprisingly little-used insight from a philosophical position called "nominalism." The nominalist's insight consists of pointing out that the notion of expressing a concept would be trivially easy to deal with if concepts were simply elements of expressions. If concepts were elements of expressions, then producing the expression (a sound–meaning pair) would be the same thing as expressing the concept: there would be no independent entity that somehow has to figure in the account. Naturally, if this suggestion is to be at all plausible, expressions must contain elements that could count as concepts or perspectives – elements that, while produced in the head, can be used to deal with the world. But if Chomsky is right that linguistic expressions are ⟨PHON, SEM⟩ pairs *and* if it is these SEMs that are used by people to deal with the world – that is, if they are perspectives that afford us ways to conceive of things – there is little reason to refuse such a therapeutic way to avoid philosophical confusion: SEMs become concepts/perspectives.

The nominalist's insight that leads to this elimination of concepts thought of as independent of linguistic items was developed in recent times in various forms by Goodman (1952, 1961, 1968), although without the complex and rich 'tools' that Chomsky's syntax provides. Goodman's conception of syntax is so crude that it cannot bear the weight of anything like meanings and concepts, and he can offer no plausible argument for how linguistic entities could do the job they are supposed to. Chomsky's sophisticated syntax can carry the weight of meanings and concepts, however, largely because in SEMs his theory provides all the texture and structure that anyone could want linguistic meanings to bear, and he offers a plausible way to conceive of these meanings as perspectives that "focus attention on selected aspects of the world as it is taken to be by other cognitive systems, and provide intricate and highly specialized perspectives from which to view them, crucially involving human interests and concerns even in the simplest cases" (1995: 20). And as we will see, he can offer a rationalist view of interpretation that makes Goodman's suggestion that language use "makes worlds" actually work.

Chomsky's arguments establish that linguistic meanings are in the language faculty, and so in the head, but not that concepts are SEMs (which he needs if they are to be perspectives). (Showing that concepts are SEMs requires showing that they are used in interpretation, which is discussed in the next section.) The argument that linguistic meanings are in the language faculty appears in Chomsky 1997. It proceeds by asking what the alternatives are to construing linguistic sounds and meanings as he does – as the SEMs and PHONs that appear at the language faculty's interfaces. The alternatives might take various forms, but they all agree in placing meanings, at least, outside the expression (as Chomsky understands it). One such alternative consists of placing meanings in another part of the mind, as 'Mentalese' entities. It does not matter what one calls a Mentalese substitute for meanings. Fodor calls them "concepts"; "ideas" would do as well. The aim is to put meanings elsewhere in the mind, outside the language faculty. Chomsky argues against this by comparing it to a proposal to place not meanings but linguistic sounds outside the language faculty. He begins by pointing out what it would be to place either sound or meaning, or both, in Mentalese.

> Consider a "Mentalese" alternative. . . . Instead of taking LI [a lexical item] to include I-sound and I-meaning [sounds and meanings in I-languages], let us assume that one or the other is missing, or perhaps both. Accordingly, either SEM, PHON, or both are missing at the interface levels. To learn a language is to acquire rules that map LI into some other system of mind, Mentalese, which is interpreted to yield (aspects of) I-sound and I-meaning. If I-sound is missing, then LI is mapped into P-Mentalese [phonetic Mentalese]. If I-meaning is missing, then LI is mapped into S-Mentalese [semantic or meaning Mentalese]. Or both. Language itself has no phonology/phonetics, or no semantics, or neither. These are properties of Mentalese. (Chomsky 1997: 10)

Notice the reminder that placing sounds and meanings outside lexical items would require a different view of language acquisition from the one Chomsky advocates, suggesting that anyone who wants to place sound and/or meaning outside a lexical item is inviting questions about how linguistic sounds and/or meanings are acquired if they are *not* in the language faculty and, furthermore, inviting questions about how language learners are supposed to be thought to be able to learn to 'index' a particular Mentalese sound or meaning to a particular lexical item. But his primary aim is to emphasize that no one wants to place sounds outside linguistic items; there are no serious proposals for doing so. Yet, in the same vein, why would anyone want to place meanings 'outside'? To make the point completely obvious, he continues:

> For concreteness, consider . . . the words of (2), or the words "persuade," "force," "remind" for X in (3):
>   (2)   chase, lace, follow
>   (3)   John X-ed Mary to take her medicine.
> Suppose the corresponding LIs lack I-sound and that Peter has learned to map them into regions of P-Mentalese that have phonetic interpretations. Peter knows a lot about the regions and their interpretations. Thus "chase" rhymes with "lace"; "persuade" and "force" begin with lip con-

striction, though in different ways, and "remind" does not; etc. Standard
approaches assign these properties to FL [the language faculty], taking
them to be represented in PHON. The P-Mentalese alternative adds an
extra layer of complexity, and raises new problems, for example: What
component of LI indicates the region of P-Mentalese to which it is
mapped, if not the I-sound (as conventionally assumed)? At what point
in the computation of an expression does the mapping of P-Mentalese
take place? How are universal and particular properties of sound
expressed in the interpretation of P-Mentalese? For good reasons, such
questions have not been raised, and we may drop the matter. (Ibid.,
10–11)

In effect, anyone who proposed this would have to demonstrate
that it is plausible to think that all the knowledge that a speaker has
about sound (which Chomsky, of course, along with everyone else,
sensibly places in the language faculty) is in fact represented elsewhere and acquired or learned in some way, and would also have
to demonstrate how this knowledge bears on the computation of an
expression. It is far simpler to assume that the sound (the relevant
kind of 'knowledge') is in the lexical item and hence the language
faculty to begin with, and that the computation that leads to an
expression simply takes it into account. Not surprisingly, no one
seriously proposes moving sounds 'outside'. The stakes are too
high. They do, however, propose it for meanings:

> Consider the semantic analogue. We now assume that LIs have only I-
> sound and uninterpreted formal properties, and that Peter has learned
> how to map them into regions of S-Mentalese, which have semantic
> interpretation. Peter knows a lot about these regions/interpretations too.
> Thus if Tom chased Bill then Tom followed Bill with a certain intention,
> not conversely; if X = "persuade" in (3), then John's efforts were a partial
> success (Mary came to intend to take her medicine, but may not have
> done so); if X = "force," John succeeded, but differently (Mary took her
> medicine, whatever her intentions); if X = "remind," John may have
> failed (Mary may not have been paying attention), but if he succeeded,
> then Mary came to remember to take her medicine. The [I-language or
> FL] picture assigns the relevant properties to FL, taking them to appear
> in SEM by virtue of operations on LIs and the constructions in which
> they appear. The S-Mentalese alternative adds an extra layer of com-
> plexity and raises new problems analogous to those of the phonetic
> component. (Ibid., 11)

The point is the same: if someone seriously proposes moving
meaning outside expressions or lexical items and the faculty of
language, he or she is going to have to answer questions about how

this knowledge is represented, how it is acquired, and how it bears on the computation of an expression.

The basic argument is easily generalized to other proposals that take meanings to be located outside the lexical item and the language faculty. One popular proposal treats a meaning as a "semantic value" that is somehow assigned to an expression/word. The same issues arise: How do semantic values represent the knowledge of meaning we have? How is knowledge of semantic values acquired? And how do semantic values bear on computations? In addition, by proposing that one place semantic values somewhere else, perhaps even outside the head, this proposal adds another problem: how are people supposed to gain and maintain access to this domain? The proposal comes to appear ludicrous, as Chomsky intends. So, he suggests, just as everyone sensible places sounds in lexical items and in the language faculty, surely the sensible person's course with meanings is to place them in expressions and thus 'in' the language faculty.

This compelling argument for placing linguistic meanings (or whatever is proposed as a substitute term for linguistic meanings) in the expression and thus in the language faculty does not speak to the question of whether meanings in the language faculty could serve as concepts – mental entities that we use to refer to and characterize the things of the world. Chomsky's calling SEMs "perspectives" presupposes that they can, and it may seem obvious that they can, but he must make the identification of concepts with SEMs in the head plausible by showing how they play a role in interpretation. To do that, Chomsky appeals to those in the rationalist tradition – Cudworth and Herbert of Cherbury are prominent examples – who have defended the constructivist view he needs.

Chomsky and Cudworth on interpretation: "innate cognoscitive power" and prolepsis

If one adopts meanings in the head and proposes that they are used to deal with the world – that is, provide perspectives that we can use in various ways to deal with this world and others – 'the world' and its things do not survive unscathed. Things are not just "out there," waiting for us to inspect them. Like Goodman, Chomsky suggests that by using language humans 'create' worlds that reflect the cognitive capacities used to deal with them. That is Goodmanian constructivism. But Chomsky has a very different view of the tools with which worlds are made. Goodman is anti-nativist; Chomsky's meanings are the products of a nativist engine. He says: "We can think of naming as a kind of 'worldmaking', in something like Nelson Goodman's sense, but the worlds we make are rich and intricate and substantially shared thanks to a complex shared nature" (1997: 15). To find others who have adopted worldmaking *and* rationalist nativist and internalist principles, one has to go back to Cudworth, Herbert of Cherbury, and Descartes. Perhaps Kant would serve too, but Chomsky does not refer much to Kant in this regard, except to mention that a familiar philosophical figure took seriously the idea that the mind informs the world. This may be because Kant, unlike Cudworth and Herbert, was reluctant to think of anything but some few "categories" of experience as a priori, or innate. In any case, Chomsky's few suggestions about how the mind configures the world are far more often expressed in quotes from Cudworth and other rationalists than in any other idiom. This is no accident. Much of what Cudworth and the others had to say – with the exception of their reliance (perhaps sometimes *pro forma*) on God's aid – is easily reconstrued in terms of SEMs as configuring tools that people use.

In what follows I use Chomsky's recent terminology and speak of SEMs as perspectives or concepts, as mental entities that people employ in their cognitive dealings with the world. This construes perspectives as tools of reference and categorization, among other things – as mental items that we use to (it is difficult to come up with another word) conceptualize experience and things. That they are used by people to deal with the world does not entail that they be defined in terms of the things of the world, derived from them, or captured in terms of how they relate to them. The aim, of course, is to clarify Cudworth or Chomsky's proposal that the perspectives used by people to make claims and think about things and themselves are products of innate capacities that provide humans with unique ways to survive – and sometimes thrive – in their environments. The concepts of central concern to Chomsky are, of course, the linguistic ones, which may or may not mesh in a cooperative cognitive enterprise with the products of other faculties. This predominantly linguistic focus would have been alien to Cudworth. Cudworth distinguished between ideas of the intellect and the 'ideas' of vision and hearing, such as visual colors and shapes, so he had something a bit like the modern notion of modularity. It is very unlikely, however, that he would have been able to accept that his ideas of the intellect – or at least some of them – could actually be produced by a *natural* organ, much less a *language* faculty (*TEIM* 215–16). Nevertheless, his examples of ideas of the intellect – <u>house</u> and others – and the way he defines them are no different from what one finds in SEMs. So we can plausibly identify his ideas or concepts with what SEMs provide.

It is crucial to Cudworth's view of the mind and its relationship to the world that what he calls "ideas" be produced by an innate cognoscitive power totally inside the head, not by experience. These ideas, he shows convincingly, *cannot* arise from things 'outside'; there is nothing in the physical world that could have the ideas (properties) that we assign to them in the form in which we conceive them. Ideas cannot even arise from semi-cognitive faculties such as the senses – vision, audition, and the like. These (in his view) add their own distinctive features to stimuli that come from the outside world, but they are insufficient for anything like <u>house</u>.

But while he locates intellectual ideas inside the head, and only there, Cudworth clearly thinks that it is these concepts or ideas that play a role in what we have been calling "interpretation." They are what we use to characterize the things of the world. There is little choice: these ideas are all we have if we are to deal with the world by use of our intellectual powers. But if they are to function in, and be relevant to how a human being deals with, the world outside, one must make sense of how they could do this. This involves constructing an account of interpretation, or 'idea application'; in Chomsky's terms, it involves speaking to how language use might be thought to be appropriate to circumstances. Cudworth focused on the role of ideas/concepts of the intellect (not the "ideas" of color and shape produced by the senses) in what we would now think of as perceptual judgment. Perceptual judgment mobilizes a concept (or concepts) of the intellect and applies it, with the aid of the sensory faculties with which, presumably, it interacts, to something 'outside'. The result is reference and perceptual categorization: "That is a house," "I hear a stream." Cudworth wanted to show how it could be plausible that the innate intellectual concept <u>house</u> could bear on (be used to refer to) and seem to properly characterize something in the outside world, even though the outside world has – strictly speaking – nothing in it which has the features that the innate concept of <u>house</u> assigns to it. Houses as understood by the intellect have the function of being fit for human habitation, because that 'feature' is contained in – or is at least definitely relevant to – the concept <u>house</u>. But, he argues, there is nothing in the physical world outside the head with the feature <u>fit for human habitation</u>; there are only atoms (Atomical Particles). There are not even bricks and beams, only atoms. What is outside the head is adequately (fully) dealt with by an "Atomical Philosophy" – basically, by physics as Cudworth understood it. To make sense of how the mind could nevertheless seem to apply to and produce experiences appropriate to circumstances that must be thought of as alien to such features, Cudworth produced his "proleptic" account of perceptual judgment. According to it, the mind generates ideas in the head and, when it successfully perceives, somehow *anticipates* circumstances. It effortlessly produces the feature <u>fit for human habitation</u> (clustered with <u>made by humans</u>, etc.) inside the head yet seems to 'find' it in things outside the head. A house is, in effect 'made'. Anticipation is a form of projection, or Goodmanian worldmaking, and, unlike Descartes, Cudworth seems to have thought that his view was defensible without relying on God's goodness to assure us that things are as they seem. For Cudworth, the inner engine that produces these concepts seems to be able to anticipate *anything*. He spoke of the "potential omniformity" of intellect, which provides sufficient concepts of sufficient complexity and richness to be able to anticipate anything that the human might encounter – anything where "Occasion serves and Outward Objects invite" (*TEIM* 135). The "Soul is in a manner All Things" (ibid., 134), he says. It awaits only occasion and invitation to produce the relevant idea/concept. Chomsky, by contrast, would distinguish the concepts provided by the language faculty from the invented concepts of the sciences. On the assumption that Cudworth's ideas of the intellect parallel Chomsky's SEMs, Chomsky would have to disagree with Cudworth's enthusiastic view that the ideas of the intellect have a "potential omniformity." They do not include scientific concepts. But they seem to be as complete as one could expect for the language faculty's contribution to common sense understanding's worldmaking: they help yield the common sense world.

Cudworth distinguishes – although not as clearly as Chomsky – the task of providing an account of where concepts are and how to produce them from the separate issue of making sense of how they come to bear on the world. The first task corresponds to Chomsky's effort to construct a theory of SEMs. Cudworth has little to say about how generation of ideas proceeds, but it is clear that he thought of concepts as the products of something like a generative device. They are not, as with Plato, 'remembered', but rather produced by what were then unfathomable mental resources – what Hume would later call "secret springs and principles." The concepts that are produced include not just those that might have a very direct bearing on perceptual judgment, such as <u>house</u>, but "Justice, Equity, Duty and Obligation, Cogitation, Opinion, Intellection, Volition, Memory, Verity, Falsity, Cause, Effect, Genus, Species, Nullity, Contingency, Possibility, Impossibility, and innumerable more such there are that will occur to any one that shall turn over the Vocabularies of any Language" (*TEIM* 140).[8] For his time, he articulated remarkably well the idea that "secret springs and principles" in the mind provide us with our intellectual capacities.

Thinking of the concept <u>house</u> as including within itself <u>fit for human habitation</u> and some of the other features outlined in chapter 3, we can put prolepsis (anticipation) into modern Chomskian dress by saying that the linguistic concept <u>house</u> (along with, perhaps, visual 'concepts') can inform perceptual judgment, and a case of successful or appropriate perception amounts not, *per impossibile*, to a matching or correspondence between inner concept and outer facts (as these are understood, presumably, in physics, chemistry, and so on), but simply to the successful, by human standards, informing of perception or experience by the relevant concept. This is a restatement of Chomsky's point that innate ideas have proved successful in informing our anthropocentrically oriented experience of the world: common sense understanding is proof positive of that. Our mind's concepts *do* seem to 'anticipate' experience. So one might think of Cudworth's anticipation or prolepsis as providing an intuitive picture of interpretation, of how meanings come to be used and useful for human purposes. SEMs thought of as concepts clearly provide a means to cope with the environments that human beings encounter in their "ecological niche." And where Descartes wanted to introduce God and clarity and distinctness to provide for a complying world outside, we can assume instead that something like evolution plays the role of reassuring us that, while strictly speaking there are no houses 'out there', nevertheless, such concepts prove useful and compelling when they appear in the exercise of cognitive capacities that constitute common sense understanding. Linguistic judgments contain concepts that a person in judging uses to describe, explain, and so on. SEMs are configurations, infinite in number (almost a potential omniformity), that with their built-in 'anticipation' of a world that suits human interests can inform perception when 'invited' or – more generally – can inform thought about things. This is why, as Chomsky remarks in *Cartesian Linguistics*, rationalistic perceptual psychology did not sharply distinguish an account of perception from an account of acquiring the capacity to produce perceptual judgments. "In both cases, essentially the same processes are at work; a store of latent principles is brought to the interpretation of the data of sense. There is, to be sure, a difference between the initial 'activation' [triggering; "inviting and occasioning" for Cudworth] of latent structure and the use of it once it has become readily available for the interpretation (*more accurately, the determination*) of experience" (*CL* 65; emphasis added).

Saying that concepts anticipate experience, or 'work', when applied in perceptual judgment, does not pretend to be a *theory* of perceptual 'interpretation'. We already know that the prospects of a serious science of interpretation of any sort are dim, at best. It is a likely story – as Plato put it in his *Timaeus* – that rearranges intuitions about the appropriateness of inner ideas to outer circumstance for one kind of interpretive activity, that of perceptual judgment, utilizing the concepts of the intellect or natural languages. It says nothing about how to construe the appropriateness of speculation about what Harriet might do tomorrow, about how well a historical novel captures a time, and especially not about how compelling a poem is – all ways in which linguistic judgment can be "appropriate to circumstances." But it offers compelling reasons to readjust intuitions and begin to see that inner ideas *must* inform experience and the world, rather than the other way around. Once again, a comparison with the phonological-phonetic domain underscores the point. Earlier the comparison led to the conclusion that natural linguistic meanings had better be seen as inherent in SEMs. Now the point is to emphasize that as children automatically hear linguistic sounds with their phonetic shapes even if there is nothing in the 'signal' that can be so described, so it should be no surprise that children automatically see (or, more generally, experience) the world with the 'shapes' provided by the configurations of features in SEMs.

Recognition of the fact that linguistic audition requires the application of specialized and innate linguistic sound concepts goes back at least to Humboldt. Paraphrasing Humboldt's *Über die Verschiedenheit des Menschlichen Sprachbaues*, Chomsky (in *CL* 70) writes:

[S]peech perception requires an analysis of the incoming signal in terms of the underlying elements that function in the essentially creative act of

speech production, and therefore it requires the activation of the generative system that plays a role in production of speech as well, since it is
only in terms of these fixed rules that the elements and their relations are
defined. The underlying "Gesetze der Erzeugung" must, therefore, function in speech perception. If it were not for its mastery of these, . . . the
mind would no more be able to deal with the mechanisms of articulated
speech than a blind man is able to perceive colors.

The mention of color perception is apt too; as indicated earlier, *our*
colors and visual spaces are the products of an inner mechanism,
not an outer colored physical world. Yet, as with linguistic sounds,
we project these features into our experience of the world. There is
no bar to reasoning in the same way for phonetic features, or even
the features of <u>house</u>. Not just color and linguistic sounds, but the
things of the common sense world, are the products of our minds.
We share these sounds, colors, and things, but that is because of the
commonality of our innate concepts. The biological rationalist has,
then, an account – not a theory – of interpretation *if* the idea or SEM
provided by the mind is also the concept used in interpretation. So
there is reason to think that SEMs are at the same time the concepts
we use to deal with the world in experience *and* products of, and
defined within, the language faculty.

Meaning guides use

Worldmaking is the long version of the story, broached in an earlier
chapter, that meanings (SEMs) guide their own use. To illustrate the
point, I return to an example mentioned but not expanded upon
earlier, the verbal concept <u>persuade</u>. The illustration depends on
Chomsky's view of the nature of our knowledge of the fact that
from the truth of "x persuade y to z" follows the truth of "y intend
to z": if someone has persuaded someone else to do something,
everyone knows that the persuaded person at least intends to do it.
This is certainly knowledge that *bears on* fact (on the things of the
world). But if Chomsky is right, it does not come from the things
of the world. It is not *learned*. No one has to learn it, for it lies in the
semantic features of the lexical item "persuade." But these features
can guide use of the concept <u>persuade</u>.

There is plenty of evidence that the feature set characteristic of
<u>persuade</u> (which would, of course, be associated with different
sounds in different natural languages) and <u>intend</u>, and the connection between them, are innate, for there is evidence that the con-

cepts and the connection are recognized across the human population. No child has difficulty automatically 'picking up' this complicated lexical item and thousands of others equally complex. It can be objected that we need independent evidence that the concept really does have this specific, complex structure. We may now have it in lexical semantic studies and in the way "persuade" and other causative verbs are dealt with in the Minimalist Program. Outlining the evidence, and especially the details of the theory, is beyond the scope of this book; it involves introducing technical concepts that even some experts in the field dispute. But it is easy to see what is at stake: is there a way to show that the concept <u>persuade</u> decomposes into something *like* <u>cause to intend</u>? Chomsky's view, expressed informally in *LPK* and much more technically in *MP*, is "Yes." <u>Persuade</u>, like a large class of other causative verbs that include <u>sink</u>, <u>wash</u>, <u>break</u>, <u>blow</u>, and <u>throw</u>, must be understood to include a causal relationship between an appropriate agent who does something and some state that is an effect of what the agent does. There is some evidence in the Minimalist Program's treatment of the assignment of theta-roles (*MP* 314–16) and in what linguists call "small verbs" that the compositional account of this and other 'causative' lexical items precisely suits the processing picture that the program insists upon. If there is both intuitive and theoretical evidence, it presents a rather convincing case that when anyone in any language has in a particular SEM the meaning/concept <u>persuade</u>, then they also have there the concept <u>intend</u> plus the relevant causal relationship. If so, it is easy to see why people across the human population who describe (say) Mary as persuading Harry to do something and hold that in doing so they are correctly describing Mary recognize that they are also committed to holding that Harry intended to do it. This further commitment is one they are enjoined to, having spoken about Mary as persuading Harry. So a lexical feature specification of a SEM can have the appearance of providing 'real world knowledge'. Of course it does, Chomsky the constructivist says, but only because such 'knowledge' is contained in the lexical specification to begin with and guides its application (in this case, quite strictly, through enjoining; in the perceptual cases earlier, less so) to – in the example – Mary and Harry. It does so because the semantic features of "persuade" are found in a SEM, and the SEM is also a concept that is a part of and configures the relevant 'thought' about Mary and Harry.

Philosophers who have tried to construct what they think are theories of meaning for natural languages are often drawn to what they think of as "the logical structure of language." This has been common since the Middle Ages, when several versions of a "language of thought" hypothesis were introduced, and it was assumed that the logical structure of thought is primary and must somehow filter into languages, giving languages their "logical form." Thought and its supposed intrinsic logic supposedly provided the key to any semantic structure that languages might contain. It is important to emphasize, then, that while natural languages have structured meanings and thus semantic structure that guides rational discourse, the structure of meanings – found, we have seen, even at the lexical level – does not follow on a more basic structure of thought. Quite the opposite: the structure of meanings seems to make linguistic thought possible. Recall that Chomsky's theory of language is not a theory of intelligent behavior. But it does help show how intelligent behavior in the form of rational speech is possible.

7

Anarchosyndicalism and the Intellectual

Getting into focus

It is impossible to discuss all Chomsky's political works. They cover a wide range of issues: terrorism, racism, state religion, rights, freedom, authority, needs, political ideals, strategies, the cold war, nationalism, council communism, anarchism, revolution, morality, the market economy, US foreign policy, imperialism, the role of intellectuals, unions, solidarity, friendship, managers, media, corporations, legal persons, and tribalism, to name some. Fortunately, there are some recurring patterns or themes that have been emphasized for years. While Chomsky dislikes labels and the creation of abstractions, he admits to being an anarchosyndicalist or libertarian socialist. He constantly reminds us that political decisions are made against a backdrop of assumptions about human nature, and he opposes an 'economic man' view of human nature to the view he supports. He insists that his 'radical politics' is in fact far more responsible to human nature and needs than many currently popular 'isms' – for instance, neoliberalism. He defends the view that citizens of democracies in which large corporations control the economy – especially the United States – are subjected to a form of mind control or propaganda by corporate-run media. He holds that the "free market economy" is anything but free, and that those who are most strident in their defense of it, such as heads of large transnationals and their elected government representatives, benefit most from both protectionism on a grand scale and a kind of welfare for the rich. "Market principles" are for the poor, not the rich.

He holds that the US invaded – committed deliberate aggression against – Vietnam. He holds that intellectuals are responsible for telling the truth in politics, although, he claims, few do. He criticizes the actions of both sides in the Arab–Israeli dispute, and he has consistently held that the better long-term solution to that particular conflict is a binational state of Israel. And he holds that US foreign policy has consistently worked to ensure that popular movements in developing countries that might be sufficiently effective to challenge the 'ideals' of a market economy are unsuccessful.

In this survey of Chomsky's intellectual project, even this relatively short list must be shortened further. I will focus on four themes that give an idea of how Chomsky approaches political issues and aid the discussion in the next chapter of how one might conceive of the relationship between his political views and his rationalist/romantic view of human nature; I also take up how both might relate to his science of language. (Note "might": I mentioned early in the first chapter that Chomsky is diffident and skeptical about these connections.)

I start with two stylistic and methodological points. First, Chomsky does not cover every social and political issue, or deal with every part of the globe. This is surely no surprise: affairs of economy, state, and human nature present an overwhelming mass of material, and Chomsky naturally emphasizes some themes and focuses on certain areas of the world to be effective in what he says. Moreover, he constantly updates his discussions of issues and areas; his work on Israel is an example. Second, he maintains high standards of scholarship even in his decidedly informal and sometimes humorously ironic discussions of political issues. He makes some mistakes, of course; even the most fastidious of scientists writing short papers in technical journals make mistakes, and Chomsky's political corpus consists of hundreds of thousands of pages. But, like the fastidious scientist, he corrects them when they are found, modifying later printings of works to do so. His care seems to be motivated by three things. First, he wants to make sure that he does "tell the truth"; discussion based on fact is the only decision procedure that everyone should respect. Second, he feels that as an intellectual concerned with political and moral social issues he has a responsibility to provide accurate information, and he does not want to let down those who are helped by his efforts by offering misleading or false information: "What I'm trying to do is simply provide the kind of service to popular dissident movements and scattered individuals that any person who has the resources, the privilege, the training, etc. should perform" (*LP* 775). He has no more training in the matter of gathering information than any other thoughtful person; this kind of work does not require any. But he does have the privilege of position and reputation, and he has access to resources that others can less easily tap. Third, in the nature of the case, he must maintain standards that those who parrot the official view and purvey ideology do not. If his data and arguments were faulty, he would be subjected to immediate efforts to discredit his integrity, resources, scholarly efforts, and so on. Remarkably, given the thousands upon thousands of citations his works contain, I know of very few cases where he has been correctly faulted for providing misinformation or for misquoting. Despite this, one famous instance "has been the subject of (literally) dozens of articles, 'proving' that nothing I say can be trusted, that I'm a conscious liar, that nothing from the left can be trusted, etc. In the first printing of *American Power and the New Mandarins*, I attributed to Truman himself a very close paraphrase of Truman's remarks given by James Warburg. In the second printing, a few months later, it's corrected" (Chomsky's personal communication, April 15, 1998). By contrast, those who criticize him often do not bother quoting his work or quote out of context and, to attack his views, ignore what he says, and create straw men that cannot be supported by Chomsky's text. Other criticisms call Chomsky's credentials into question: it is said that he's not an expert on political matters, unlike (say) Henry Kissinger or someone who happens to have a PhD in political science. The answer to this form of attack is clear from the first chapter: politics is not science, but a domain of concern where we all can and do rely upon a massive number of shared assumptions and concerns. We also know his opinion of claims of expertise in this domain. In *Language and Politics* he puts an ironic cast on his point: "I don't think international affairs are harder [than sport commentaries and 'expertise' in analyzing a team's play and chances against others]. I don't think that national security policy is intellectually more challenging ... That's a pretense of the social sciences – that they're dealing with deeply complex issues that are beyond the level of the ordinary person. That's mostly fraud" (*LP* 717). The fraud, Chomsky holds, is that the intellectual – perhaps especially in the case of the social sciences and the media – pretends to objectivity and to telling the truth, but is actually part of a very effective form of thought control: the intelligentsia "which includes historians and other scholars, journalists, political commentators, and so on, undertakes to analyze and present some picture of social reality. By virtue of their analyses and interpretations, they serve as mediators between the social facts and the mass of the population: they create the ideological justification for social practice" (*LR* 4). Because everyone has common sense understanding, given a bit of healthy skepticism and open-mindedness, the *only* additional thing the ordinary person lacks is information. "In the analysis of social and political issues it is sufficient to face the facts and to be willing to follow a rational line of argument. Only Cartesian common sense, which is quite evenly distributed, is needed" (*LR* 5). Typically, that information is denied, through lack of opportunity aided by apathy (propaganda-induced, Chomsky holds) and lack of will. "The social sciences generally, and above all the analysis of contemporary affairs, are quite accessible to anyone who wants to take an interest in these matters. The alleged complexity, depth, and obscurity of these questions is part of the illusion propagated by the system of ideological control, which aims to make the issues seem remote from the general population and to persuade them of their incapacity to organize their own affairs or to understand the social world in which they live without the tutelage of intermediaries" (*LR* 4–5). Chomsky sees his task as providing the information and encouraging individuals to overcome their apathy. Given that there is so much information, but that it is too often deliberately hidden, he has to be – in his words – "a fanatic" to get it. "This information is accessible, but only for *fanatics*: in order to unearth it, you have to devote much of your life to the search" (*LR* 30).

The few (because of limitations of space) examples of government actions and policy decisions discussed in what follows are drawn primarily from Chomsky's more recent political works and illustrate three of the four themes I mention. There are no current illustrations of the social and political consequences of the romantic/rationalist conception of human beings because it has seldom been implemented, although Chomsky sees signs of what an implementation might look like in relatively open, self-governing communities, including (some) universities. The few clear historical cases are Israeli kibbutzim (some forms, especially in their beginnings) and the brief aftermath of the Spanish Revolution.

The "liberal" economic conception of humans and US domestic and foreign policy

When noted MIT economist and Nobel prize winner Paul Samuelson's book *Economics* was the standard text in undergraduate economics courses in the US, Chomsky quoted from it to illustrate some of the assumptions built into the reigning version of "economic man." He noted that when Samuelson spoke of the range of possible economic systems, he simply assumed that the spectrum was defined by freedom from state constraints on exploitation on the one side and complete government control on the other. He saw a "spectrum with complete *laissez faire* at one extreme and 'totalitarian dictatorship of production' at the other." Assuming this scale, " 'the relevant choice for policy today' is to determine where along this spectrum our economy should properly lie" (*PKF* 62; the inner quotes are from p. 39 of Samuelson's *Economics*). Chomsky continues: "There are other dimensions, however, along which Samuelson's polar opposites fall at the same extreme: for example, the spectrum that places direct democratic control of production at one pole and autocratic control, whether by state or private capital, at the other" (*PKF* 62). The same point is taken up in "Some Tasks for the Left," reprinted in *Radical Priorities*. There, Chomsky notes:

> The assumptions that guide the mass of [economic and political] scholarship hardly differ from those expressed in manifestoes of the American ruling elite, for example the report of the study group on *Political Economy of American Foreign Policy*, which identifies "Western civilization" with capitalist forms (as contrasted to the collectivist denial of freedom, initiative, and progress) and defines 'the aim of economic activity in the West (as) the maximization of money income – in one or another of its forms – by individuals through the investment of capital or labour on one's own account or for, and under the direction of, others.' (*RP* 226; inner quotes from a report from the Woodrow Wilson Foundation and National Planning Association)

Then Chomsky comes to his primary point:

> Surely this concept of economic man is a psychological absurdity which leads to untold suffering for those who try to mould themselves to this pattern, as well as for their victims. "Look out for number one" is a prescription for demoralization, corruption, and ultimately general catastrophe, whatever value it may have had in the early stages of industrialization. Cooperation for the common good and concern for the rights and needs of others must replace the dismal search for maximization of personal power and consumption if the barbarism of capitalist society is to be overcome. (Ibid.)

Chomsky holds that, so conceived, "economic man" is a distortion, and that (by implication) the concept of freedom that this conception of human beings presupposes is not that of the "free and creative use of one's capacities" but only the lack of constraint against exploitation, or what Chomsky calls "accumulation and domination" (*PP* 77). In fact, on a different scale, drawn from a different conception of the human being, *both* Samuelson's "polar opposites" are at the same extreme. Both represent autocratic or clearly nondemocratic forms of control of capital; they differ only in whether the control of capital is private or state-based, as neither puts control in the hands of the people. The conception of economic man that Samuelson relies upon is typical of contemporary 'liberal' economic doctrine that has some roots in Locke and Smith but is due primarily to Malthus and Ricardo. In 1690 Locke held that the pursuit of fortune (property) is, along with life and liberty, among the basic rights of human beings. Smith, in 1776, thought that human nature shows a "propensity" to "truck, barter, and exchange one thing for another" (*An Inquiry into the Nature and Causes of the Wealth of Nations*, bk I, ch. 2); for Smith this propensity, along with reason and speech, distinguishes human beings from beasts. But – as Chomsky sometimes emphasizes to undermine the 'liberal' claim that Smith is the parent of current doctrine – Smith himself held in contempt "the 'mean' and 'sordid pursuits' of 'the masters of mankind' and their 'vile maxim'" (*PP* 77). It was only in the eighteenth century with Ricardo and Malthus that accumulation and domination became the critical aims for defining economic values and modern 'liberal' economic doctrine. *Classical* liberal economic doctrine valued freedom and the opportunity for individuals to find fulfillment in their labor.[1]

Economic man conceived of in terms of accumulation and domination has been an important part of US economic and political faith from the beginning. James Madison, fourth president of the US, put the rights of property ahead of the rights of persons, holding that the rights of property must take precedence because "the rights of property will constantly be under threat from 'the will of the majority', who may, by their power in a democracy, 'trespass on the rights of a minority' . . . The rights of the 'opulent minority' that government must protect as its primary duty are . . . quite unlike 'the rights of persons'; the latter are to be granted uniformly under the Constitutional system, whereas 'the rights of property' are narrowly held in the hands of the 'opulent minority'" (*PP* 118). Chomsky goes on to point out the basic confusion in this rhetoric. Property has no rights, people do. So Madison is saying that the rich have the right to be rich. To guarantee this, only the wealthy may run a government; this is only fair because, as Madison says, property "chiefly bears the burden of government." It is clear where the emphasis is to be among the three rights Locke assigned to all people. And it is clear whose liberty, and of what sort, is to be taken seriously. In fact, in the US's early days, the right to life was also denied to some citizens, as it was in industrial England, no doubt in accordance with Malthus's view that someone who is not independently wealthy and does not survive in the labor market has "no claim of right to the smallest portion of food, and, in fact, has no business to be where he is" (*PP* 89). Chomsky ironically mentions Ricardo on the market economy's devotion to the "happiness of the people." The relevant people are the rich, and, strictly, only they should be allowed to vote, for " 'limiting the elective franchise to the very narrowest bounds' would guarantee more 'security for a good choice of representatives'." To be sure, some others might generously be allowed to vote – " 'not, indeed, . . . all people, but . . . that part of them which cannot be supposed to have any interest in overturning the right of property' " (*PP* 89–90).

There were dissident voices from the start – virtually all of them genuine conservatives, unlike today's post-Reaganist and post-Thatcher conservatives, who are in fact nonclassical 'liberals'. In his later years Thomas Jefferson, third president of the US, recognized that democracy was in danger if the "aristocrats" (the bankers, etc.) who "fear and distrust the people" were allowed to take all powers unto themselves. He preferred the democrats who "identify with the people, have confidence in them, cherish and consider them as the honest & safe, altho not [always] the most wise depository of the public interest." Furthermore, he declared that "widespread poverty and concentrated wealth cannot exist side by side in a democracy" (*PP* 87–8). Jefferson's remark echoes Enlightenment emphasis upon a crucial connection between free and creative labor and self-development and self-worth. As mentioned, Smith – unlike Malthus and Ricardo – recognized this connection and the constraints it introduces when he wrote:

> The man whose whole life is spent in performing a few simple operations, of which the effects are perhaps always the same, or very nearly the same, has no occasion to exert his understanding or to exercise his invention in finding out expedients for removing difficulties which never occur. He naturally loses, therefore, the habit of such exertion, and generally becomes as stupid and ignorant as it is possible for a human creature to become. . . . But in every improved and civilized society this is the state into which the labouring poor, that is, the great body of the people,

must necessarily fall, unless government takes some pains to prevent it.
(*Inquiry*, bk 1, ch. 2)

These seeds of a state concerned for the welfare of all its citizens
had a mixed reception in the nineteenth century. Along with steady
growth of the new "manufacturing aristocracy" that worried de
Tocqueville, one also finds a labor movement that honored Enlightenment ideals and a Republican Party that thought of wage labor
as like chattel slavery. While the 'laws' of the market and the acceptance of domination in the form of wage slavery did not completely
control domestic policy for most of the period, matters began to
change near the end of the century with the corporatization of the
US – something that Jefferson and other Enlightenment thinkers did
not anticipate. With the exception of a period after the Depression,
when welfare policies were introduced as part of the New Deal, and
advances in some rights legislation after that, corporatization has
generally increased.

In recent years, US domestic accommodation to Enlightenment
ideals of free labor and self-fulfillment, equality of opportunity, and
democratic principles has suffered some serious setbacks. For
instance, the disparity in net worth between rich and poor has
become extreme. A 1997 report from Kennickell and Woodburn,
based on the 1995 Survey of Consumer Finances provided by the
US Federal Reserve, reveals that "the richest 1% of the U.S. population has a larger share of total worth (defined as net worth, that
is, assets less debts) than the bottom 90% of the population, and
the top 10% has just over twice as much as everyone else" (reported
in *Left Business Observer* 80, Nov. 17, 1997, p. 8). From the Reagan
recession in 1982 until 1994, report Mishel and Bernstein in their
The State of Working America, wages for entry-level jobs fell 30
percent for male high school graduates and 18 percent for female.
Chomsky also mentions information from the 1994 *Report of the President* that indicates one result of the Clinton recovery: poverty rates
in the US are twice those of any other industrialized country, and
children are particularly heavily affected (*PP* 128). To be sure, public
largesse has not disappeared, but the recipients have changed.
Chomsky notes that among the most strident defenders of the principle that governments must get "off our backs" and let the "free
market" reign was former Speaker of the House Newt Gingrich.
Gingrich represented Cobb County, Georgia, an opulent district
that derives much of its income from aerospace (Lockheed–Martin,
primarily military aircraft) and high-technology industries. Because

these industries are directly subsidized by the government, it receives the third highest amount in subsidies of any suburban district in the United States. (The other two are Arlington, Virginia, and the county in Florida where the Kennedy Space Center is housed – in both cases, federal enclaves.) The result is, as Chomsky points out, protection of the rich from "market discipline" by "a powerful and interventionist welfare state" (*PP* 121). Of course, if Gingrich were to use the term "welfare" in connection with these subsidies for the rich, neither he nor any of the other defenders of the "Contract with America" would have been elected, much less taken seriously and widely admired in the press.[2] So instead of calling such funds "subsidies," they are held to be necessary for 'security', as the first secretary of the US Air Force, Stuart Symington, noted in 1948. Symington, himself a representative of the aerospace industry, demanded that the military budget "meet the requirements of the aircraft industry" (*PP* 122). Since then, security, rather than subsidy, has been the watchword and has led to the US devoting (in 1995 dollars) 85 percent of its average cold war budget to military spending, even though there were no discernible enemies that justified such an extraordinary expense; in fact, military spending in 1995 was $30 billion *higher* than under Nixon. The extraordinary phenomenon of elected officials openly spending billions in funds that cannot be justified by need and that demonstrably line the pockets of the rich can be sustained only by maintaining the illusion that there *is* a need and that representatives are acting in the interests of the governed. So a significant feature of US government domestic spending after the cold war's demise has been the concerted effort to foster the illusion that there is need. For example, the Air Force sold Lockheed F-16s to Third World countries with taxpayer-subsidized loans (US arms sales to the Third World represented about half of all arms sales to this market), so that the Air Force could pay Lockheed, while Lockheed developed F-22s with taxpayer subventions so that they could be sold to the US Air Force to allow the US to protect itself against weapons it sold in the first place. The threat to national security from Third World countries and other imagined enemies was so great that Gingrich and other supporters put through an "emergency" $3.2 billion appropriation for the Pentagon. Chomsky notes, "House Democrat David Obey proposed in committee to replace a planned US$5–US$7 billion of cuts in child nutrition, housing, and job training by a five-year delay in deployment of Lockheed F-22 advanced fighters, a (surely underestimated) welfare program [for Lockheed] of $72 billion: *delay*, not discontinuation of the taxpayer giveaway. The suggestion was summarily rejected, and scarcely reported" (*PP* 123). Incidentally, military subsidy has benefited the rich in more than these direct ways. Virtually all research in electronics and computers from the 1950s on has been heavily subsidized by the US government with the nominal intent of producing better military equipment. Consumer equipment built by corporations relying on discoveries and techniques developed under public subvention is then sold to the public that paid for the research and development costs through taxes.

There is ample evidence, Chomsky points out, that sales of arms to most foreign states are opposed by the US populace. He notes: "Arms sales to undemocratic countries – most of the recipients – are opposed by a mere 96 percent of the population" (*PP* 124). What about other aspects of Gingrich's "Contract with America?" At the time of the Republican victory, over 60 percent of the populace wanted an *increased* degree of social spending, not the so-called Contract's severe cuts (*PP* 114). Apparently the vast majority of people at the time of the election had never heard of Gingrich's "Contract." No doubt considerable support was and is shown in polls for a "balanced budget," another item in the "Contract"; a balanced budget sounds good to anyone who has had to contend with their own finances. But when people are asked if they want a balanced budget if it means reduction in spending for education, health, and the environment, support "dwindles to a small minority – in the 20–30 percent range" (*PP* 115). Chomsky quotes the *Wall Street Journal* (June 8, 1995) in this regard: "A strong 72 percent oppose any reduction in education whatever . . . [and] solid majorities oppose any substantial cuts in Social Security, the Medicare health program for the elderly and the Medicaid health program for the poor" (*PP* 116). What gets emphasized in reporting, however, is support for a balanced budget, without mention of the fact that this is impossible (*given* US defense spending) without cutting what solid majorities want.

If emphasis on accumulation and domination is sometimes mitigated in US domestic policy, this is not the case in foreign policy. The Gulf War provided an unprecedented opportunity for the US to gain more control over a region that contains a large part of the world's oil reserves. The background to this event included prior US support for Saddam Hussein and a decision by the Bush administration to continue trade with Iraq until the war – certainly consistent with standard policy, for Saddam's repressive, cruel rule was seen as more 'stable' than Iraqi dissident elements, who would have upset the status quo. That this form of stability was an aim was clear after the war, when Bush provided "aid and support to Saddam Hussein as he mercilessly crushed the Shi'ite and Kurdish uprisings under the eyes of the victorious allied forces, who refused to lift a finger" (*PP* 13). US postwar support for this policy was seconded by Turkey, itself concerned with the Kurds, and Israel, "fearing that Kurdish autonomy in Iraq might 'create a territorial, military, contiguity between Teheran and Damascus', a potential danger for Israel (Moshe Zak, senior editor of the mass-circulation daily *Ma'ariv*, explaining the support for Saddam on the part of the top military command and a broad range of political opinion, including leading doves)" (*PP* 135).

Weeks before the war actually began, faced with the threat of US direct involvement, Iraq had offered to withdraw from Kuwait. This was ignored by the US government and effectively went unreported in the press. It was not in the interests of a government that wanted to establish control to let its citizens know that there was a way out that would make the outcome less decisive: "on the eve of the bombing, the American population, by about 2 to 1, supported a settlement based on withdrawal of Iraqi troops in the context of consideration of regional issues, not knowing of an Iraqi proposal to this effect a few weeks earlier, or its summary rejection in Washington" (*PP* 136; *WOON* 10). Keep in mind that this region is a rich prize if policy is driven primarily by an attempt to control the market. It had been apparent since the end of World War II that this region would be a "strategically important area in the world," as Eisenhower noted, and US foreign policy for the region has consistently been devoted to gaining and maintaining hegemony. Israel too has been a part of this policy: maintaining a pro-US stance in Israel and earlier in Iran was crucial to maintaining control of the resources, keeping things appropriately 'stable'. Before Khomeini, support was directed to the Shah. After that, Chomsky remarks, "it should come as no surprise that after the fall of the Shah, Israel and Saudi Arabia at once began to cooperate [with the willing compliance of the US] in selling US arms to the Iranian army . . . These are the initial stages of what later became known as the 'arms for hostages' scandal" (*PP* 139). The aim was to support the military in Iran in the no doubt correct belief that if the Ayatollah were to be removed and the old regime replaced, the army would have to be involved in the replacement and re-establishment. It is clear where the US stood throughout: maximize control so that things remain as 'stable' as possible, where stability is deemed to be what is needed for control of a market.

Since President Wilson's time it has been important for the US to try to appear to be acting in the interests of a target state that corporate US interests want to control. Wilson set the US on an 'idealistic' course – one that served the interests of 'freedom', by which was meant – inspection reveals – the freedom of the rich to do what they want. Wilson was no slouch in protecting market principles in domestic policy – his Red Scare (which brought J. Edgar Hoover to prominence and led to the US's aversion to even the word "Communism") and attacks on unions were very successful in the early twenties (cf. *NI* 187) – and his foreign policy included several efforts to provide for the 'self-determination' of various states. It included, that is, a successful effort to turn Venezuela (then a primary oil producer) into a client of the US, eliminating British influence in the area in order to do this (*PP* 139). It included also outright invasions of Haiti and the Dominican Republic. Chomsky notes: "This exercise in 'Wilsonian Idealism' killed thousands, restored virtually slavery in Haiti, and dismantled its parliamentary system because legislators refused to accept a 'progressive' Constitution written in Washington that allowed US investors to turn the country into their private plantation, and perhaps most important, left both countries in the hands of terrorist armies dedicated to 'internal security' and trained and armed for the task" (*PP* 97; *WOON* 44f). Notice that these invasions preceded Vietnam, and there was no cold war to fight; nor was there yet the "Scourge of Communism" to serve as an excuse for intervention. Intervention was for market interests alone. Wilson's Secretary of State Robert Lansing admitted privately that the motivation behind the doctrine was "selfishness alone," and in presenting it, the US (quoting Lansing from *PP* 137) "considers its own interests. The integrity of other American nations is an incident, not an end." Recent US activities in Haiti reconfirm the policy (*WOON* 64f).

It was, however, only after World War II led to the emergence of the US as a great power that interventionist efforts in favor of maintaining markets began to proceed on a grand scale. Chomsky notes that US policy makers decided that while other capitalist economies would be allowed to develop within what was called a Grand Area of economic influence, they would be constrained to development that responded to the needs of the US economy: "only the United States would be permitted to dominate regional systems" (*NI* 25). He continues: "The United States moved to take effective control of world energy production and to organize a world system in which its various components would fulfill their functions as industrial centers, as markets and sources of raw materials, or as dependent states pursuing their 'regional interests' within the 'overall framework of order' managed by the United States (as Henry Kissinger was later to explain)." Given this policy, it was clear that the primary enemies to its full implementation would be those "indigenous populations" who "fall prey to the wrong ideas" (*NI* 27). One example is Vietnam, another Nicaragua. The then Soviet Union was another matter, of course. The Soviet Union had emerged as another powerful nation that resisted incorporation in the Grand Area and that had aggressive expansionist ideas of its own. The remedy for this nuisance had both an international dimension and a domestic one. Internationally, the aim was to slowly weaken the Soviet Union by "containment" (supporting heavy arms emplacements in surrounding states, such as Turkey, maintaining an arms race, and supporting any armies or groups willing to resist – for example, supporting armies "established by Hitler in the Ukraine and Eastern Europe, with the assistance of such figures as Reinhard Gehlen, who headed Nazi military intelligence on the Eastern front and was placed in charge of the espionage service of West Germany under close CIA supervision, assigned the task of developing a 'secret army' of thousands of SS men to assist the forces fighting within the Soviet Union" (*NI* 27)). Domestically, the idea was to maintain voter support for 'security' (and subvention) and intervention in the affairs of other states by insisting that the Soviet Union represented the Evil One who was responsible for propagating the Scourge of Communism. The Korean War was very useful for the purpose of establishing the evil intentions of Communist hordes and the view that – continuing Wilsonian "idealism" – the intentions of the US are pure: the United States intervenes only in the interest of 'self-determination'. With the agenda set, it came to seem obvious that if any countries showed signs of developing popular movements that might resist accepting market values and US control within the Grand Area, intervention was required to enable them to see the right path, that of self-determination as understood in Washington. The idea was to make it appear that the US was justified in invading (Vietnam) or in providing support to local armies (Nicaragua) because these countries were set on a path that could not possibly be freely chosen. Notice that Chomsky certainly does not deny that the Soviet Union also invaded and intervened. Nor, obviously, does he approve of the

Soviets' actions. He is careful to point out that it "is unnecessary to make up reasons to oppose the brutality of the Soviet leaders in dominating their internal empire and their dependencies" (*NI* 27). The point is rather that one should not be under the illusion that the US's invasions and aggression against movements that had broad popular support but showed signs of denying the values of accumulation and domination were somehow unselfishly motivated, or that they ever deviated from the market control policies of the Grand Area.

The idea of the Scourge of Communism resuscitated the Wilsonian Red Scare's great success in inducing an aversion to "Communism," an aversion generalized to socialist and independent capitalist policies. Aversion to such notions had waned while the US was deep in recession in the 1930s, and its revival was welcomed by the captains of industry, who encouraged an effort to repeal many of the rather modest reforms of the New Deal. But the Scourge proved useful above all in offering a postwar excuse to divert funds and to present subversion against foreign states as 'idealistic' efforts in the interest of those states' 'self-determination'. Containment of the Scourge required massive arms investments at public expense. However, because building and developing arms were supposed to be necessary for self-defense, what was in fact a wasteful use of public funds and a boon for certain industries that might otherwise have had to retool or reorient could be presented as an understandable effort to ensure that all would rest secure at night. The cold war also provided a convenient excuse for intervention where there was no actual or even potential physical threat but only a threat to market values because of popular reformist movements. Vietnam is one example, Nicaragua another.

The Sandinistas (Washington's 'bad guys') took power in Nicaragua in 1979 by toppling the US-backed Somoza regime. In elections held in 1984 the Sandinistas won by a two to one margin. There was good evidence by 1984 that the Sandinistas were engaged in efforts generally supported by the people – improved health care, agrarian reform, improved education, and the like – and that the vote was a strong endorsement of continuation. José Figueres, the "founder of Costa Rican democracy," expressed his view that "for the first time, Nicaragua has a government that cares for its people" (*NI* 62). He was seconded by Edgar Chamorro, a CIA-appointed spokesperson for the *opposition* contras (Washington's 'good guys'), who reported: " 'What I have seen here is very, very positive, people are walking on their own two feet', regaining the 'dignity and nationalism' they had lost under Somoza'. . . . He saw 'very little militarization' and 'a deep sense of equality', 'one of the accomplishments of the revolution'. 'I didn't see people hungry'; 'most people look very healthy, strong, alive', and he saw few beggars, unlike [US-backed and run] Honduras 'or even in city streets in the US'" (*NI* 63). But one got a very different picture of conditions in Nicaragua under the Sandinistas from the US mainstream press. James LeMoyne of the *New York Times* saw "a brutal and repressive state under 'one-party rule' with 'crowds of pot-bellied urchins in the streets', state security agents 'ubiquitous' and the army 'everywhere'." Mainstream media aside, there is reason to think that the Sandinistas were popular and were busy putting in place in Nicaragua – in spite of strong US opposition (including heavy support for the contras) – a reform that benefited the great majority, but not US "interests." Chomsky summarizes:

> There are two very striking differences between the Sandinistas and the U.S. favorites who adhere to 'regional standards'. The first is that the Sandinistas, whatever their sins, had not conducted campaigns of mass slaughter, torture, mutilation, and general terror to traumatize the population. . . . The second major difference is that the Sandinistas diverted resources to the poor majority and attempted measures of meaningful social reform – quite successfully, in fact, until U.S. economic and military warfare succeeded in reversing the unwelcome improvement in health and welfare standards, literacy, and development. (*NI* 64)

Chomsky calls the US actions against this apparently popular regime "economic and military warfare." To support this, he points to the Reagan administration's claim, echoed by virtually every mainstream media writer or speaker, that there were no elections in 1984: there could not have been, because had there been, a socialist government would have been legitimized. The evidence is strongly to the contrary. Chomsky also mentions the military supplies provided to the contras, including US flights into Nicaraguan territory and the terrorist techniques in which the contras engaged. He mentions the US's simple dismissal of a World Court judgment against the US – a judgment that demanded that the US cease aiding the contras, cease illegal economic warfare, honor existing treaties, and pay reparations to the Sandinista-run government. He mentions the effort to dismantle the peace accord reached in 1987 among the presidents of the various Central American states. Among other things, it called for an immediate cessation of CIA flights to supply the contras; the response was to increase the number of flights, already at one a day. After a cease-fire was signed in March of 1988, the US did not stop. It continued to provide 'aid' to the contras. The threat of continued intervention undoubtedly played a role in the 1990 Nicaraguan election that established a pro-US government. Chomsky remarks:

> As the campaign opened in November 1989, the White House and Congress at once made it clear that the terror and economic warfare would continue unless the U.S. candidate was elected. In the United States – indeed, the West generally – none of this was considered an interference with "the democratic process." The U.S. candidate was duly elected in February 1990. In Latin America, the outcome was generally interpreted as a victory for George Bush, even by those who celebrated it. In the United States, in contrast, it was hailed as a "Victory for U.S. Fair Play." (*WOON* 47)

It was not until 1994, during the Clinton administration, that the US finally accepted the Sandinistas as a "legitimate political force in Nicaragua." Earlier, of course, the US had done everything it could to ensure that Nicaragua be anything but the unaligned country it had tried to be.

Another aspect of US 'idealism' in foreign affairs since Carter has been a "concern for human rights." Arguably, the Sandinistas *were* concerned about them: they saw to arranging what appears to be a reasonably fair election, and they tried to see to the basic needs of individuals even when they had to devote very considerable resources to fighting heavily subsidized (by the US) contra actions. In contrast, the human rights records of El Salvador and Guatemala – both touted as democracies (although beleaguered by rebellious guerrillas) – show how well Washington has managed to instill a respect for human rights in its client states. Chomsky reports:

> The Costa Rican-based Commission for the Defense of Human Rights in Central America reported to the U.N. in November [1987] on the continuing terror by the Guatemalan security services and death squads, documenting some 175 cases of abductions, disappearances, and assassinations from August 8 to November 17, 1987, in addition to grenade attacks, a bomb thrown into a church, etc. The Guatemalan Human Rights Commission had recorded 334 extrajudicial executions and 73 disappearances in the first nine months of 1987. (*NI* 227)

These records should be seen in the following context: the Central American presidents, angered at US interference in their affairs, had signed an accord known as Esquipulas II on August 7, 1987. Nicaragua was a signatory. The accord

> called for "an authentic pluralistic and participatory democratic process to promote social justice, respect for human rights, sovereignty, the territorial integrity of states and the right of each nation to determine, freely and without any kind of external interference, its own economic, political and social model" as well as steps to ensure "justice, freedom and democracy," freedom of expression and political action, and opening of the communication media "for all ideological groups." They also called for "dialogue with all unarmed political opposition groups within the country" and other steps to achieve national reconciliation. Furthermore, "amnesty decrees will be issued setting out the steps to guarantee the inviolability of all forms of life and liberty, material goods and the safety of the people to benefit from said decrees." (*NI* 226–7)

El Salvador immediately 'respected' the amnesty decree by declaring its own security forces free from prosecution for their actions; not surprisingly, their terrorist activities increased. "Tutela Legal, the human rights monitoring office of the Archdiocese of San Salvador, reported that recorded death squad killings doubled to about ten a month immediately after the accords, continuing through January" (*NI* 228). As for Guatemala, security forces managed to pick up the pace that they had maintained in the first nine months of 1987. From August 7 to January 1988, Guatemalan security forces were responsible for over 500 dead and 160 disappearances. In stark contrast, Chomsky notes, "not only the pro-contra internal opposition, but even contra military leaders who decide to return to Nicaragua live and work there without concern for their lives. To cite only one of several cases, contra leader Fernando Chomorro returned to Nicaragua from Costa Rica and was named regional president of the Conservative Party, which openly supports the contras" (*NI* 230). Nicaragua apparently did respect the accords.

More recent developments indicate a continuing Grand Area policy. The US changed its tune after the end of the cold war, but in no way modified its overall foreign policy of maintaining hegemony for US corporations – now often transnationals based in the US and heavily invested in by US nationals – in what amounts to a greatly expanded Grand Area without Soviet resistance. As Chomsky notes, the aim seems to be to conquer by 'free trade' agreements and other means: the general intention is to use government to eliminate any constraints on corporate power. This set of developments emphasizes that corporations are in fact in charge, and that governments that hope to survive must do their will. Chomsky said in 1994:

> U.S. attitudes towards "free trade" are illustrated by its reliance on embargo and sanctions against its Third World enemies from democratic capitalist Guatemala and Chile to Cuba, Vietnam, Nicaragua, and other transgressors. Of 116 cases of sanctions used since World War II, 80 percent were initiated by the United States alone. These measures, which radically violate free trade doctrine, have often received international condemnation, including decisions of the World Court and GATT council. GATT rules do offer recourse to victims of such measures: they may retaliate in kind. Thus the United States may retaliate if it feels that Nicaragua discriminates against it, and Nicaragua can impose sanctions on the United States and even demand the reparations called for by the World Court, abandoned by Nicaragua under U.S. threat. As recognized by the founders of the Chicago school [of economics] before it was taken over by ideological extremists, "freedom without power, like power without freedom, has no substance or meaning" – another truism drowned out in the enthusiastic "free market" chorus. (*WOON* 184)

"In the New World Order, the world is to be run by the rich and for the rich. The world system is nothing like a classical [free] market; the term 'corporate mercantilism' is a closer fit. Governance is increasingly in the hands of huge private institutions and their representatives" (ibid., 185). National borders have lost much of their interest, except as ways of locating which governments are willing to, and have the power to, carry out the corporate will. So have the trade statistics; much 'trade' is in fact intra-corporate transfer of goods, hardly trade at all. In 1994, some 40 percent of US trade was in this form (ibid., 180). Northern industrial countries, especially the United States, benefit. Or, rather, the transnational corporations benefit, and those who happen to be in charge of these corporations benefit disproportionately more. Chomsky notes: "Resource transfers from South to North amount to 'a much understated $418 billion' from 1982 to 1990, Susan George estimates, the equivalent in today's dollars of some 'six Marshall Plans for the rich through debt service alone'. In the same years, the debt burden increased 61 percent, 110 percent for the 'least developed' countries" (ibid., 130). The penalties for not playing the game, by being unaligned, are great: Cuba's and Nicaragua's infant mortality figures indicate this. The embargo on medical supplies to Cuba "has contributed to an increase in hunger, illness, death and to one of the world's largest neurological epidemics in the past century," Chomsky quotes from "health experts writing in US medical journals in October 1994. The author of one says, 'Well, the fact is that we are killing people', by denying them food and medicines, and equipment for manufacturing their own medical products" (*PP* 81).

In this New World Order, not even the US can now afford to take the initiative (including perhaps assuming increased debt, though simple reallocation of resources would be more than sufficient) that social reform might require. Everyone except for large corporations is subject to "market discipline" – that is, the will of the corporation. Chomsky remarks that the

> mechanisms are straightforward. With capital highly mobile and labor immobile, the globalization of the economy provides employers with means to play one national labor force against another. The device can be used to diminish living standards, security, opportunities, and expectations for the great mass of the population, while profits soar and privileged sectors live in increasing luxury. Note that the mobility of capital and immobility of labor reverses the basic conditions of classical economic theory, which derived its conclusions about the benefits of comparative advantage and free trade from the assumption that capital is relatively immobile and labor highly mobile, assumptions that were realistic in Ricardo's day. (*WOON* 160)

The result is that US labor is forced to decline to Third World standards, which the *Wall Street Journal* calls "a welcome development of transcendent importance." "The guiding doctrine is straightforward: profit for investors is the supreme human value, to which all else must be subordinated. Human life has value insofar as it contributes to this end" (*WOON* 162).

The outcome of all this is that what are known as "legal persons" – corporations – have become the only agents, and real persons come to be defined in terms of their "use value" for the corporation – by their roles or functions in the corporation. The lucky few who have sufficient (economic) power to control or play a part in the control of the corporation receive the rewards that 'market discipline' gives them. This goes against traditional Enlightenment-inspired conceptions of the human being, of course, including traditional conservative and anarchosyndicalist concepts of the person, to say nothing of the fact that it is completely undemocratic. What one gets instead is what political economist Robert Brady described a half a century ago. Quoting from *PP*: "Within the corporation, all policies emanate from the control above. In the union of this power to determine policy with the execution thereof, all authority necessarily proceeds from the top to the bottom and all responsibility from the bottom to the top. This is, of course, the inverse of 'democratic' control; it follows the structural conditions of dictatorial power" (p. 71).

The anarchosyndicalist conception of the person

Anarchosyndicalism might seem to some to be a contradiction in terms. Isn't anarchism the complete absence of any obligations towards others? It might appear so to those who have in mind as a model of the person something like economic man. This view of anarchism and its value is represented in economist James Buchanan's account of the ideal society. Buchanan holds that "the ideal society is anarchy, in which no one man or group of men coerces another" (1975: 92). This is glossed by Buchanan in the following way: "any person's ideal situation is one that allows him full freedom of action and inhibits the behavior of others so as to force adherence to his own desires. That is to say, each person seeks mastery over a world of slaves." The definition of anarchy as the absence of coercion by others is on the right track, but Buchanan's gloss is pathological. Yet it is what the conception of economic man in terms of accumulation and domination leads to, represented for us now in Brady's corporations as "the union of . . . power to determine policy with the execution thereof" – as an agent without responsibility. Unlike Buchanan, Chomsky is an anarchosyndicalist, and the "syndicalist" side of anarchosyndicalism reminds us that Chomsky's conception of anarchism and anarchy is by no means like Buchanan's gloss. In fact, he says, "In today's world, . . . the goals of a committed anarchist should be to defend some state institutions from the attack against them, while trying at the same time to pry them open to more meaningful public participation – and ultimately, to dismantle them in a much more free society, *if* the appropriate circumstances can be achieved" (*PP* 75; emphasis added). The institutions he has in mind are those that limit the powers of corporations to pollute, to eliminate or severely restrict unions, to restrict trade, avoid taxation, and the like.

"Anarchosyndicalism" is interchangeable with "libertarian socialism." In an interview on London Weekend TV in 1976 Chomsky said:

[A]narchism can be conceived as a kind of voluntary socialism, that is, as libertarian socialist or anarcho-syndicalist or communist anarchist,[3] in the tradition of say Bakunin and Kropotkin and others.[4] They had in mind a highly organized form of society, but a society that was organized on the basis of organic units, organic communities. And generally they meant by that the workplace and the neighborhood, and for these two basic units there could derive through federal arrangements a highly integrated kind of social organization, which might be national or even international in scope. And these decisions could be made over a substantial range, but by delegates who are always part of the organic community from which they come, to which they return and in which, in fact, they live. (*RP* 245)

The result for anarchosyndicalism/libertarian socialism is a form of representational government, but very much unlike what one finds in the US or the UK. In these latter forms, representation is "limited to the political sphere and in no serious way encroaches on the economic sphere." Chomsky continues: "Anarchists of this tradition have always held that democratic control of one's productive life is at the core of any serious human liberation, or, for that matter, of any significant democratic practice" (*RP* 246). This is the context for Chomsky's insistence that people need free and productive activity in order to fulfill themselves. If they do not have it and must 'rent' their labor to others, who treat them solely in terms of their part in production without giving them effective control, the result is "coercion and oppression." Coercion and oppression take their standard meanings (doing things against one's will and unjust exercise of power), but because he takes free and creative activity to be a fundamental need of humans, Chomsky presumably intends some of the psychological aspects of oppression too – depression, failure to thrive. In fact, as is clear from the above, this aspect is quite important to him: the result of taking accumulation and domination as the basic values, particularly in the form these values now take in the operations of transnational corporations, affects both victim and those in charge of the corporations. It is, as quoted above, a "psychological absurdity which leads to untold suffering for those who try to mould themselves to this pattern, as well as for their victims." This connection to the psychological is tied to the fact that Chomsky holds that anarchosyndicalism is defensible as an empirical claim about the nature of a society in which human beings cannot just survive but thrive, by fulfilling their natures.

It is important to see that for Chomsky anarchosyndicalism/libertarian socialism is both an outgrowth of the Enlightenment and a response to a specific problem that was not anticipated when Enlightenment thinkers began to deliberate about implementing the humanistic ideal of the autonomous and responsible person. There is no question but that Jefferson, Thoreau, Humboldt, and Rousseau (in some works, at least) had in mind a society of uncoerced individuals that met the bare description of anarchy that Buchanan offered, a society in which "no one man or group of men coerces another." But they did not have in mind the pathological gloss that Buchanan put on it; nor, crucially, did they have in mind anything like the concept of private power in corporations that has emerged. For them, the power to coerce was held by Church or State, and – as Jefferson put it – government is best that governs least. Today, concentration of private power in corporations represents for Chomsky, as we have seen, the most serious challenge to the basically anarchist principles of Jefferson and others. He sees anarchosyndicalism as a modification of the basic Enlightenment conception of the person as a free and responsible agent, a modification required to meet the challenge of private power. Empowering individuals by putting control back into their hands is the best way to meet this challenge and provide a meaningful form of freedom.

Chomsky is no Luddite. The technological advances of industrial society could well be turned to aid the anarchosyndicalist. He remarks:

> I think that industrialization and the advance of technology raise possibilities for self-management over a broad scale that simply didn't exist in an earlier period. And that in fact this is precisely the rational mode for an advanced and complex industrial society, one in which workers can very well become masters of their own immediate affairs, that is, in direction and control of the shop, but also can be in a position to make the major substantive decisions concerning the structure of the economy, concerning social institutions, concerning planning regionally and beyond. At present, institutions do not permit them to have control over the requisite information, and the relevant training to understand these matters. A good deal could be automated. Much of the necessary work that is required to keep a decent level of social life going can be consigned to machines – at least in principle – which means humans can be free to undertake the kind of creative work which may not have been possible, objectively, in the early stages of the industrial revolution. (*RP* 248–9)

This projection of ways in which technology might be appropriated by the anarchist thinker is at best a gesture in a direction, but that is excusable. In fact, it may be best. Arguably, it is best to maintain well-founded principles of human nature at the core of one's "vision" (in Chomsky's terminology) while allowing for differences in implementation and, at a particular time, differences in specific "goals" (again his terminology) or plans of action. If nothing else, different societies with different problems and at different stages of industrialization, health care provision, and so on will require different specific proposals. These remarks reflect Chomsky's practical core. He is no pie-in-the-sky idealist. He wants to move towards what can be accomplished at a particular time in a particular society, given a good understanding not just of what one eventually hopes for (the vision) but of how people think and act at a particular time.

Chomsky has made specific suggestions for implementing worker control of the "means of production":

> Beginning with the two modes of immediate organization and control, namely organization and control in the workplace and in the community, one can imagine a network of workers' councils, and at a higher level, representation across the factories, or across branches of industry, or across crafts, and on to general assemblies of workers' councils that can be regional and national and international in character. And from another point of view one can project a system of governance that involves local assemblies – again federated regionally, dealing with regional issues, crossing crafts, industries, trades and so on and again at the level of the nation or beyond, through federation and so on. (*RP* 249)

He explicitly refuses to provide more details about how these forms could develop and how they would interrelate. Presumably, though, given his complete antipathy to the Leninist strategy of implementing a system from 'on high', he would reject any proposal along these lines. Indeed, no self-respecting anarchist *could* propose anything like Leninist or other forms of top-down implementation, for that would undermine the anarchist's own declared principles. This points to the use of anarchosyndicalism/libertarian socialism as a critical tool, at the very least. It also has the merit of leading to healthier societies: it rules out autocratic forms of control that demonstrably – in Chomsky's view – lead to depression on the part of those who are used and to becoming "moral monsters" on the part of the users. It would require that individuals no longer abandon control of their societies to the 'experts', but accept individual responsibility for their direction, something Chomsky thinks is not only desirable but possible. The feeling of helplessness before the complexity of modern society is, as we will see, in part fostered by those forces most interested in maintaining their control.

The principles of anarchosyndicalism rule out political parties as part of the vision:

> I think it is fair to say that insofar as political parties are felt to be
> necessary, anarchist organization of society will have failed. That is, it
> should be the case, I would think, that where there is direct participa-
> tion in self-management, in economic and social affairs, then factions,
> conflicts, differences of interests and ideas and opinion, which should
> be welcomed and cultivated, will be expressed at every one of these
> levels. Why they should fall into two, three, or *n* political parties, I don't
> quite see. I think that the complexity of human interest and life does
> not fall in that fashion. Parties represent basically class interests, and
> classes would have been eliminated or transcended in such a society.
> (*RP* 250)

On the other hand, elsewhere he seems to be happy enough to speak
of class interests and of classes organizing to defend those interests
(cf. *RP* 59). So, while he thinks that parties are ruled out as a vision,
they are allowed as a sensible goal. A similar attitude is found in
recent emphasis of the point that the aim in democratic societies
should not be to overthrow government, but to take control of government from corporations and make them responsible to people
(e.g., *CG* 138f).

The more interesting aspect of this quotation, however, is
Chomsky's emphasis on differences of interests, ideas, and opinions. This reflects an important feature of his view of Cartesian
common sense understanding – its nonsystematic and highly
flexible character. This is the basic framework that people use in
dealing with political matters, and anarchosyndicalism has the
merit of recognizing not just diversity in individuals (specific interests and talents at various stages of development) but diversity in
specific, local form of organization (communities, industries).
Chomsky seems to think that there is a connection between individual and communal diversity and his view that governance
should not be a specialization in which only some people participate: specialization leads to too great a concentration of interests
and a skewed view of what needs to be done. On the other hand,
he allows that governance may be a specialized skill that requires
specialized training, training that may require too much time and
effort to provide to everyone. "It may be that governance is itself a
function on a par with, say, steel production. If that turns out to be
true – and I think that is a question of empirical fact that has to be
determined, it can't be projected out of the mind – but if it turns out
to be true then it seems to me that the natural suggestion is that
governance should be organized industrially, as simply one of the
branches of industry, with their own workers' councils and their

own self-governance and their own participation in broader assemblies" (*RP* 251).

Chomsky's London TV interviewer Peter Jay pressed him on several issues concerning the viability of anarchism. His answers to questions concerning how the anarchist deals with the problem of work that needs to be done but that people might find uninteresting or unappealing – cleaning sewers, for example, or maintaining electrical circuits in an ice storm – are particularly helpful in understanding the connection he sees between work, fulfillment, and control. A lot of this work could and should be automated, Chomsky assumes, and he suggests that if more serious attention were paid to dealing scientifically with ways to perform the undesirable tasks (something not done now because people have always assumed that there would be "wage slaves" who needed to do the undesirable work in order to live), it is possible that there would be very few onerous tasks that required human workers. Moreover, some such tasks might, with sufficient technological support, prove sufficiently challenging and interesting – or could be made so – that people might want to do them. Nevertheless, *if* there still remain some undesirable tasks that need to be done, Chomsky suggests that one solution is to share them (*RP* 254–5) on a part-time basis. Another solution is to provide additional remuneration to those who do the unpleasant jobs (*RP* 256). Chomsky prefers the first solution, in which people receive approximately equal pay and the residue of unpleasant tasks that must be performed is shared, but grants that the second solution is consistent with anarchism. Both solutions would be very different from today's arrangements, where the people who do the unpleasant work are those who are lowest paid. Pressed about whether such solutions are feasible while still maintaining the standard of living that people are used to, Chomsky's reply reveals an important assumption – that people find work that produces things that are useful to others fulfilling and meaningful. He says:

> Now, you speak of work freely undertaken as a hobby. But I don't believe that. I think work freely undertaken can be useful, meaningful work done well. Also you pose a dilemma which many people pose, between desire for satisfaction in work and a desire to create things of value to the community. But it's not so obvious that there is any dilemma, any contradiction. So it's by no means clear – in fact I think it's false – that contributing to the enhancement of pleasure and satisfaction in work is inversely proportional to contributing to the value of the output. [Most of] the occupations that exist – specially the ones that involve what are

called services, that is, relations to human beings – have an intrinsic satisfaction and rewards associated with them, namely in the dealings with the human beings that are involved. That's true of teaching, and it's true of ice-cream vending. (*RP* 257–8)

Chomsky seems to think that the connection between self-satisfaction and fulfillment in one's work and producing something useful for the community is empirically based. He mentions interviews with assembly line workers which indicate that their greatest complaint is that they cannot do their job well at the pace they are forced to do it; he also mentions that the most successful predictor for a long life, other factors being equal, is job satisfaction. And he claims that an important part of the satisfaction has to do with "knowledge that you are doing something useful for the community. . . . I think the feeling that what one is doing is important, is worth doing, contributes to those with whom one has social bonds, is a very significant factor in one's personal satisfaction" (*RP* 258). That is not all, of course; there is the satisfaction of pride and self-fulfillment in the job well done. But it is obvious that he holds that free, creative activity and contributions to the community are by no means unrelated; that the satisfaction obtained from the use of one's talents, skills, and intelligence in producing things that are useful to others is part of the fulfillment one gets from free, creative activity. People find that control over their own labor is a matter of freedom and self-fulfillment, and, far from being a matter of mastery over others, Chomsky holds, this self-fulfillment is closely tied to contributing to others by producing things that are useful to them. Buchanan's gloss of anarchy in terms of mastery over a world of slaves really does appear to be pathological.

Chomsky grants that a successful society run along lines that are consistent with anarchosyndicalism would have to be one in which everyone is well educated and capable of dealing with the business/industrial issues on which he or she will be asked to make decisions (so be able to understand basic mathematics and statistics, say, and be sufficiently informed about what others are doing). Moreover, he holds, one must suppose that the success of such a society would require a "transformation in the way humans conceive of themselves and their ability to act, to decide, to create, to produce, to enquire." This is not, presumably, a transformation in human nature but a matter of reorienting the values that one puts on what one produces and on relationships to others – their importance, significance, and the like. Furthermore, Chomsky says, the point is to introduce institutions that will assist this transformation and maintain it – that will "permit new aspects of human nature to flourish" (*RP* 260), recalling the theme that human nature and particular talents provide for unexplored avenues.

Perhaps we will be guided to anarchosyndicalism by our natures (unless we destroy ourselves first). Chomsky concludes:

> [I]t seems to me that the development towards state totalitarianism and towards economic concentration – and of course they are linked – will continually lead to revulsion, to efforts of personal liberation and to organizational efforts at social liberation. And that'll take all sorts of forms. Throughout all Europe, in one form or another, there is a call for what is sometimes called worker participation or co-determination, or even sometimes worker control. Now most of these efforts are minimal. I think that they're misleading, in fact may even undermine efforts for the working class to liberate itself. But in part they're responsive to a strong intuition and understanding that coercion and oppression, whether by private [capitalist] economic power or by the State bureaucracy, is by no means a necessary feature of human life. And the more those concentrations of power and authority continue, the more we will see revulsion against them and efforts to organize and overthrow them. Sooner or later they'll succeed, I hope. (*RP* 260–1)

The continued growth of transnational corporations and the globalization of the economy may well make this more difficult than he had hoped at the time, although it might be argued that this further concentration of private power could hasten the process. Chomsky, however, would probably decline to speculate about this: "I don't think I'm wise enough, or informed enough, to make predictions and I think predictions about such poorly-understood matters probably generally reflect personality more than judgment" (*RP* 260).

The manufacture of consent

Media actions

Chomsky's view of mainstream US media is an instance of his more general view of the "intelligentsia" (academics, media), especially in the US. He thinks that anyone who uses nothing more than Cartesian common sense, a bit of open-mindedness, and a healthy skepticism can see that the intelligentsia serve as purveyors of the ideology of the state (*LR* 3f). This is not because there is a conspiracy between them. The explanation is much more straightforward: the intelligentsia go where the rewards of their professions are to be found and, in a corporate-run system, these are gained by not questioning the presuppositions of the system. Chomsky and Herman note in the second volume of their *Political Economy of Human Rights* (*PEHR* ii. 29): "The will to believe patriotic truths and a positive desire to aid the cause of one's own state are dominant forces, and those abiding by such principles may also anticipate corresponding rewards and privileges." In the case of the intelligentsia in the media, the system seems to be particularly effective. Chomsky remarked to Mitsou Ronat in 1976, "To my knowledge, in the American mass media you cannot find a single socialist journalist, not a single syndicated political commentator who is a socialist. From the ideological point of view the mass media are almost one hundred percent 'state capitalist'" (*LR* 9). The situation has not changed. Remarkably, this homogeneity is not the result of government oppression or control, as it was in the Soviet Union at the time. It is the result of the fact, Chomsky notes, that "mass media are capitalist institutions" (*LR* 29). It is no more surprising than that no socialist is to be found on the board of directors of General Motors: they do not 'belong'. And just as members of the board of directors of General Motors decide and act in ways that respect the aims of their institution, so do mainstream journalists. Journalists, however, unlike members of boards of directors of corporations, are expected to be dedicated to the pursuit of the truth: their profession would not be taken seriously otherwise. Furthermore, they declare themselves to be professionals dedicated to digging for and presenting the truth; they pride themselves on their supposed autonomy and dedication to freedom of the press. This explicitly raises moral obligations that members of boards of directors might deny (although in doing so, they cease to be fully human, since these are responsibilities any human must respect). Journalists, however, cannot make such a denial: they are committed to telling the truth. Nevertheless, Chomsky shows, they too often lie and misrepresent. They do not consciously intend to do so. Indeed, Chomsky acknowledges that most journalists are hardworking, honest, dedicated individuals who meet high standards of professionalism and exhibit "courage, integrity, and enterprise" (*NI* 11) and fully believe that they are defenders of a free, independent press. It is not their honesty or their integrity that is at stake but their unexamined "choice of topics and highlighting of issues, the range of opinions permitted expression, the unquestioned premises that guide reporting and commentary, and the general framework imposed for the presentation of a view of the world" (*NI* 12). The scope of their inquiries and the kind of issues they discuss are, on inspection by an open, skeptical eye linked to normal intelligence, limited in ways that clearly reveal a uniform, dominant ideology. Thus, they fail to fully tell the truth and become purveyors of ideology. In this respect they are seriously at fault, for they, like other US (and, generally, Western) intellectuals, are "in a position to expose the lies of governments, to analyze actions according to their causes and motives and often hidden intentions. [They have] the power that comes from political liberty, from access to information and freedom of expression. For a privileged minority, Western democracy provides the leisure, the facilities, and the training to seek the truth lying behind the veil of distortion and misrepresentation, ideology, and class interest" (*CR* 60). They acknowledge that they have the responsibility to tell the truth; they have the means to uncover it; they have the freedom to express it; yet they fail to do so. Chomsky highlights this point by focusing on the question of how free the 'free press' really is. It turns out that it is not free, that in the US (and other countries) the press is corporate-owned and reflects the priorities and interests of corporations. So, in fact, those who declare that the press is free are deluding themselves. They are engaging in a form of self-deception.

Chomsky has written numerous books (sometimes with Edward Herman) demonstrating that the media misrepresent. Perhaps it is not surprising, then, that he has not enjoyed the best of relationships with the mass media, including and especially the "elite" US media – the *New York Times*, for example, or the *New York Review of Books* – that, as the most powerful 'opinion makers', are in the best position to influence people's views. The *New York Times* is often the target of Chomsky's ire, perhaps because it claims to print all that is fit to print and purports to be the "newspaper of record." In one respect it is – it is the "most important newspaper and the one that provides the quasi-official record for history" (*NI* 225), says Chomsky with hard-to-miss irony. He notes that it was thanked by Schlesinger for willingly suppressing information in the Bay of Pigs fiasco (*CR* 60; *APNM* 325); that even at the end of the Vietnam conflict the editors were unable to conceive that the US might have been wrong to invade Vietnam (*LR* 36–8); that the *Times* (with all other major newspapers except for some in Chicago where it happened) virtually ignored the murder of Fred Hampton of the Black Panthers, and, like all the others, ignored clear evidence of

FBI complicity, concentrating instead on Watergate, which was in Chomsky's view a far less important crime, involving no harassment or murders by agents of the state. In more recent times, he has mentioned the *Times*'s efforts in the 1980s in Palestinian–Israeli affairs to ignore reports and letters concerning Arafat's call for negotiations aimed at mutual recognition (*NI* 290f) because this went against official US policy. For instance, on December 10, 1986, the *Times*'s Jerusalem correspondent Thomas Friedman insisted that there was no "Arab negotiating partner," although six days before this the mass-circulation Israeli *Ma'ariv* headlined "Arafat indicates to Israel that he is ready to enter into direct negotiations" (*NI* 293). (The Israelis under Peres rejected the offer.) Another instance: on January 14, 1988, "Arafat stated that the PLO would 'recognize Israel's right to exist if it and the United States accept PLO participation in an international Middle East Peace conference' based on all UN resolutions. . . . Once again the *New York Times* refused to publish Arafat's statement, or even to permit letters referring to it – though the facts were buried in an article on another topic nine days later" (*NI* 295–6). In 1990 Chomsky summarized the situation as: "*Times* history follows the official [US] line [on Israel] throughout. In its news reports and commentary, the major Arab initiatives are down the memory hole, apart from that of Sadat in 1977 – which is admitted into 'history' because it could be molded by Washington into an arrangement that satisfied US–Israeli needs. The 'peace process' is defined as whatever the US proposes: blocking the peace process for 20 years, in the present case. The *Times* regularly refused to report Arafat's offers; even letters referring to them were banned" (*LL* 6). Nor did the *New York Times* see fit to condemn the atrocities committed by Israeli death squads early in 1995, although it expressed outrage at the mindless murder of Israelis by Hamas. As of May 1995, Chomsky cited reports that put the toll at 124 Israeli dead, 204 Palestinians (*PP* 156).

As for Nicaragua and other Central American countries, there are instances of mis-emphasis, overlooking, and even fabrication. Recall the difference between what José Figueres reported concerning the apparent vitality of the population of Nicaragua under the Sandinistas compared to the *Times*'s James LeMoyne's "pot-bellied urchins." LeMoyne also failed to report that the Sandinistas had not, unlike the governments of El Salvador and Honduras, engaged in terrorist tactics and killing to keep their population in line. Nor does he report that the contras *are* engaged in just these kinds of tactics (*NI* 66). He also leaves out the role of the US in the matter while emphasizing the roles – supposed and real – of others. LeMoyne's cover story in a 1986 *New York Times Sunday Magazine* provided a perspective on the guerrilla movements in Central America. Chomsky notes that LeMoyne correctly points out that poverty and failures to bring about political reform played important roles in guerrilla activities, but then devotes considerable space to the roles (supposed and real) of "Cuba, the Soviet Union, North Korea, the PLO, Vietnam, and so on" (*NI* 81). But, Chomsky continues,

> one participant in the drama is missing, except for the statement that in El Salvador, "the United States bolstered the Salvadoran Army, insisted on elections and called for some reforms." Also missing is the fact that the army we "bolstered" conducted a program of slaughter and torture to destroy "the people's organizations fighting to defend their most fundamental human rights," to borrow the words of Archbishop Romero shortly before his assassination as he vainly pleaded with President Carter not to "bolster" these forces, which "know only how to repress the people and defend the interests of the Salvadorean oligarchy."

The skew is also obvious in the *Times* reports of what happened after the peace accords were signed in 1988. While terrorism continued in El Salvador, Honduras, and Guatemala – and indeed, increased, as noted – this was "barely noted [in the *Times*], apart from guerrilla terror in El Salvador, to which the government sometimes 'responded', James LeMoyne commented with regret. In October 1988, Amnesty International released a report on the sharp increase in death squad killings, abduction, torture, and mutilation, tracing the terror to the government security forces. The *Times* ignored the story, while the Senate passed a resolution warning Nicaragua that new military aid would be sent to the contras if the *Sandinistas* continued to violate the peace accords" (*NI* 94). Another of Chomsky's examples emphasizes the role of the *Times* in establishing and maintaining official history. It was important to the US propaganda effort to insist that, in providing massive support to the contras, the US was doing only what Nicaragua was doing for the rebels fighting the terrorist regime of El Salvador. This apparently nonexistent 'symmetry' was established by LeMoyne. First, he and all other correspondents of mainstream media ignored the extraordinary scale of the US's aid to the "proxy army" in Nicaragua – what Chomsky calls the contras. Second, on Nicaraguan aid to El Salavador, LeMoyne stated that "ample evidence shows it exists, and it is questionable how long they could survive without it" (*New York Times*, August 13, 1987). Chomsky notes: "LeMoyne presented no evidence, then or ever, to support this claim. He has yet to comment on the failure of the US government, which is not entirely lacking in facilities, to provide any credible evidence since early 1981 – and little enough then – as was noted by the World Court. . . . The claim is a propaganda necessity; therefore, it is true" (*NI* 199).

In sum, Chomsky documents many cases of media bias in favor of the official line from Washington. His documentation indicates media support for a continuation of the policy of the Grand Area, especially revealing in cases – such as Vietnam, Haiti, Cuba, and Nicaragua – where the US fears grass roots efforts to establish an indigenous unaligned government, outside US market control. (It is not important for US policy decisions that there actually be progress; what is important is that it be thought that there might be.) Further documentation of bias and misrepresentation of various sorts appears below as part of a summary of the "propaganda model" that Chomsky and Herman constructed to predict media reactions to claims by them and others that mainstream US media are biased in favor of US government policies and that correspondents such as Friedman and LeMoyne are "intellectual commissars" who serve the same function in a democracy that the propaganda machine does in a totalitarian state.

Keep in mind that most of the 'opinion leaders' and probably most of the US public firmly believed in the US's good intentions in Nicaragua: LeMoyne, for example, did not consciously lie. It is remarkable how few mainstream and especially elite media journalists actually criticized US intervention in Nicaragua, and even those who did assumed without question that the US's course was idealistically motivated. The *New York Times's* Tom Wicker was one of the critical few, and he, Chomsky points out, "condemned the application of the Reagan Doctrine to Nicaragua because 'the United States has no historic or God-given right to bring democracy to other nations'" (*NI* 51). But the basic presupposition remains – it was assumed that the US's motivation was to support democracy; criticism was directed only against involvement. Chomsky often expresses amazement at the extraordinary success of this propaganda machine that always remains silent on the basic ideological presuppositions: no one is coerced as regards to what to think or believe, but they do it anyway and are extremely offended when informed of their bias and their unwillingness to examine it. As an Enlightenment thinker, Chomsky perhaps expects that thought control ought to be much more difficult than control of actions.

Looking for reward is part of the explanation of the system's effect-iveness, of course. In fact, this alone seems to be enough to support the predictions in Chomsky's and Herman's propaganda model, discussed below. But this explanation does not seem to be quite enough where, as in this case, we find people who claim to be devoted to the pursuit of truth. Another piece of the explanation may be found in what Chomsky has to say about Orwell's problem, discussed in the next chapter.

The propaganda model

In introducing the propaganda model, which predicts the phenom-enon of US (and generally, Western) media actions and their reac-tions to criticism, Chomsky points out that the model fits only mainstream media in democratic but corporate-run states. In these democracies, as John Stuart Mill's father James Mill suggested early in the nineteenth century, those in power will want to use state edu-cation and any other means they can (such as the media) to "'train the minds of the people to a virtuous attachment to their govern-ment' [to authority], and to the arrangements of the social, eco-nomic, and political order more generally" (*NI* 13). They cannot do so by telling media personnel what to print and say; that is pos-sible in a dictatorship, but not in a democracy. Instead, what they do is provide power and privilege to those who do not question the basic values of the system.

Brady saw the corporation's 'need' for propaganda:

> "What in political circles would be called legislative, executive, and judi-cial powers" is gathered in "controlling hands" which, "so far as policy formation and execution are concerned, are found at the peak of the pyramid and are manipulated without significant check from its base." As private [corporate] power "grows and expands," it is transformed "into a community force ever more politically potent and politically con-scious," ever more dedicated to a "propaganda program" that "becomes a matter of converting the public . . . to the point of view of the control pyramid." (*PP* 71–2)

Chomsky expands on Brady's propaganda theme: "That project, already substantial in the period Brady reviewed, reached an awesome scale a few years later as American business sought to beat back the social democratic currents of the postwar [World War I] world, which reached the United States as well, and to win what its leaders called 'the everlasting battle for the minds of men', using the huge resources of the public relations industry, the entertainment industry, the corporate media, and whatever else could be mobilized by the 'control pyramids' of the social and economic order" (*PP* 72). While the actions of mainstream media in corporate-run democracies differ from those in dictatorships, both forms are autocratically controlled. In one case the press is responsive to government policy; in the other to the basic policies of the corporate state. Chomsky points out that there is an alternative, a genuinely democratic press. It is represented in *NI* (p. 1) by a proposal by Brazil's Catholic bishops that the existing system – in Brazil, TV is owned by five corporations, and almost all advertising is done by eight transnational corporations – be replaced by a system that encourages grass roots participation. On this democratic model, the press would be responsive to the truth and, in being so, also responsible to the individual who must make decisions about how he or she and others are to act in society. Arguably, Chomsky's own political 'journalism' offers good examples of what this kind of press might look like – it represents positions fairly and speaks to the need for information by citizens who must make informed decisions concerning how to best meet their needs and hopes.

The propaganda model itself contains three orders of prediction. The first is that "the media serve the interests of state and corporate power, which are closely interlinked, framing their reporting and analysis in a manner supportive of established privilege and limiting debate and discussion accordingly" (*NI* 10). The second is that: "media debate will be bounded in a manner that satisfies these external needs [of corporate and state power], thus limited to the question of the alleged adversarial stance of the media" (*NI* 153). The third is that if there are inquiries into the supposed freedom and lack of bias of the press (such as those presented by Chomsky and Herman), "such inquiry will be ignored or bitterly condemned, for it conflicts with the needs of the powerful and privileged" (ibid.). "The general prediction, at each level, is that what enters the mainstream will support the needs of established power" (ibid.). This is only what Cartesian common sense accompanied by an open mind and a healthy skepticism would lead one to expect when considering the motivations of people whose service of authority provides them with a privileged place in society.

Evidence of first-order predictions is provided by simple and obvious paired examples. We have already seen some, such as the way in which the *New York Times* presents the situations and actions of the 'democracies' of El Salvador, Guatemala, and Honduras – all US client states in the same region of the world as Nicaragua, at the same time, at similar levels of development, and facing similar problems – in contrast to the way it presents the situation and actions of Nicaragua under the Sandinistas. In every instance, Washington's view is presented. Terrorism in the client states is ignored, the benefits provided under the Sandinistas ignored, the US's support of a proxy army downplayed or ignored. Similar evidence of media bias is seen in the way Palestinian atrocities are presented, as opposed to Israeli ones, and in the way Iraq's willingness to comply is ignored, not to mention the 'historical' case of Vietnam.

A particularly useful illustration of first-, second-, and third-order predictions of the model is provided by noting the ways in which corporate media present "bloodbaths." In *PEHR* Chomsky and Herman distinguished constructive, benign, and nefarious bloodbaths. Summarizing this classification in *NI*, Chomsky says: " 'Constructive bloodbaths' are those that serve the interests of US power; 'benign bloodbaths' are largely irrelevant to these concerns; and 'nefarious bloodbaths' are those that can be charged to the account of official enemies and are thus useful for mobilizing the public" (*NI* 153–4). The first-order prediction of the model is that constructive bloodbaths will be welcomed, benign ignored, and nefarious "passionately condemned" (*NI* 154). As the model predicts, the Khmer Rouge atrocities in Cambodia were presented by the media as nefarious, the invasion of East Timor by US-backed Indonesia as benign, and the Gulf War as constructive. The second-order prediction is that the mainstream media will not study media bias or present information concerning media bias. As predicted, there are no mainstream media studies of how media present bloodbaths. The third-order prediction is that where studies such as Chomsky and Herman's occur, "exposure will be ignored in the case of constructive bloodbaths; it may be occasionally noted without interest in the case of benign bloodbaths; and it will lead to great indignation in the case of nefarious bloodbaths" (ibid.). As predicted, their criticism of neglect in the case of East Timor was, after several years of persistent effort on their parts and on the parts of others, acknowledged by the *New York Times* with a shrug, while exposure of patent fabrication of evidence by the media in the case of the Khmer Rouge atrocities raised an immediate hue and cry.

The atrocities committed in the US-backed Indonesian invasion of East Timor parallel in almost every way those committed by Pol Pot and the Khmer Rouge – in "accessibility [to the press], credibility [from reports], and character [slaughters of people]" (*NI* 155). They were even alike in scale or numbers killed, although – Chomsky remarks – "larger in East Timor relative to the population" (ibid.). The obvious difference was that Cambodia's slaughter was "conducted by an official enemy and was, furthermore, highly functional at the time in helping to overcome the 'Vietnam syndrome' and to restore popular support for US intervention and violence in the Third World 'in defense against the Pol Pots'. In fact, a few months after [Chomsky and Herman] wrote about this prospect, the deepening engagement of the US government in Pol Pot–style terror in El Salvador was being justified as necessary to save the population from the 'Pol Pot left'" (ibid.).

It is important to keep in mind that Chomsky and Herman do not assess the facts of the case when they present this and other paired examples; they do not go out in the field and do on-the-spot interviews and statistical studies. But they do what anyone could do; they depend on what anyone with common sense would allow are the more reliable sources of information. In the case of East Timor, they rely on refugee and church accounts that were available (little else was), and in the case of Cambodia, on US State Department reports. Sources like these are, in the circumstances, difficult to deny. They provide as good evidence of media bias and fabrication as one could expect. As for the first-order predictions in the East Timor/Cambodia pairing, the results are clear.

> In the case of Cambodia under the Khmer Rouge [not when there was US involvement, of course] there were [from US mainstream media] denunciations of genocide from the first moment, a huge outcry of protest, fabrication of evidence on a grand scale, suppression of some of the most reliable sources (including State Department Cambodia watchers, the most knowledgeable source at the time) because they did not support the preferred picture, reiteration of extraordinary fabrications even after they were openly conceded to have been invented, and so on. In the case of Timor, coverage declined from a substantial level before the US-backed Indonesian invasion to flat zero as the atrocities reached their peak with increasing US support. (*NI* 156)

The very considerable details that this summary encapsulates appear in *Manufacturing Consent*. (Some of the most striking evidence appears in graphic form in Achbar and Meltonick's CBC film of the same name; they display, for example, the number of column inches in the US's "newspaper of record" (the *New York Times* in 1975–9) devoted to the Pol Pot atrocities (about 1,175 column inches total) as opposed to the Indonesian invasion of East Timor (70 for the same period).) Characteristically, Chomsky berates himself for not emphasizing in print the mainstream media's suppression of information from East Timor, saying, "I published my first word about [East Timor] nineteen months after writing about Khmer Rouge atrocities, though the Timor massacres were far more important by any moral criterion for the simple and sufficient reason that something could be done to terminate them. Thanks to media self-censorship, there were no substantial efforts to organize the kind of opposition that might have compelled the United States to desist from its active participation in the slaughter" (*NI* 156–7). This concern reappears in the discussion of the responsibility of the intellectual below; there, he remarks of the East Timor atrocities: "To terminate them has always been very easy, given the locus of responsibility. This is not Bosnia, or Rwanda, or Chechnya. There has been no need to send troops, bomb Jakarta, impose sanctions, even issue warnings. It would have been enough to turn off the tap [of US aid]" (*PP* 57). The responsibility of the press in this is striking: Chomsky's "article was the first in the US (or, to my knowledge, Canada) devoted specifically to East Timor, only the second that dealt with the topic at all, after three years of huge atrocities, perhaps the worst relative to population since the Holocaust, funded mainly by the American taxpayer" (*PP* 58).

In the case of East Timor/Cambodia, Chomsky says, the "second-order predictions [of limitation of media debate] were not only confirmed, but far surpassed; the doctrine that was concocted and quickly became standard, utterly inconsistent with readily documented facts, is that there was 'silence' in the West over the Khmer Rouge atrocities. This fantasy is highly serviceable, not only in suppressing [awareness of] the subordination of educated elites to external power [corporate control], but also in suggesting that in the future we must focus attention still more intensely and narrowly on enemy crimes" (*NI* 157). The only kind of permissible debate of mainstream media's motivations and actions within these media themselves concerns whether the press might be "too free," and thus capable of undermining the proper execution of the state/corporate will. As Landrum Bolling put it in 1982, "Can a 'free-press', democratic society defend itself and its friends and allies, in a dangerous world, against the totalitarian adversaries that do not have to contend with a free press and uncontrolled television?" (quoted in *NI* 162). Bolling seems to assume that the press must serve state/corporate interests, and that when it is "too free," it cannot do so.

The third-order prediction in the case of East Timor (benign bloodbath) and Cambodia (nefarious bloodbath) was also confirmed. Herman and Chomsky's criticism that the mainstream press had ignored East Timor was eventually acknowledged in a dismissive way. It was "conceded that what had happened was problematic, even 'the shaming of Indonesia' (as the *New York Times* described it)" (*PP* 58) – but not, of course, the shaming of the press for not providing information in a case where US citizens could do something about the atrocity. As for their allegation that the press had exaggerated and created evidence in the form of greatly exaggerated death counts in press reporting of the Khmer Rouge atrocities, it aroused a flood of protest. Chomsky and Herman had used the only reliable evidence available at the time, that provided by the US State Department. The press had apparently thought nothing of increasing the few thousand reported deaths to two million, apparently ignoring the obvious sources, and were then offended when it was pointed out to them what they had done and – much worse – why.

It is important to recognize that the propaganda model does not claim that the press will never be critical of what Chomsky calls the "current state managers." It has been critical: the obvious cases are the eventual recognition that US involvement in Vietnam was wrong (inexpedient) and Watergate. The claim is rather that "the media reflect the consensus of powerful elites of the state–corporate nexus generally, including those who object to some aspect of government policy, typically on tactical grounds. The model argues, from its foundations, that the media will protect the interests of the powerful, not that it will protect state managers from their criticisms" (*NI* 149). The press follows the consensus of the powerful, and in a corporate-based state that consensus is represented by those who make the basic market decisions. Thus, criticism of involvement in Vietnam never amounted to criticism of the US's 'right' to invade a country that seemed to be developing a grass roots effort to address human needs, or of the Grand Area principles that govern this 'right'. Criticism appeared in the form of doubts about the viability of the effort and its cost-effectiveness. In the Watergate case, Chomsky suggests that Nixon had dared to challenge the real masters by including IBM's Chairman Tom

Watson, the *Washington Post*, and McGeorge Bundy on his 'enemies list' and by authorizing a foray against another 'domestic power', the Democratic Party (*LP* 720), thus pitting "men of power against men of power" (*LR* 21). No doubt, too, Nixon's extraordinary foolishness in maintaining the list, keeping tapes, and authorizing a foray persuaded the power elite that he was expendable and replaceable – particularly given the fact that US administrations, whether Democrat or Republican, have diligently maintained the principles of the Grand Area since the end of World War II.

Notice that the propaganda model relies on what Chomsky calls "the interests of the powerful." It reflects interests rather than specific decisions, so is not committed to the idea that control of the media is a matter of a few conspirators getting together and deciding how to convince the press to reflect their point of view. It should be obvious that Chomsky could not accept a conspiracy view in any case. If media acted as they do as the result of a conspiracy, they could be at least in part excused of their responsibilities because they have been deceived. Chomsky does not want to excuse these intellectuals, or any others, from their obligation to pursue and tell the truth. Corporate media do as someone with common sense would expect them to: serve the interests of the power elite to preserve their own privileged status in society. Such a press is democratic only if one construes a citizen as a consumer, not a free agent. Chomsky remarks: "Our political culture has a conception of democracy that differs from that of the Brazilian bishops. For them, democracy means that citizens should have the opportunity to inform themselves, to take part in inquiry and discussion and policy formation, and to advance their programs through political actions. For us, democracy is more narrowly conceived: the citizen is a consumer, an observer but not a participant" (*NI* 14). If so, mainstream corporate media, and particularly the elite media, are "vigilant guardians protecting privilege from the threat of public understanding and participation" (ibid.) by providing only filtered information and by encouraging public apathy. Chomsky allows that criticisms could be raised against his alternative genuinely democratic model of the media – media that "tell the truth" so that free agents can decide. For example, "the call for democratizing the media could mask highly unwelcome efforts to limit intellectual independence through popular pressures" (ibid.) – everything from certain forms of "political correctness" to censorship by self-appointed defenders of morality and "family values" (the "moral majority"). But while this problem is "not easily dismissed, . . . it is not an inherent property of democratization of the media" (ibid.). By allowing a voice to various points of view, a democratized press might well provide a form of self-correction. Chomsky also assumes that people share a human nature and certain basic needs, so that, once the external influence of efforts to advance "economic man" are corrected by serious efforts to tell the truth, they will probably converge in their judgments. He holds out hope for such change in the belief that "any system that's based on lying and deceit is inherently unstable" (*CR* 49).

The responsibility of intellectuals

The propaganda model's assessment of certain intellectuals – press reporters, correspondents, and editors – is a special case of Chomsky's more general assessment of intellectuals in the 'guided' free speech communities provided by capitalist economies. It is a special case of Bakunin's prediction regarding any form of society in which authority resides in a few. Bakunin's particular target was the Leninist-inclined Marxist:

> According to the theory of Mr. Marx, the people not only must not destroy [the state] but must strengthen it and place it at the complete disposal of their benefactors, guardians, and teachers – the leaders of the Communist party, namely Mr. Marx and his friends, who will proceed to liberate [mankind] in their own way. They will establish a single state bank, concentrating in its hands all commercial, industrial, agricultural and even scientific production, and then divide the masses into two armies – industrial and agricultural – under the direct command of the state engineers who will constitute a new privileged scientific-political estate. (Quoted in *CR* 84)

The "new privileged scientific-political estate" would consist of managers who have access to information and distribute it as the system needs, to their benefit. The intellectuals would be among them, constituting a new class that uses its access to information to gain control of economy and society. They will form, Bakunin said, "the reign of scientific intelligence, the most aristocratic, despotic, arrogant, and elitist of all regimes. There will be scholars, and the world will be divided into a minority ruling in the name of knowledge, and an immense ignorant majority. And then, woe unto the mass of ignorant ones" (quoted in *RP* 24).

Chomsky includes most social scientists among managers and points out that much of the "alleged complexity, depth, and obscurity of [the analysis of contemporary affairs] is part of the illusion propagated by the system of ideological control, which aims to make the issues seem remote from the general population and to persuade them of their incapacity to organize their own affairs" (*LR* 4–5) – to persuade them that they should cede control to those who claim to know. Such mystification is characteristic of the irresponsible intellectual, for it involves the misuse of truth.

Chomsky has emphasized the theme of the responsibility of the intellectual from the very beginning of his political work. At one level, his view is simple and has not changed. In a recent speech to the Writers' Centre in Sydney, Australia, in January 1995, he says, "the intellectual responsibility of the writer, or any decent person, is to tell the truth" (*PP* 55; cf. *APNM* 325). More specifically, he adds, "it is a moral imperative to find out and tell the truth *as best one can*, about things *that matter*, to the *right audience*" (ibid.). This "is often hard, and can be personally costly, particularly for those who are more vulnerable. That is true even in societies that are very free; in others, the costs can be severe indeed" (*PP* 55–6). His remark, "as best one can" should be read "as best one can, given that one is operating within the common sense framework." The truths that are relevant here are practical truths, those that involve humans and their social and political affairs. The truths of the various serious sciences are not *directly* apropos. The qualification allows for the possibility, explored in the next chapter, that Chomsky's science of language might bear in some way on his political views, through the mediation of its implications for human nature.

What about "things that matter" and "right audience"? Chomsky points out that there are certain ways to explain what matters that are irrelevant to discussion of political and social questions. To illustrate, he mentions the question of whether the brain sciences have anything to say about various mental phenomena. This question matters to numerous people, and the puzzle about what the brain sciences might have to say about consciousness, for example, has a certain intellectual interest to virtually everyone. But philosophical questions of this sort have little, if anything, to do with practical human affairs. Chomsky conceives of the human being as involved in practical affairs as an *agent*. So when the writer or other intellectual acts as *moral agent*, he or she is supposed to bring "the truth about *matters of human significance* to *an audience that can do something about them*" (*PP* 56). This is "part of what it means to be a moral agent rather than a monster." Unfortunately, "the standard practice of the intellectual communities to which we (more or less) belong rejects this elementary moral principle, with considerable fervor and passion, in fact. We may even have sunk to historical lower depths, in this regard, by the natural measure [of] comparison of standard practice to opportunities available" (ibid.). "We" have access to extraordinary amounts of information and live in societies that allow freedom of expression but, more often than not, "we" become willing members of Bakunin's new class, as Chomsky shows with his data comparing press activities in regard to Indonesian atrocities in East Timor and Khmer Rouge atrocities in Cambodia.

> The responsibility of Western intellectuals [in this case] has been to tell the truth about the "shaming of the West" [East Timor] to a Western audience, who can act to terminate the crimes effectively, easily, and quickly. Simple, unambiguous, and plainly correct. If [these intellectuals] chose to condemn K[hmer]R[ouge] atrocities, well and good, as long as they tried to keep to the truth. But it was a matter of limited importance, unless they had some proposal about what to do; no one did. One should also tell the truth about Genghis Khan, but the task hardly rates high on the moral scale. (*PP* 60)

We have no moral responsibility for Genghis Khan's actions, but we do for those where we can affect the outcome.

Naturally, the audience plays an important role here, and Chomsky illustrates his view of how one chooses an audience to whom one tells the truth by comparing his own efforts to those of Quaker friends with whom he has participated in various protests. Quakers adhere to the principle that one must speak the truth to those in power. Chomsky disagrees, calling this a form of self-indulgence. "It is a waste of time and a pointless pursuit to speak truth to Henry Kissinger, or the CEO of General Motors, or others who exercise power in coercive institutions – truths that they already know well enough, for the most part" (*PP* 61). If one could find such a person in a situation in which he or she is not playing an institutional role but acting as a human being with normal human concerns and sympathies, then this technique might be effective. But "as people who wield power, they are hardly worth addressing, any more than the worst tyrants and criminals, who are also human beings [and should be held responsible for their actions], however terrible their actions" (ibid.).

Moreover, Chomsky insists, while one should seek out an audience that matters, "it should not be seen as an audience, but as a community of common concern in which one hopes to participate constructively. We should not be speaking *to*, but *with*. That is second nature to any good teacher, and should be to any writer and intellectual as well" (ibid.). This recalls Chomsky's view that libertarianism (or anarchy) cannot properly be conceived apart from socialism (syndicalism).

Nor can it be claimed that the intellectual does not recognize the elementary principle that one should speak of things that matter morally. "Western intellectuals . . . understand the point very well, and have no trouble applying elementary moral principles in at least one case, [to] official enemies, say, Stalinist Russia" (ibid.). Specifically, Western intellectuals applied elementary moral principles to their counterparts in Stalinist Russia in the following ways (quoting from *PP* 62–3):

1 If Soviet intellectuals told the truth about American crimes, well and good, but they won no praise from us. . . .
2 If a Soviet intellectual exaggerated or fabricated American crimes, then he became an object of contempt.
3 If a Soviet intellectual ignored American crimes, it was a matter of no consequence. . . .
4 If Soviet intellectuals denied or minimized American crimes, . . . it was also a matter of minor or even null significance.
5 If Soviet intellectuals ignored or justified Soviet crimes, that was criminal.

Applying the same reasonable moral standards to Western intellectuals, we should find:

1 If Western intellectuals told the truth about the crimes of the USSR, Pol Pot, [and] Saddam Hussein (after he was designated an enemy in August 1990), that's fine, but has no moral standing.
2 If they exaggerate or fabricate such crimes, they become objects of contempt.
3 If they ignore such crimes, it is a matter of little significance.
4 If they deny or minimize such crimes, it is also a minor matter.
5 And if they ignore or justify the crimes in which their own state is implicated, that is criminal.

But Western intellectuals judge their own actions in the opposite way: those who uncovered the crimes of Baghdad and Pol Pot were praised, and there was no recognition of the fact that ignoring or justifying the crimes of one's own state is criminal. Chomsky grants that points 3 and 4, while parallel to the Soviet case, are, strictly, inapplicable to the Western intellectual: he or she should *not* ignore or minimize the crimes of Saddam, Stalin, or Pol Pot. But point 5 applies, unequivocally. Chomsky allows that one could argue that it is unfair to compare Soviet and Western intellectuals. But the unfairness is to the Soviet commissars, "who could at least plead fear, not mere servility and cowardice" (*PP* 65). The culpability of Western intellectuals is greater, because of their much greater freedom and opportunity. Moreover, at least the Soviet commissars, "however corrupt, generally *were* able to recognize that the invasion of Afghanistan was just that: an invasion of Afghanistan." But in the case of Vietnam, Chomsky notes, he has been looking for 30 years, but has not found "one accurate reference in the mainstream to John F. Kennedy's escalation of US intervention in Indochina from support for a standard Latin America-style terror state to outright aggression against South Vietnam, which bore the brunt of US aggression in Indochina throughout" (ibid.).

In matters directly related to issues of human concern, Western intellectuals adopt a double standard and subordinate their responsibility to the truth to satisfying the demands of the state/ corporation. Chomsky and a few others are exceptions, of course: in matters of human concern, he tries to tell the truth about things that matter to anyone who is, or can be prompted to become, a moral agent who might try to do something about them.

8

Human Nature and Ideal Social Organization

Language and politics

In chapter 7 Chomsky's anarchosyndicalist/libertarian socialist political views and the ideals they respect (autonomy and free association) were contrasted with 'liberal' values (accumulation and domination). Chomsky extends these ideals to criticism, practical short-term goals, and a vision of a society of free agents with rich natural endowments and particular talents and interests. His view is that the current system prevents the vast majority of people from developing their capacities and talents, and that even those who benefit economically from the system – the power elite – are warped by it, becoming inhuman (moral monsters) in the exercise of power. He holds that there are many things people can do to modify current practices, that *everyone* can and should make decisions about how society is to be run, and that the intellectual's responsibility is to provide full information so that individuals can make up their own minds. The vision of a society of free agents in supportive communities can help in making choices and decisions about which goals are feasible.

Chomsky expresses diffidence, even skepticism, when asked to speak about the relationship between his political views and his linguistics. No doubt part of the reason for this is that too many who ask – such as media personnel – want a quick and ready answer, as well as one that suits their presuppositions about how such a question should be answered. ("You remark that French intellectuals have a totalitarian streak, Prof. Chomsky (cf. *LP* 308–9). Could this be because they speak French?") Because, however, he holds that the issue is a difficult one and may well be unresolvable, the diffidence is real, not feigned. Nevertheless, his version of anarchism assumes the possibility of a stable free association of individuals that meets human needs and avoids the pathological "state of nature" as understood in some traditional political thought – the absence of all social ties and obligations and war as the means to resolution of conflict. He holds that people will naturally converge on a kind of order that respects what Bakunin called an "instinct for freedom," a natural desire/need to overcome the "constraints of external authority" (cf. *LP* 468–9) while cooperating with others. If asked why he holds this, he has to provide *some* justification, and, given that his biologically based rationalist conception of mind seems to be well-founded and his linguistics makes a rich contribution to understanding why and how the human mind is unique, a plausible route is to seek justification in known, discernible features of human nature. He often takes this route, appealing to basic human "instincts" and needs. And he makes the point that there is *some* connection between his work in linguistics and his politics. In dealing with a hostile French interviewer in connection with the Faurisson affair,[1] Chomsky began by saying that there was "no connection" between his political and scientific views, but continued "apart from some very tenuous relations at an abstract level, for example, with regard to a concept of human freedom that animates both endeavors" (*LP* 318). In general, anyone who, like Chomsky, adopts Enlightenment ideals must hope to show that reason can appeal to properties of human nature to point the direction for moral and political decisions. The connection that reason needs may not be deductive: "I wish it were possible, as it obviously is not, to deduce from our understanding of human nature that the next stage in social evolution ought to be such and such" (*LP* 245). But there had better be some rationally justified connection, at least between human nature and a *vision* of an ideal form of social organization.

Chomsky often appeals to fundamental human needs when asked how one might justify an argument in favor of a vision of an ideal society, because he adopts a principle so obvious that it is difficult to deny: a good society must satisfy fundamental human needs. The principle offers a lot to someone who wants to connect political ideals to a nativist theory of language via human nature: it suggests justifying moral claims about an ideal form of social organization by appeal to "natural instincts" lodged in human nature. Assuming the principle, to implement it Chomsky needs to develop (by appeal to science, not faith or hope) a list of what the fundamental human needs are, and then argue that these are best satisfied by a particular kind of society. Because the principle on which it is based seems to be sufficiently obvious that anyone would accept it, call the strategy that relies on it a "default" strategy.[2] The problem is that there is at present no science of human nature, only Chomsky's suggestive rationalist view of the mind (which does, however, incorporate several sciences). Since we do not know what is and what is not "lodged in human nature," it is not obvious how to come up with a naturalistically justified list of fundamental needs.

In a debate with Chomsky in 1971, the relativist Michel Foucault underscored an aspect of the problem. He pointed out that it is difficult to determine whether a particular need is part of human nature or an artifact of some form of political arrangement or society. Then he argued, in effect, that there are no fundamental needs; the needs that are relevant to politics and morality depend on the form that power and authority relationships take within a particular society. There can be no fundamental needs, only needs that *seem* fundamental, given the form of power and authority at a time. If no (socially or politically relevant) need is demonstrably fundamental, the default strategy fails.

Given that at present there is no science of human nature, it may be better to try to find another, but still naturalistic, way to construct a list of fundamental human needs. It can appeal to some of the conclusions of Chomsky's linguistics (such as that SEMs provide an inexhaustible source of perspectives that can serve human interests) and to general characteristics of the biological rationalist's conception of mind – modularity, stimulus freedom, the nativist origins of common sense understanding, etc. And it can use these conclusions and characteristics to analyze massive amounts of data provided by history, sociology, anthropology, economics, . . . to see if there are patterns in the way that people behave that support a list of fundamental needs. The patterns might suggest limits to how people can conceive of organizing themselves and what justifications they will accept for one course as opposed to another. They might also indicate what people generally aim at and get satisfaction from doing. In the 1970 essay "Language and Freedom"[3] Chomsky spoke of a new form of social science that would do this and possibly more. It would gather data and seek patterns, but it would also project an ideal form of social organization. That would be in line with the default strategy and might provide as good a form of rational justification as can now be offered.

The needs of human nature

Mention of a new social science appears near the end of "Language and Freedom," where Chomsky asks how a science of human nature that discovers and establishes the fundamental properties of the human mind – among others, the language faculty in all its detail – might have a bearing on matters of freedom and action. As always, he expresses puzzlement about how language and freedom might be related, but he writes these few intriguing sentences:

> Conceivably, we might . . . develop a social science based on empirically well-founded propositions concerning human nature. Just as we study the range of humanly attainable languages, with some success, we might also try to study the forms of artistic expression or, for that matter, scientific knowledge that humans can conceive, and perhaps even the range of ethical systems and social structures in which humans can live and function, given their intrinsic capacities and needs. Perhaps one might go on to project a concept of social organization that would – under given conditions of material and spiritual culture – best encourage and accommodate the fundamental human need – if such it is – for spontaneous initiative, creative work, solidarity, pursuit of social justice. (CR 155)

Ignoring until later what a new social science might look like, let us examine the list of fundamental needs in the last sentence and ask how Chomsky could choose such a specific list and justify his choice. He says that humans need "spontaneous initiative, creative work, solidarity, pursuit of social justice." The list is not canonical. In other places he says that freedom is *the* fundamental human need – often, though, in the form of a need for "free and creative activity." In different contexts, he emphasizes solidarity. In 1969's "Some Tasks for the Left," in the course of rejecting calls from some in the radical Left for revolution with little thought for its aftermath, Chomsky insists that one must pursue a "new social order," building his argument on the claim that "compassion, solidarity, friendship are also human needs. They are driving needs, no less than the desire to increase one's share of commodities or to improve working conditions. Beyond this, I do not doubt that it is a fundamental human need to take an active part in the democratic control of social institutions" (*RP* 224). Emphasizing freedom again, but relating it to solidarity, in *PKF* Chomsky quotes Russell approvingly: " 'There can be no real freedom or democracy', Russell wrote, 'until the men who do the work in a business also control its management.' " Chomsky continues: "Socialism will be achieved only insofar as all social institutions, in particular the central industrial, commercial, and financial institutions of a modern society, are placed under democratic control in a federal industrial republic of the sort that Russell and others envisioned, with actively functioning workers' councils and other self-governing units in which each citizen, in Thomas Jefferson's words, will be 'a direct participator in the government of affairs' " (*PKF* 61). Should we add control of management of production to the list of fundamental human needs? Arguably, this specific a need is not a direct product of human nature but arises only in an industrialized economy with forms of social organization that require coordination of one person's work with another's, including under "coordination" various considerations such as control of resources, distribution of goods, and avoidance of oversupply. It would be more accurate to say that in an industrialized society one or more fundamental human needs *express themselves* in a need for the worker to control management. This grants that control of management of production is a need for those in an industrialized society but leaves open what the fundamental needs that express themselves this way are. In this case, they are plausibly those contained in Chomsky's conception of freedom: it is likely that control of one's workplace and production (direct participation in the government of industrial affairs) is a specific expression of one or more of the fundamental needs for "spontaneous initiative, creative work." More generally, we have a plausible assumption: fundamental needs can express themselves in a variety of ways in different circumstances.

To clarify matters, consider the status of needs in an account of mind or human nature. It is unlikely that Chomsky or anyone else seriously thinks of human needs – whether fundamental or not – as somehow lodged in a 'need box' in the mind. It is much more likely, given the architecture of the mind outlined in chapter 2, that he would hold that all needs arise from the basic structure of the mind when it is placed within a particular set of physical and social circumstances and presented with the task of coping with them – with the world that that set of circumstances presents. In *LP* (p. 145), in the context of a discussion of how a mind with limited faculties and capacities not only provides great advantages to humans but undermines the plasticity claims of behaviorism, he says: "Naturally I hope that it will turn out that there are intrinsic structures determining human need and fulfillment of human need." On this way of looking at it, human nature, in the form of the various faculties, arranged and interconnected as they are, "determines" – under given circumstances – what counts as need and as fulfillment of need. (Needs for food and sex are not specifically *human* needs; the fundamental human needs are, plausibly, those due to the distinctive human mind.) Needs would arise when minds with a given structure confront the contingencies of life. If so, the various needs that humans have in various circumstances are likely to display a relatively stable pattern, for, even though circumstances change, the human nature represented by the mind remains the same. And the needs should be detectable by looking at what people get fulfillment or satisfaction from.

Chomsky undoubtedly has something like the idea of looking to satisfactions to decide upon a list of needs when, in discussing moral, political, and aesthetic "instincts," he appeals to history for evidence of how people secure satisfaction over time. We can think of satisfaction of distinctively human needs as providing self-fulfillment. Fundamental human needs would then be those in which *any* human being finds fulfillment over history: uniformity in intellectual, moral, aesthetic, and/or social and political satisfactions over time would suggest that one is on the trail of a distinctively human need. With this kind of data in mind, I suggest tentatively that Chomsky's list of fundamental human needs be reduced to two. One is freedom, which is satisfied in various ways – creative work, spontaneous initiative, play, creative language use, poetry, . . . generally, what he calls "free and creative activity." It can also be seen in control of oneself and one's circumstances – as autonomous thought and action. It represents the individualistic aspect of human needs. The other is community.[4] This is satisfied in friendship, solidarity, compassion, pursuit of social justice, fellowship, sympathy, support, nurture, love, companionship. It is the social aspect of human need: satisfaction is found in association and cooperation involving family, friends, industry, team, township, neighborhood, village, etc. Compressing the list of needs to two, which represent social and individual aspects, is no doubt both regimenting and restrictive. It might also appear to set up an opposition within human nature itself – the need to be solitary versus the need to be social, something Chomsky would not want. Among other things, it does not make much sense to think in terms of purely individual satisfactions: an individual's satisfaction in work well done or a product well made has its social side in acknowledgment and perhaps praise, as well as in recognition that one has made a contribution to others. But such regimentation and restriction provide a way to organize Chomsky's list of needs and at the same time present a tentative hypothesis about the fundamental human needs. Emphasizing both an individual and a social aspect also makes sense of why Chomsky endorses anarchosyndicalism, or libertarian socialism, not anarchism-libertarianism alone, or syndicalism-socialism alone. It is because human satisfactions – and thus needs – have both individual and social aspects.

Neither of these (tentatively suggested) basic needs covers "desire to increase one's share of commodities" or control of others (domination). As we have seen, Chomsky considers domination pathological, perhaps a perversion of the need to control one's affairs. Desire to increase one's share of commodities read as unlimited accumulation in the "economic man" sense, however, poses a puzzle, for Chomsky speaks of it as a "driving need." It is, then, a useful test case, for if this "driving need" for commodities is unlimited accumulation, and if a driving need is fundamental, it would seem to provide some support for a 'liberal' vision of an ideal society. Before dealing with this, we need to look more closely at the historical and anthropological evidence which Chomsky offers for the hypothesis that freedom and community are fundamental human needs.

In the argument leading up to the "Language and Freedom" quotation, Chomsky summarizes observations of human action and motivation made by other rationalist/romantic thinkers. This tradition focuses on freedom and sees the satisfactions of exercising freedom in *self-respect* when exercising one's own freedom and *admiration* in the case of others. The implicit assumption is that persons who have sold out – who have chosen rewards from authority over freedom and autonomy – recognize that they have done so and that, while they may try to justify what they have done by listing rewards received and treating them as accomplishments, these claims ring hollow. They do not respect themselves; nor can they command admiration: one might envy the riches and power, but not admire the person. Chomsky quotes Rousseau in his *Discourse on Inequality*: they "do nothing but boast incessantly of the peace and repose they enjoy in their chains ... But when I see ... others sacrifice pleasures, repose, wealth, power, and life itself for the preservation of this sole good which is so disdained by those who have lost it; . . . when I see multitudes of entirely naked savages scorn European voluptuousness and endure hunger, fire, the sword, and death to preserve only their independence, I feel that it does not behoove slaves to reason about freedom" (*CR* 144). Kant makes similar claims in arguing in favor of the French Revolution after the Terror had begun. Responding to complaints by those who said that the Terror showed that those who rebelled were not "ripe for freedom," he said: "If one accepts this assumption, freedom will never be achieved; for one can not arrive at the maturity for freedom without having already acquired it; one must be free to learn how to make use of one's powers freely and usefully. . . . To accept the principle that freedom is worthless for those under one's control and that one has the right to refuse it to them forever, is an infringement on the rights of God himself, who has created man to be free" (quoted ibid.). Self-respect and admiration are here being used to justify revolution and its aftermath: people's need for these override concerns even for their survival. Chomsky continues: "No rational person will approve of violence and terror. In particular, the terror of the post-revolutionary state, fallen into the hands of a grim autocracy, has, more than once, reached indescribable levels of savagery. Yet no person of understanding or humanity will too quickly condemn the violence that often occurs when long-subdued masses rise against their oppressors, or take their first steps towards liberty and social reconstruction" (*CR* 144–5).

Chomsky notes that Humboldt makes freedom out to be the "first and indispensable condition" of self-fulfillment and self-development. Freedom is not granted when one is "ripe" for it; it has to be exercised from within. Humboldt argues that it is lodged in "the very nature of man. The incapacity for freedom can only arise from a want of moral and intellectual power; to heighten this power is the only way to supply this want; but to do this presupposes the exercise of the power, and this exercise presupposes the freedom which awakens spontaneous activity" (*CR* 148). Nevertheless, "a variety of situations" is needed for its stimulation and development. Education plays an important role – not, of course, education as indoctrination, but education as providing opportunities for the exercise of freedom. This cannot be refused to any person. Chomsky quotes Humboldt and remarks further:

> "There is something degrading to human nature in the idea of refusing
> to any man the right to be a man." [Humboldt] is, then, optimistic about
> the effects on all of "the diffusion of scientific knowledge by freedom and

enlightenment." But "all moral culture springs solely and immediately from the inner life of the soul, and can only be stimulated in human nature, and never produced by external and artificial contrivances." "The cultivation of the understanding, as of any of man's other faculties is generally achieved by his own activity, his own ingenuity, or his own methods of using the discoveries of others . . ." Education, then, must provide the opportunities for self-fulfillment; it can at best provide a rich and challenging environment for the individual to explore, in his own way. (*CR* 149)

The common theme in these observations is that people need to exercise freedom in order to develop as people – as free agents. Positive evidence that there is a need for freedom built into human nature is found in the rejection of slavery, the fact of revolution, and the awakening of powers of self-understanding, self-development, and self-fulfillment through education that refuses to instill and control but rather occasions and invites, to use Cudworth's phrase.

The satisfactions of community are sufficiently obvious that they need less attention. They are found in working together, solidarity in performing a task, conversation and gossip, teamwork, community projects, joint planning, friendship, love, and so on. Denial of these satisfactions leads to alienation, loneliness, disaffection. Like Humboldt and unlike Rousseau, Chomsky is not a primitive individualist. He holds with Humboldt that "[t]he isolated man is no more able to develop than the one who is fettered" (*CR* 152). But if humans need community as well as freedom, Chomsky claims, the community must be one of "free association without coercion by the state or other authoritarian institutions," a form of free association where "free men can create and inquire, and achieve the highest development of their powers" (ibid.) – in effect, a form of association that is Chomsky's preferred form of social organization, anarchosyndicalism. In Western democracies, elements of this form of free association are found, for example, in guarantees of individual rights; hints about what such a form of free association would look like are found "in the Israeli Kibbutzim; in the experiments with workers' councils in Yugoslavia; in the effort to awaken popular consciousness and create a new involvement in the social process which is a fundamental element in the "Third World" revolutions, coexisting uneasily with indefensible authoritarian practice" (ibid.). Community can, of course, be misconstrued – largely when it is detached from freedom and individuality. It might, for example, be construed as blind loyalty or, within a statist system, in terms of jingoist sentiments – a denial of differences between individuals within a state and a refusal to recognize commonality with people in others. At its worst, it can be seen – as by Hegel and some of his followers – to absorb freedom. But when both it and freedom are satisfied, the result is the free and responsible individual.

Chomsky allows that in special circumstances the "instincts" for freedom and solidarity might be forbidden expression in self-fulfillment because of a need for survival, thereby making a person's actions inhuman and – in these special circumstances – less responsible and accountable. He also points out that most people in modern industrialized democracies are *not* in these circumstances. He illustrates: "I've very rarely talked about atrocities committed by soldiers. I've explained why. The reason is that soldiers, in a situation of conflict, are frightened. The options open to them are few. They can be enraged. These are situations in which people can't use their normal human instincts" (*LP* 772). This excuse is open to very few. In an article in the *New York Review of Books* on the My Lai incident (in which US soldiers slaughtered civilians in Vietnam), he wrote three sentences pointing out that no one could say much that was sensible about the actions of a bunch of "half-crazed GI's in the field" and about their responsibilities. He remarks on this article: "The much more serious question, I think, is how people who are subject to no threat, who are comfortable, educated and if they don't know what's going on it's because of a conscious decision not to know what's going on, how such people can, in the quiet of their living rooms, tolerate and support and back horrifying atrocities, and plan them in their well-appointed offices. That's the real evil, far worse than what's done by soldiers in the field" (ibid.). Those sitting at home in a democratic state who have the information and are not in combat have the opportunity to exercise their moral instincts and are thus more responsible for the atrocities than the soldier in the field. They are, and were, in a position to reject the policies that led to the atrocities.

This is related to a general claim about the nature of evil: that it can be institutionalized and that, when it is, it leads to results far worse than those perpetrated by the occasional evil individual. Chomsky notes that while individual humans are capable of evil actions, they are also capable of good. They have "lots of capacities and options." Problems arise when those capacities and options are channeled in such a way that, in order to survive, one must emphasize those that lead to causing harm. War would be one example. It is possible even to conceive of institutional war. "If we had institutions which permitted pathological killers free rein, they'd be running the place. The only way to survive would be to let those elements of your nature [presumably, an instinct for survival and so not essentially human] manifest themselves" (*LP* 773).

These observations about the role of institutions with regard to needs complement a passage that suggests a picture of needs that supports the idea that, in addition to freedom and community, the "driving need" to accumulate (which, if unlimited, can be read as greed) is among fundamental needs. "If we have institutions which make greed out to be the sole property of human beings and encourage pure greed at the expense of other human emotions and commitments, we're going to have a society based on greed, with all that follows. A different society might be organized in such a way that human feelings and emotions of other sorts, say solidarity, support, sympathy, become dominant. Then you'll have different aspects of human nature and personality revealing themselves" (ibid.). On one reading, the picture is this: humans have various needs, only some of which will be revealed (allowed expression in satisfactions) by particular institutions. But, presumably, if a need is revealed, it is 'there' from the start. So, if unlimited accumulation is encouraged by some institutions, it must be among the needs that are 'there' in human nature. If so, however, the default strategy returns the result that the ideal form of social organization should provide for the satisfaction of a central 'value' of "economic man."

Clearly, Chomsky would not *want* this result. Not only does it offer support to institutions that provide for the satisfaction of greed but, by the same argument, domination of others (which Chomsky takes to be pathological) ends up among the needs 'there' in human nature too, and the default strategy provides justification for "market ideals." Indeed, any satisfaction encouraged by any historical institution will end up among the needs 'there' in human nature; the result is hardly different from Foucault's view that institutions make needs. But wanting to reject the result and actually doing so are very different; the argument must rest on empirical, naturalistic grounds. Let us see if more data might support a different picture.

In *LPK* Chomsky looks at what certainly should be a relevant form of human behavior – moral judgment and moral argument – and at the range of agreements and disagreements allowed within it. He points out that moral argument is "not always pointless, merely a matter of 'I assert this' and 'you assert that'" (*LPK* 152). It is not, then, merely relative – a matter of what society one happens to be in or what one's individual interests happen to be. If so, it is plausible to postulate a common basis to all human moral systems. The argument is like other poverty of stimulus arguments that take observations provided by common sense and appeal to inner capacities and faculties to make sense of the data. "The acquisition of a specific moral and ethical system, wide ranging and often precise in its consequences, cannot simply be the result of 'shaping' and 'control' by the social environment" (*LPK* 152–3). That is, particular systems involve a highly specific texture and structure – what is right and wrong, what one's obligations are, to whom one is responsible, what kinds of excuses are permitted, what is just – and while one finds diversity, it is hardly credible that a system of rights and obligations, permissions and excuses, that is acquired as readily by children as human moral/ethical systems seem to be is learned by some generalized learning procedure or induced by some form of training. Apparently, as "in the case of language, the environment is far too impoverished and indeterminate to provide this system to the child, in its full richness and applicability. Knowing little about the matter, we are compelled to speculate; but it certainly seems reasonable to speculate that the moral and ethical system acquired by the child owes much to some innate human faculty. The environment is relevant, as is the case of language, vision, and so on; thus we can find individual and cultural divergence. But there is surely a common basis, rooted in our nature" (*LPK* 153).

One of Chomsky's favorite examples – he uses it in several of his writings and interviews – is a case of convergence in moral judgment and argument that seems to indicate that freedom is a need of all human beings and domination is not – that it really is pathological. It also seems to support a picture of fundamental needs that justifies some institutions as better than others, a picture that is different from the one above. He remarks: "Not long ago, slavery was considered legitimate, even estimable; slave owners did not characteristically regard what they were doing as wrong but rather saw it as a proof of their high moral values. Their arguments were, furthermore, not absurd, though we now regard them as morally grotesque" (ibid.). Slave-owners in the early years of industrialization argued that if a person owned a piece of machinery, he or she would be more likely to care for it than the person who rented one for temporary use – as with wage slaves. "The argument was that it would have been improper to allow the slaves to be free. They

were much better off if their owners were able to take care of them"
(*LP* 469). Chomsky then claims that, since the time when arguments
like this were taken seriously and accepted, there has been an
observable form of moral progress that is reflected in convergence
of moral judgments that reject the earlier argument: "No sane
person would now accept this argument, though it is not entirely
absurd by any means. As civilization progressed, it came to be
understood [accepted by everyone] that slavery is an infringement
on essential human rights," so the slave-owner's argument would
no longer be accepted by any decent person. Everyone has the right
to be free. Chomsky hopes for more progress in what he think of as
the same direction: "We may look forward to the day when wage
slavery and the need to rent oneself to survive may be seen in a
similar light, as we come to have better understanding of the moral
values rooted in our inner nature" (*LPK* 153).

To clarify "moral values rooted in our inner nature" we can look
to *LP*, in which Chomsky presents the same illustration, makes a
similar remark about moral progress consisting in coming to a
"better understanding of the moral values rooted in our inner
nature," but then adds a point about "natural morality." Speaking
of slave-owners who provided moral justifications for keeping
slaves, he says: "The people who put this forth were civilized
people, but now from our point of view, they're moral monsters.
And, in fact, from the point of view of a natural morality, they were
moral monsters, except that moral and cultural evolution had not
reached the point where they could perceive that. I'm sure that the
same is true about us today. If history goes on for another hundred
years, which is dubious, I imagine that people will be looking back
to practices that we accept and condone and will regard them as
morally monstrous" (*LP* 469). He predicts that "wage slavery" will
be seen as among these practices: that we will find it too to be
an infringement of "fundamental human rights." The picture that
emerges from this is that there is a natural morality that requires
satisfaction of distinctively human needs (including freedom) for
everyone, and that it is correct and applies even if societal practices
make it difficult to realize what that natural morality is, thereby
making it appear deniable and perhaps even wrong.[5]

Evidence from data of both moral structure and moral progress
certainly suggest that there is a fixed form of human nature that
some institutions serve better than others. And evidence from the
slavery example – that we would now reject out of hand the slave-
owner's justification for enslaving humans – suggests that domi-

nation is not a fundamental need. Further evidence is provided by the fact that even now very few, if any, would count wage slavery as a *morally justifiable* form of human behavior; we seem already to recognize that "natural morality" rules it out, for it is a form of domination – of some controlling the lives of others. What, then, of our test case, unrestricted accumulation of commodities – greed? It is not difficult to imagine morally justifying accumulating commodities in the event of disaster, loss of income, provision for children or parents, loss of capacity, and so on. These kinds of activities can be seen to satisfy a need to survive – surely a fundamental need, if not a distinctively human one. But it is difficult to imagine moral justification for accumulation without appeal to survival. Nor can one simply ignore justification; it is needed. Even the slave-owner in offering his "better treatment" argument recognized that. Without justification – or without an argument that seems to provide it – one loses dignity and self-respect and perhaps even fails to be a human being. Moral justification must, however, proceed in the public domain and aim towards agreement.[6] Assuming this, anyone who accumulates must justify doing so to others living in an environment with limited resources. It is extremely unlikely, then, that one could morally justify greed or accumulation for its own sake, any more than one could justify domination as a way to satisfy the need for freedom. This casts a different light on what Chomsky called the "driving need to increase one's share of commodities." The "driving need" is survival, and it expresses itself in accumulation, *some* of which can be justified, although greed cannot. Both greed and domination distort natural morality; they are pathological. And, returning to an earlier point, institutions that enshrine "market discipline" and condone and even celebrate this pathology are more evil than the occasional pathological individual. On this picture, there 'are' fundamental needs, although unlimited accumulation is not among them; fundamental needs can be used to justify some institutions over others (none that deny freedom or condone greed can be justified); and there can be moral progress – though this is not guaranteed.

The correctness of this picture of needs and its ability to appeal to the default strategy to project a vision of an ideal form of social organization and justify some institutions over others depend on whether it provides a better empirical account than the other picture. There is always uncertainty in empirical matters, of course; but there is even more here because of the massive amounts of data needed, the lack of a completed science of human nature, the fact that needs are not in a 'need box' but arise in circumstances, and the difficulty of disentangling fact from ideology. It is sufficiently important to Chomsky to establish the picture on empirical grounds, however, that – I suggest – he has tried to do so for most of his career.

The relativist's challenge, the new social science, and projection

Unlike Plato, Chomsky does not try to provide a nonnaturalistic grounding for his vision of the good society but rather one based on empirical data and empirically justified theories – currently, on available social science data and a plausible view of the mind, but eventually, perhaps, with the aid of a theory of human nature. Because he wants to provide a naturalistic argument, he must, unlike Plato, reject moral relativism on naturalistic or empirical grounds. The problem – as is evident from the discussion of the last few pages – is that discerning patterns and defending one account of them as opposed to another is not easy and relies on distinctions that can be challenged. Where Chomsky sees moral progress, the relativist claims to see only changes in 'moral' evaluation. Where he sees some satisfactions as satisfactions of fundamental needs and others as pathological perversions, the relativist would claim to see undistinguishable pleasures. Where he sees evidence of a fixed human nature with a moral component, the relativist sees the drifts and currents of historical change.

One of the most interesting of Chomsky's encounters with a moral relativist is that with Foucault in 1971, in a debate on the topic "Human Nature: Justice versus Power."[7] In that debate, Foucault replies to Chomsky's attempt to construct naturalistic arguments in the moral domain by claiming that moral concepts such as justice are all relative, mere artifacts. "I will be a little bit Nietzschean about this: . . . it seems to me that the idea of justice . . . is an idea which in effect has been invented and put to work in different types of societies as an instrument of a certain political and economic power or as a weapon against that power. But it seems to me that, in any case, the notion of justice itself functions within a society of classes as a claim made by the oppressed class and as justification for it" (*RW* 184–5). The remark "and as justification for it" might suggest that Foucault is willing to allow that not only do members of an oppressed class *appeal* to a concept of justice to justify revolution, but that they in fact *offer a justification* for revolution when they do. But it soon becomes clear that he has nothing like this in mind; if a concept of justice is an artifact of a society ("is . . . invented"), the most that members of an oppressed class could do is use the concept as a form of persuasion, where persuasion is nothing more than another form of power or coercion. That for Foucault there is no independent concept of justice to which one can appeal is clear from his statement that "notions of human nature, of justice, of the realization of the essence of human beings, are all notions and concepts which have been formed within our civilization, within our type of knowledge and our form of philosophy, and that as a result form part of our class system . . . [O]ne can't however regrettable it may be, put forward these notions to describe or justify a fight which should – and shall in principle – overthrow the very fundaments of our society. This is an extrapolation for which I can't find the historical justification" (*RW* 187). Generalizing to other moral principles, including the principle on which the default strategy rests, it follows that no social change can, strictly speaking, be said to be an improvement or to result in a better form of society, for there is no independent measure of what a good society is. So, in the final analysis, there is no rational justification for revolution or change; revolution and change are just matters of one power usurping another, established power.

Chomsky expresses his position: "I really disagree. I think there is some sort of an absolute basis . . . ultimately residing in fundamental human qualities, in terms of which a 'real' notion of justice is grounded." He points out that even in today's society there is an embodiment of a "kind of groping towards the true, humanly concepts of justice and decency, . . . which I think are real," and follows this with an expression of hope that in a future society, whatever elements of justice and decency can be found "will come closer to incorporating a defence of fundamental human needs, including such needs as those for solidarity and sympathy" (*RW* 185). His remarks presuppose that, even though our current notion of justice and our current understanding of human needs are far from perfect, they can be justified, and that in proposing that one move to a better – here, more just – society, one is not merely mouthing words as a preface to bringing out the cannon, but stating on the basis of the best evidence available that what one proposes *is* justified.

Foucault presents a comparison that is interesting for two reasons. First, he has an explanation of sorts for why people construct moral arguments in the way they do. Second – and much more important, as it turns out – his detailed work on the concept of madness relies heavily on historical data – just the kind of data that Chomsky appeals to in order to defend some needs as fundamental human needs – and he came to a different, relativist conclusion. The first is less important because, in the absence of a response to poverty of stimulus observations in the moral domain, the "Nietzschean" principle that moral values and moral justifications are artifacts of power and authority relations amounts only to badly motivated stipulation. The second is more important, because it makes an opposing claim on what purport to be empirical grounds.

This is why the empirically based argument presented in the last section is so important to Chomsky's project. But someone could rightly object that very little data was taken into consideration there, particularly compared to the mass that Foucault offers in several books. One response to this is to discuss more data. And that is exactly what Chomsky has been doing in his political works, amassing material from history, sociology, anthropology, and economics. More important, he has been doing this against a backdrop of an improving science of language and an independently justifiable biologically oriented rationalist view of the human mind. He has, then, without calling it that, been developing what in "Language and Freedom" he called a social science that would "study the forms of artistic expression or, for that matter, scientific knowledge that humans can conceive, and perhaps even the range of ethical systems and social structures in which humans can live and function, given their intrinsic capacities and needs," and on that basis has projected an ideal form of social organization. If so, Chomsky did not suggest a new social science in the late 1960s and early 1970s just to drop the idea, but has been advancing the social science he suggested all along. With the aid of a large network of individuals, he has gathered detailed economic, social, and cultural information and, with the aid of collaborators such as Edward Herman, has presented it in texts, speeches, and interviews, providing information about what people do and think now, as well as the history of what people have done and thought, to get a grip on what they consider acceptable behavior and the ways they are prepared to justify it. He has suggested what he thinks the fundamental human needs are. And he has projected an ideal form of social organization. One measure of success is whether, after looking at his data and (relatively thin) analysis, one agrees that an anarchosyndical policy or practice is obviously better than another policy or practice. Put it this way: if you agree that the Brazilian bishops' proposal for how to organize media in society (to respect freedom and cooperative decision making) is better than what one finds in corporate-run democracies, if you agree that the intellectual's responsibilities include providing correct information to others even if it undermines corporate and government aims, and if you agree that moral justification by appeal to sheer gain or to domination is pathological, you have come to agree with Chomsky's assessment of fundamental human needs and, given the principle behind the default argument, their implications. Crucially, moreover, you have come to these conclusions not by being told that you must believe them, or by an effort to overpower your critical faculties with mystification and 'expertise' but by exercising your critical sense and using native common sense – aided, perhaps, by some knowledge of an independently justifiable conception of human nature. That is why it is plausible to maintain not only that these conclusions are reasonable, given the data, but that others exercising their native cognitive powers ought to accept them too – provisionally, of course, as with any conclusion reached by empirical argument.

Arguably, Chomsky's new social science represents the best *form* of rational argument that one can now hope for in the moral and political domain. It appeals to a developing science of human nature, welcomes as much data as can be provided, calls on a principle that is hard to deny, and rests on argument techniques as old as common sense. Showing that it is the best is beyond the scope of this book; all I have done is indicate Chomsky's response to Foucault's rival view. This is not to say that the form has been executed as well as it could be. Its execution can be improved with more data, but that goes without saying. Among other things, the few practicing it have tended, like Chomsky, to focus on contemporary issues and circumstances, and a restricted set of them at that.[8] And it could be better grounded; it doubtless would be if one could appeal to a science of human nature. But if it is plausible that the form is as good as one is likely to find, there is reason to think that the connection between Chomsky's linguistics and his politics is tighter than he allows.

There are important differences between Chomsky's new social science and current understandings of social science. For one thing, his version abandons the idea that the goal of social science is to "explain human behavior" in the sense of predicting it (typically accompanied by the suggestion that one can then control it); for another, it is fully compatible with a fixed human nature, in contradistinction to the idea that human nature might be plastic. Furthermore, it is not committed to the concept of rationality embedded in "rational choice theory." It also differs in that it makes no pretence to be value-free. It does, of course, aim towards as much objectivity as one can currently hope for in the domain of human action and behavior, where this is obtained by taking into account as much data as possible over as long a time as possible, while employing as good statistical techniques as are available. But objectivity in this sense has nothing to do with being value-free. The new social science both takes values ("ethical systems") to be within its subject matter and, in relying on the principle that connects fundamental human needs to ideal forms of social organization, takes projection of an ideal form of social organization to be part of its task. In doing the latter, it openly engages in moral argument – but not advocacy.

Incidentally, in Chomsky's current terminology, ethnoscience seems to carry out at least the descriptive task that the new form of social science of "Language & Freedom" was said to do: it looks at and organizes data concerning what people do through the lens of what is known about human nature, largely by investigating common sense understanding (cf. 1995: 28–9). Chomsky's few discussions of ethnoscience do not give it the task of projecting a best form of social organization. Nevertheless, the two projects seem consistent.

Orwell's problem

Orwell's problem, unlike Plato's problem, is not a serious intellectual problem (cf. *KL*, p. xxix). But it is a serious *practical* problem that calls for a great deal of analytic work and effort, not to mention a willingness to overcome illusion. It is, Chomsky says suggestively, "an analogue in the domain of social and political life of what might be called 'Freud's problem'" (*KL*, p. xxv). If so, it is a social and political version of the issue of how people manage to deceive themselves about themselves – the devices that lead to inattention, prejudice, bias, and the like. Chomsky puts it this way: "Plato's problem . . . is to explain how we know so much, given that the evidence available to us is so sparse. Orwell's problem is to explain why we know and understand so little, even though the evidence available to us is so rich. Like many other twentieth-century intellectuals, Orwell was impressed with the ability of totalitarian systems to instill beliefs that are firmly held and widely accepted although they are completely without foundation and often plainly at variance with obvious facts about the world around us. The problem is far broader, as the history of religious dogma suffices to show" (*KL*, p. xxvii).

The allusion to religious dogma provides another clue to Chomsky's understanding of Orwell's problem. It is associated with a kind of secular faith – an unreasoning form of loyalty to one's nation or 'people' characteristic of tribalism and its modern form, nationalism. To undermine this unreasoning faith and solve the problem, one has to analyze the mechanisms that bring it about – the psychological/social/political devices that induce it and maintain it. These mechanisms are open to view to anyone with common sense understanding, fully within the scope of a folk psychology. Even children have no difficulty recognizing favoritism, bias, prejudice, and the workings of power and authority. Applying these concepts to social and political life and discerning the mechanisms involved take a bit more sophistication perhaps, but no adult is incapable of doing these things.

The mechanisms, however, are more difficult to detect in nontotalitarian societies – posing more of a challenge and requiring more work to analyze and, apparently, more effort to overcome. In totalitarian societies, the mechanisms of control are straightforward: governments induce conformity and obedience by force or the threat of force. As Hume noted in his *Dialogues Concerning Natural Religion*, the threat of punishment for not conforming to the tenets of the faith – trial, torture, exclusion, and (according to some doctrines) eternal punishment after death – has proved to be a powerful tool in the history of religious faith. Rational argument is unnecessary; people conform. In Western non-totalitarian democracies, direct threat of injury or punishment is excluded. Intriguingly, though, it turns out that rational argument plays no role here either. If it did, people would see the untruths and faulty reasonings for what they are and, if rational, would determine not to be taken in. Various nonviolent forms of nonrational persuasion and control have come into use, in ways that Orwell did not anticipate. They consist in the creation of necessary illusions – for example, fostering the illusion of a free, democratic press, vigorously devoted to informing the citizen of "all the news that's fit to print." To foster the illusion, debate of a very restricted sort is permitted and performed in a ritualistic manner: the press debates solemnly whether they are "too free." But there is no investigation of the means by which conformity is induced, and – crucially – no questioning of the basic presuppositions that define the secular faith.

Nor did Orwell anticipate the degree of success of nonviolent thought control. Even among those who declare themselves the most free of indoctrination – those who have access to information, freedom to pursue more information, and opportunity to reflect – one finds, with very few exceptions, obedience and conformity to the state religion. One of the more intriguing of Chomsky's thousands of examples is his comparison of US intellectuals' reactions to Soviet radio newscaster Vladimir Danchev's denunciation of the Soviet invasion of Afghanistan on Moscow radio five times during a week in May 1983 with their reactions to the US's invasion of Vietnam. It lies in the background of the discussion at the end of the last chapter. We saw the inconsistency – praise from US intellectuals for Danchev and other Soviet dissidents and not a word about their own Afghanistan, Vietnam. Notice that reason plays no role in explaining this difference in reaction; reason requires a consistent reaction, or what was earlier described as the reaction one ought to have to Vietnam, given that one approves of Danchev's actions. Notice too that the US intellectual was perfectly able to assess the facts of the case of Afghanistan, as was Danchev, and to come to Danchev's conclusion, with all its moral burden. It was clear to Danchev that the invasion was immoral, and he rightly condemned it. And any number of US intellectuals correctly and quickly came to the same conclusion as Danchev; it was obvious to anyone of reason. One must suppose that US intellectuals are equally capable of looking at the facts in the case of Vietnam, of coming to the conclusion that the US invaded Vietnam, and of accepting the moral burden to inform others of this. Yet, except for Chomsky and a few others, very few US intellectuals (and no mainstream press) drew the conclusion and accepted the burden. Notice that this is not selective blindness or refusal to draw a simple conclusion in one's own individual case; it is not "Freud's problem." Although there are parallels, it is in many respects more puzzling. It is selective blindness and refusal to draw a simple conclusion on the part of a group of highly sophisticated, trained intellectuals who have the tools and opportunity to seek the truth and make the simplest judgments, but consistently and uniformly do not do so. Even those with the highest reputations fail to make use of reason in such cases, and do so routinely. In one of his earliest studies, "The

Responsibility of Intellectuals," Chomsky notes that Arthur Schlesinger spoke of US Vietnam policy in 1954 (when Eisenhower was threatening the use of nuclear weapons) "as part of our [US] general program of international goodwill" (*CR* 63). Chomsky notes also in *KL* that in his history of the Kennedy administration Schlesinger described 1962, when Kennedy escalated involvement in Vietnam to direct aggression, as "not . . . a bad year," with "aggression checked in Vietnam" (p. 279).

The solution to Orwell's problem, unlike Plato's problem, does not require profound thought and the construction of a scientific theory. It requires instead a practical program of "intellectual self-defense." One part of this program is to develop an ear for Newspeak and to provide plausible translations. One can find Newspeak easily enough: for instance, after World War II, the US War Department was renamed the Department of Defense; the "defense" of Vietnam is the attack of Vietnam. And translation is easy enough. Chomsky notes that this part of the program of intellectual self-defense is straightforward: "one has to defend oneself against it [Newspeak], but once one realizes what's going on it's not very hard to do" (*LP* 617). The other part of the program is, as noted above, more challenging, at least for citizens of modern democracies. In general, says Chomsky, to "solve Orwell's problem we must discover the institutional and other factors that block insight and understanding in crucial areas of our lives and ask why they are effective" (*KL*, p. xxvii). In the case of totalitarian governments, explaining the effectiveness is straightforward: the institution is the government itself, and it is effective through force. In the case of democracies, it is less straightforward. Still, the challenge is not intellectual, but practical, and anyone with common sense is capable of carrying it out. "The patterns that lie behind the most important phenomena of political, economic, and social life are not very difficult to discern, although much effort is devoted toward obscuring the fact; and the explanation for what will be observed by those who can free themselves from the doctrines of the faith is hardly profound or difficult to discover or comprehend." Hume carried out such an investigation into the institution of religion in his *Dialogues*, Chomsky's investigation of the secular religion of the state – the priests, the powers, the motives, the practices – is no more complicated. He continues (*KL*, p. xviii): "The study of Orwell's problem . . . is primarily a matter of accumulating evidence and examples to illustrate what should be fairly obvious to a rational observer even on superficial inspection, to establish the conclusion that power and privilege function much as any rational mind would expect, and to exhibit the mechanisms that operate to yield the results that we observe." In other words, trace the origin and history of development and growth of the conception of "economic man" and its current embodiment in transnational corporations, and you have the key to this particular form of secular religion and to the role of its secular priesthood, the serviceable intellectual. As with the investigation of any faith, discussion of the folk-psychological mechanisms by which the faith is maintained will be met by incomprehension, denial, scorn: "the evidence and examples accumulated and the principles under which they fall will, virtually by definition, be unintelligible, misconstrued, distorted, dismissed, or otherwise irrelevant, however powerful the case that is made with regard to the highly systematic behavior of the state and other dominant institutions, including the ideological institutions." A crucial element in explaining the extraordinary success of faith with the intellectual lies in allowing debate to proceed, but only within certain bounds. By fostering the illusion of rational inquiry, the intellectual can pretend that he or she is subjecting the faith to constant scrutiny, while its basic tenets remain untouched.

Notice that much of Chomsky's moral/political discussion of "necessary illusions" has, in its critical role, been carrying out the journeyman intellectual worker's job of describing the phenomena and sketching the mechanisms by which the intellectual in a corporate-run democracy is suborned by the system. Notice also that, as in other cases in which reason opposes faith, the reaction of the faithful is what one would expect: ignore the nuisance as long as possible and then insist that one is in fact a stalwart, free, unbiased provider of information to the citizen – providing as evidence of that one's openness to debate. Fortunately, because the intellectual does recognize the demand that he or she tell the truth, a system built on lies and on ignoring the obvious is inherently unstable: Chomsky's journeyman work as a new social scientist can, in principle, succeed in detaching the goals of the serviceable intellectual from the corporate system. (But, if so, it seems to be working rather slowly.)

On the matter of faith and reason, Chomsky is clear. When asked by James Peck, in the interview with which *CR* begins, "Do you have a deep faith in reason?," Chomsky answers: "I don't have a faith in that or anything else." Peck presses: "Not even in reason?," to which Chomsky replies: "I wouldn't say 'faith'. I think . . . it's all we have. I don't have faith that the truth will prevail if it becomes known, but we have no alternative to proceeding on that assumption, whatever its credibility may be" (*CR* 48). On the fact that people do recognize the truth (at least in the relevant social/political cases, within the domain of common sense understanding) he adds: "It's of more than a little interest that ideological managers act in ways that indicate that they share this belief [that truth will prevail]. This is shown, for example, by the substantial efforts to conceal the obvious. After all, it would be easier just to tell the truth" (ibid.). He does not mention that telling the truth does not serve the interests of those in power; that is obvious.

Why does Chomsky continue to devote so much time and effort to the journeyman's intellectual task? His linguistic work would be much more than enough to occupy most people, and his continuing accomplishments in it would be more than enough to satisfy most. He has a home and a family and large numbers of students with all the obligations that these entail and – as his actions indicate – that he honors. Why does he spend so much time on political and social matters? Avoiding psychological analyses and personality profiles, we might find some answer to this kind of question by comparing Chomsky to another intellectual hero, Plato's Socrates.

Socrates and Chomsky

Comparison with Plato's Socrates is complicated by the fact that the historical Socrates was not quite as Plato depicts him and he seems to have at least a slightly different character in different dialogues. But, so long as it is clear that the aim is to compare Chomsky's intellectual project with some reasonable approximation to Plato's Socrates, the exercise can be illuminating.

One parallel is that both Socrates and Chomsky make use of irony. The stylistic fact is not interesting in itself. The interesting feature is that irony presupposes that participants in a conversation or discourse know that what is being presented is false, not because they have been told what the truth is but because they know it already. This suits both Chomsky's and Socrates' assumption that the kind of knowledge that is under discussion is innately specified. There are, however, important differences. First, Socrates' interesting uses of irony (those that put a very different cast on a whole dialogue, for example) take considerable sophistication to appreciate. Chomsky's – at least in his political work – do not. Second,

Chomsky argues that some knowledge that human beings are capable of is not innate – scientific knowledge, for example. One must have some innate equipment in order to develop scientific knowledge – a concept of explanation and/or some kind of idea of what constitutes a plausible hypothesis for a given domain, plus mathematics/geometry and/or formal reasoning capacities. But, unlike innate concepts and the common sense understandings that they largely enable, the details of (serious, not social) science must be gained through hard intellectual work. Correlated with the difference between science and common sense, Chomsky makes little use of irony in his scientific work. (It appears sometimes in his philosophical work.)

A third, related difference is found in differences between kinds of knowledge. When Plato's Socrates speaks of attainable knowledge, because he has no distinction between the kind of knowledge at which he aims and scientific knowledge, and because he thinks that the knowledge he deals with (in effect, common sense understanding) is much more systematic than it is, he naturally adopts the optimistic view that knowledge of all there is, is attainable, at least in principle. Chomsky, by contrast, begins with a biologically limited mind with various faculties that enable common sense understanding and, to a lesser extent, science. Common sense understanding provides an efficient, but not a systematic, way to deal with the world. And while one can hope for some sort of accommodation between the sciences, like that finally accomplished within Chomsky's lifetime between physics and chemistry, there is no guarantee that this will be possible across the board. So a single, unified science is a hope, at best. Indeed, Chomsky allows that there may be forms of understanding that are different from those available to humans and treats success in *any* science as a bit of a miracle. In the case of common sense understanding, it is no miracle that the world 'fits' our descriptions, although – paradoxically – common sense understanding is no sure guide to what is 'really' out there: depending upon concepts that have undoubtedly evolved, common sense is virtually designed for use by human beings to deal with *their* world. The cost of this 'fit' is that these innate concepts are anthropocentric, and, while common sense understanding certainly yields truths on which people agree ("Jerry's Volvo is dented," "Harriet wants to leave the company") – that is, humans with the relevant information agree in their use or application in various circumstances, they are not the kinds of concepts one tries to apply when constructing a science. The world of dented Volvos, companies, and Harriet's intentions is not necessarily 'the' real one or the only one (*PP* 43f).

Second, both think that it is in principle possible to construct a theory of human nature, or of the nature of humans. Socrates' theory, however, amounts to a definition of the "Form" of a human being. He treats humans as having certain functions, from which he hopes to extract a definition of the good human being: a good human being is one who fulfills the functions of a human being, as defined. The procedure for discovering this definition is dialectic – discourse directed towards producing an account of how the Form of human beings both differs from and is like the Forms of all other things. Chomsky's (possible) theory of human nature is arrived at by empirical science or, more plausibly, through various empirical sciences that jointly contribute to a science of human mental faculties and capacities. For each domain with which it deals (language, vision, etc.), this science must respect not just standard desiderata for a theory (simplicity of the 'external' sort) but the demands of explanatory and descriptive adequacy for that domain. There is no direct route, at least yet, from a science of human beings to an account of "the good human being." But, as we have seen, there is a rationally and naturalistically defensible connection even now. In any case, any foundation for an account of ethics/morality based on a naturalistic account of human nature would be unlike Socrates' recourse to an eternally existing abstract Form of human beings, lodged (as later religious doctrine would have it, and as Plato's *Timaeus* very tentatively suggests) in the mind of a God. Perhaps it is no surprise that Socrates' picture of a science of human nature and its foundation yields an authoritarian view of what it is to be a good person. It lodges the standard of the good person elsewhere. Chomsky's naturalistic approach avoids this. Nor does it make the more basic mistake of identifying the good person with a single set of functions or functionings. If it had, the result might have been some variation of Plato's attempt to impose a single form of society, as appears in the *Republic*.[9] Chomsky can allow room for various ways in which small communities could organize and, one hopes, flourish. There is a tight connection between underspecifying societal function (largely by focusing on fundamental needs) and democratic and anarchist principles. Plausibly, it is only if one underspecifies societal function that one can seriously allow for the full development of an individual's specific talents and abilities, as well as recognize cultural and societal differences.

Third, both Socrates and Chomsky tie action tightly to thought. Socrates (keeping in mind that his portrayal may be a bit of a caricature) seems to have honored Plato's principle that those who know the good do it. Chomsky comes as close to honoring the principle as any person I know. But again, there are differences. Socrates' field of action was the rather small, isolated community of Athens, and, judging by the dialogues Plato relates, at least, he frequently spoke with the elite. (Granted, his field was necessarily limited by the contemporary state of communication techniques: he could hardly appear on community radio, for example.) Chomsky's target is anyone who will listen. He has said that he only expects to be effective in certain areas, so focuses his attention on topics and areas with which he is familiar. But his potential audience is virtually anyone in the world. And, apparently unlike Socrates, with respect to social and political matters, he really is willing to talk to anyone. The qualification reflects his view of the differences between the sciences and common sense understanding. In the case of science, he is quite selective in those with whom he deals.

Fourth, both Socrates and Chomsky are strongly committed to telling the truth in the social/political/moral domain. Socrates, on trial for his life and accused of impiety and corrupting youth, both told the truth and refused to seek clemency from the court. Chomsky, in a society that grants rights to freedom of speech and association, is in little legal danger, but as a result of attempting to tell the truth uncompromisingly as best he can in the social/political domain, he has been subjected to criticism from the analog of Socrates' sophists with their secular faith and even to threat from practitioners of other, non-secular faiths. Again, there are differences – in this case crucial. Socrates, at least when justifying his not seeking clemency, argued for the immortality of the soul, and in doing so made his commitment to the truth appear to be not quite unrewarded, and therefore not quite the uncompromising commitment one finds in Chomsky. Because of this, it rings a bit hollow to say that Chomsky's motivation in telling the truth is like Socrates' – Chomsky's motivation seems to be genuinely uncompromising.

Rationalist philosophy and the new social science

In the first chapter I raised the question of whether Chomsky's intellectual project is unified and suggested a strategy for showing that it is. His linguistic work can be seen as a contribution to a biologically based science of a distinctively human nature. That science of human nature can reasonably be expected to yield an understanding of fundamental human needs, given the kinds of environments in which people live. Accepting the principle that fundamental needs should be satisfied, one can argue from fundamental needs to an ideal form of social organization. If these needs are best satisfied by an anarchosyndicalist form of social organization, moreover, there is a definite connection between Chomsky's linguistic science with its nativist, internalist, and constructivist features and his political vision.

Chomsky himself, we saw, expresses diffidence, even skepticism, about whether there is a connection. He suggests that there might be a tenuous, abstract one, having to do with freedom, but avoids further commitment. Some of his assumptions and claims, though – I have argued – imply something more than a tenuous, abstract connection. If he is serious about anarchosyndicalism, even if only as a vision rather than a goal, he should provide justifiable reasons for thinking that people cannot just survive, but actually thrive, without authoritarian structures. The only plausible way to defend this claim is to appeal to human nature.

My investigation of the goals and prospects of a new social science – a very different creature from standard social science – suggests a way to establish a connection between human nature and social ideals. This new social science does not just wait for a completed science of human nature. It gathers as much data as it can about the ways humans behaved and behave now in various circumstances, and, given what we can reasonably suppose about human nature now, searches for patterns in these data. It adopts a reasonable principle about the relationship of fundamental human needs to the best form of social organization. It draws up a list of needs. Then it projects an ideal form of social organization as best it can. This new social science thus seems to carry out as well as can now be expected the task of establishing a connection between what is known about a distinctive human nature (to which Chomsky's linguistics makes a very important contribution) and a vision of an ideal form of social organization that can inform short-term goals and strategies.

But where does this new social science fit in Chomsky's intellectual projects: is it a science, or is it 'in' common sense? Neither and both, I suggest; it is part of the rationalist philosopher's effort to bridge the two domains. The techniques, assumptions, and aims of this new form of social science can be identified with what a scientifically sophisticated rationalist philosopher could be expected to adopt, given the current state of knowledge, if he or she wanted to establish a rationally justified connection between a linguistics that is part of a (very incomplete) science of human nature and political and moral ideals. The suggestion that this new social science is biological rationalism applied to the issue at hand, and that it provides the best available answer to that issue, raises in an interesting way the question of whether one can ever hope (as Chomsky sometimes seems to) to *deduce* what we ought to do from knowledge of what we are. At least for the new social scientist's project, this is not a matter of predicting what people *will* do next. Nor is it a matter of deducing the specific strategies to follow in the next few months; that is a matter of setting goals, once the vision is clear. It is not even a matter of deducing what "the next stage in social evolution ought to be." It is a matter of reasoning from what we know and can reasonably assume to a vision of an ideal, given the principle on which the default strategy is based. If so, we have seen that we can already engage in rational argument to this end. As Chomsky emphasizes in making empirical evidence the basis of his arguments and their conclusions, we will need to continually reassess our data to ensure that the list of fundamental human needs we draw up is correct and complete, that our principles are the best we can manage, and that what we say about human nature is right. But, given this, the default strategy lets us deduce a vision. If the alternative is faith and appeal to authority, perhaps our rational natures demand that we take the path of deduction.

Notes

Introduction

1 Chomsky speaks of I-languages as "states," because he holds that all people are born with Universal Grammar (UG), so that when they develop a language (an I-language), it counts as a state of development of UG or (alternatively) a state of development of the language faculty.

Chapter 1 Common Sense and Science

1 Two comments to avert misunderstanding: first, Chomsky is not a socio-biologist. His view that our biologically based minds make free action possible must not be confused with the idea that our biological natures somehow determine human action. Second, Chomsky takes a science of language to be a crucial contribution to a science of human mind and human nature (as it surely is), but he in no way holds that a science of language tells us everything about the mind. See ch. 2.

2 Robert F. Barsky mentions this article and outlines some of the influences on Chomsky's early development in his *Noam Chomsky: A Life of Dissent* (Barsky 1997). He gives Chomsky's age as ten. Chomsky's statement in a BBC interview that he was "about 12" is probably a misremembering.

3 This work was written and revised over several years in the mid-1950s. It was not published until 1975, but was circulated in mimeographed form and on microfilm during the intervening 20 years.

4 Guglielmo Cinque reports this in n. 18 of his "On the Connections between Chomsky's Work in Linguistics and Cognitive Science, and His Social Views and Attitudes." Chomsky's remark, *LSLT* 108, is: "The program of developing a general linguistic theory is reminiscent, in certain respects, of much earlier attempts to develop a universal grammar."

5 This is not an accident, Chomsky suggests: social scientists are among the more prominent members of what Chomsky calls the "secular

priesthood." Academics in general are tempted to become "managers" (individuals who use authority to control others), but those who portray themselves as expert in human behavior and, furthermore, offer the power elite the tempting idea that people are basically plastic beings that need to be molded are particular targets of his ire. Speaking of Kissinger the manager in response to a question from James Peck (*CR* 42–3), Chomsky says: "His ignorance and foolishness really are a phenomenon. I've written about this in some detail. But he did have a marvelous talent, namely, of playing the role of the philosopher who understands profound things in ways that are beyond the capacity of the ordinary person. He played that role quite elegantly. That's one reason I think he was so attractive to the people who actually have power. That's just the kind of person they need."

Other prominent targets of Chomsky's ire are the behaviorists. It is easy to understand why. Here is the behaviorist Watson in 1925: "Give me a dozen healthy infants, well-formed, and my own specified world to bring them up in and I'll guarantee to take any one at random and train him to become any type of specialist I might select – doctor, lawyer, artist, merchant-chief, and yes, even beggar-man and thief, regardless of his talents, penchants, tendencies, abilities, vocations, and race of his ancestors" (quoted in Pinker 1994b: 406–7). Chomsky often comments on Skinner, probably the most prominent of behaviorists and once almost a deity among psychologists: "As far as the Skinner thing is concerned . . . I think it's a fraud, there's nothing there. . . . I think that there are two levels of discussion here. . . . First you ask, is it science? No, it's fraud. And then you say, OK, then why the interest in it? Answer: because it tells any concentration camp guard that he can do what his instincts tell him to do, but pretend to be a scientist at the same time. So that makes it good, because science is good, or neutral, and so on. . . . [Behaviorism gives] a kind of cloak of neutrality to the techniques of oppression and control. . . . That is the behaviorists' contribution: to take the standard techniques of control and oppression and coercion, and try to make them disappear, to insulate them from criticism or understanding by assimilating them to science" (*LP* 190–1). The emptiness of behaviorism (and empiricism) in its effort to construct a science of mind is discussed later.

6   The targets could as easily have been continental philosophers such as Heidegger and Habermas; they too almost universally adopt a plastic view of mind. His arguments against Foucault (discussed in ch. 8) are *a propos* here. Note that Chomsky uses empiricism to refer to a view of the nature of mind. Empiricism should not be confused with 'empirical'; he is an empirical scientist, but not an empiricist.

7   Chomsky is not the only or the first person to use irony when discussing moral and political issues. A precedent is Plato's Socrates. The parallel is instructive. Socrates, like Chomsky, constructs political (moral) arguments on the assumption that the people with whom he speaks know what the right answer is, even if it may be difficult to discern that answer due to the complicated nature of the issues and the distorting effects of interest and deliberate deception. Socrates and Plato had nothing like our modern sciences in place, of course; the closest approximation is Plato's stab at

mathematical physics in his "likely story" in the *Timaeus*. For what it is worth, there is little irony in that dialogue (but little in the late, un-Socratic *Laws* too).

8 Compare: "[T]he search for theoretical understanding pursues its own paths, leading to a completely different picture of the world, which neither vindicates nor eliminates our ordinary ways of talking and thinking. These we can come to appreciate, modify, and enrich in many ways, though science is rarely a guide in areas of human significance. Naturalistic inquiry is a particular form of human enterprise that seeks a special kind of understanding, attainable for humans in some few domains when problems can be simplified enough. Meanwhile, we live our lives, facing as best we can problems of radically different kinds, far too rich in character for us to hope to be able to discern explanatory principles of any depth, if these even exist" (1995: 8).

9 Philosophers and others might insist that "in the final analysis" (or in a millennial science, or . . .) all the sciences are one. Perhaps they will all turn out to be reducible to one science, or perhaps there are interesting accommodations ahead. We all hope for the accommodation of mental sciences like those for vision and language to some brain science or another. But, as it stands, there is little more than that hope to drive the idea that there *must* be – there has been success at accommodating parts of physics to parts of chemistry and progress at incorporating some of molecular biology and a few suggestions about aspects of sensory capacities like vision, but not even a plausible suggestion about how to begin with language. Furthermore, each science now and probably in the future *does* deal with a specific subject matter. Physics and chemistry and their parts do, even though some of their respective parts have been united.

10 Other commonly used orthographic devices include capitalization (HOUSE) or a different font or typeface (**house**).

11 I put scare-quotes around 'noun', 'verb', and 'sentence' to warn that there is no *prima facie* reason to think that concepts like <u>noun</u> defined by linguists for the investigation of natural languages automatically apply to scientific symbol systems like physics (or to the symbols of formal linguistics (N, PP, IP), for that matter).

12 This is not to say that they come configured in exactly the same ways in all natural languages; different natural languages might 'lexicalize' concepts in different ways, and – trivially – any concept might be paired with virtually any natural language sound (so that the concept <u>arthritis</u> might be paired with "arthritis" or with "grinch"). The important consideration is that the *features* (defined later) that make up natural language concepts be innate (1997: 17–18). The features of <u>kaon</u> are not.

13 It is important to be very careful here. There are too many people who – for reasons that cannot be scientific, because they are unsupported by any evidence, and perhaps any possible evidence – enthusiastically substitute "evolution" and even "natural selection" (not identical with evolution, even for Darwin) for "God" when it comes to explaining where human cognitive capacities come from. Chomsky admits only what the empirical evidence allows – among other things that there is reason to hold that

evolution plays a role in making sense of why "words" and natural language sentences provide anthropocentric perspectives that serve human interests. This gives evolution a role in explaining why human language is innate and why language (and common sense) are so readily acquired and used, but it in no way depends upon a thesis about language being selected because it offers reproductive success.

14 One of Chomsky's targets here is the philosopher Quine. It is important to keep in mind that Chomsky *includes* a theory of meaning within the science of language. See ch. 6.

15 Perhaps Chomsky should go even further and speak of two different worlds or (for the scientific domain, which has many theories) a common sense world and several scientific ones. He says almost as much in "Internalist Explorations" when he speaks, as does his teacher Goodman, of "making worlds" (1997); this also suits his rationalist constructivist views, explored later.

16 I do not discuss his review of Skinner; that would require speaking to Skinner's meretricious terminology – not the familiar and reasonably well-defined "stimulus," "response," and "reinforcement," but the terminology he specially introduced to deal with language, including the arcane "mand" and "tact" and the code terms "control," "evoke," "aversive control," "echoic operant," "textual behavior," etc., which are at best only pretentious forms of traditional unscientific terms, such as "refer."

17 A recent group of empiricists who call themselves "connectionists" claim that they have found that mechanism in training procedures applied to neural nets, perhaps making a science of what earlier had been – as Chomsky calls it – speculation. This is not the occasion for a critique of connectionism as an account of concept and connection acquisition; those familiar with it can judge whether Chomsky's criticisms of empiricist assumptions – the claims above – apply to connectionist empiricism too. He thinks they do.

One must distinguish whether connectionism explains learning from the issue of whether neural nets carry out the linguistic processing done by the language faculty. At the current level of understanding of neural processes, I doubt that there is a sensible answer to the second question. Arguably, though, linguistic processing, even as Chomsky's theory construed it, could be instantiated in something like a neural net. The first issue – the one of concern here – is whether language is learned or simply develops. Chomsky holds that it develops; the learning-connectionists think they can show that it is learned, largely by training. Looked at in this way, learning-connectionism is behaviorism with neural nets, and it is not obvious that neural nets add anything to the idea that the mind learns by training.

Chapter 2 Mapping the Mind

1 For a contrary view, see Bracken 1984: ch. 1.

2 Granted, vision is not the knowledge-representing faculty that language is, and it is not plausible to speak of 'knowing' Gaussians, whereas it

might be plausible to speak of 'knowing' the linguistic principle mentioned before (cf. *LPK* 160). But the cases are parallel in other ways.

3 In lectures Chomsky has pointed out the various ways in which Newton tried to avoid the consequence that his own theory committed him to. Contact mechanics apparently has a strong appeal. This is connected with Chomsky's suggestion, mentioned in the last chapter, that dualism might have a grounding in common sense understanding. In *PP* (4f) Chomsky also pursues the point that Descartes saw contact mechanics and a mechanical world as key to getting rid of the medieval period's occult qualities and mysterious forces. It is no wonder that Newton found it difficult to accept action at a distance: to those anxious to shed medieval thinking, this looked to be the reintroduction of mysterious forces.

4 Chomsky makes this point in several ways in his 1994, 1995, 1997, and elsewhere. One way is this: the language faculty in its expressions provides perspectives for people to use; it does not (and no other faculty of the mind does) apply them. See the beginning of ch. 4 for another reason: language use is a matter of pragmatics.

5 In recent lectures at MIT Chomsky has distinguished reference applied to the symbols of science from reference by people who use natural language terms (cf. *PP*: 45–6). Reference in the sciences approximates a two-term relationship between a "symbol" (which is not a natural language "expression") and a theoretically specified thing or class of things, *because* it is one of the essential features of scientific inquiry to aim for such a relationship. Nevertheless, even in the sciences reference is something people do, not a "factual relationship"; thus it is still nothing that a science can contend with. It is just that it is an aim of scientists to ensure that their symbols always 'speak of the same thing'. Because they are sometimes successful, one gets something like a term–thing relationship.

6 There are parallels in Kant's view that agents and their freedom cannot be dealt with within the domain of science or theoretical reason, but only within the domain of practical reason.

7 Putnam tried a move like this in his "The Innateness Hypothesis and Explanatory Models in Linguistics" (1967).

8 The Greeks, like the Egyptians, had some interesting technology – astrolabes and such. However, technology is not science. Second, most technology – this was certainly true until well into the nineteenth century – is the product of engineering which proceeds in terms of principles that any person of common sense has and can easily understand. A lot of engineering is still of this sort – mechanical, architectural, etc.

9 Chomsky's terminology varies. Sometimes "the language faculty" includes not just the computational system for which there is currently a science, but the various "performance systems" with which the computational system that produces SEMs and PHONs "interfaces" or which it gives instructions to – perceptual and speech production systems in the case of PHON. It is assumed that there can be (internalist) sciences of these performance systems inside the head too, although it is not even clear (particularly in the case of what Chomsky calls the "conceptual and

intentional" systems on the other side of SEM) what these systems might be. For more details, see chs 5 and 6. For my purposes (unless otherwise indicated), the language faculty can be identified with the cognitive or computational system, or what Chomsky in *MP* calls the computational system of human language (C_{HL}). Chomsky sometimes speaks of the language faculty in this way too, or at least of "the language faculty in a narrow sense of the term" (*LGB* 18).

10 PET scans have demonstrated this, although there is still considerable dispute about precisely what such evidence shows.

11 The conception of how to educate the mind that underlies it is pernicious to boot. The "culture does it" story is often lodged in the apparently inno-cent technical notion "rule of language." "Rule" is readily given a pre-scriptive and normative gloss: rules dictate correct behavior. Then a community's role in 'maintaining' these prescriptions comes to seem all too natural. Perhaps the dominance of this prescriptive reading of "rule of language" among philosophers (e.g., Wittgenstein, Dummett, Kripke) and others is one reason why Chomsky has virtually abandoned use of the word. It used to figure prominently in his linguistic work (where it was given a technical application, of course); it now appears only occasionally.

12 Famously, Kant argued that the limits of our cognitive powers could *not* be determined by empirical inquiry.

Chapter 3 Poverty, Creativity, and Making the World

1 Dominic Scott argues in *Recollection and Experience* (1995) that Plato focuses on the theorem because he holds that "recollection" is needed *only* for non-ordinary concepts, such as those found in geometry and ethics. I have my doubts about Scott's claim, but it does not matter for my purposes. The *Meno* case nicely illustrates the issues.

2 I am not speaking here of cases where a child has to cope with irregular constructions in a language – cases where a child must learn (that is the right word) language-specific rules, such as that 'bought' is the past of 'buy'. See below.

3 These data are well supported. For informal discussion see Pinker 1994b.

4 The figure is from Pinker 1994b: 150–1 and is perhaps too modest. Chomsky's apparently different assumptions provide for a vocabulary of about 35,000 words by age eight (about a word per waking hour between two and eight).

5 The specific case, that of "Simon" (studied by Singleton and Newport), is cited and discussed by Pinker (1994b: 38–9).

6 The topic is taken up briefly in ch. 6.

7 He used this terminology to characterize his Minimalist Program ac-count of language in the last of a series of lectures on syntax at MIT on December 7, 1996; the discussion at the end of chapter 5 may suggest why. The general point about science, though, is obvious now: scientific success is not due to God; nor (*pace* Peirce) can one gesture towards evolution, as one can to make sense of the practical success of common sense concepts. So it is difficult to conceive of scientific success as anything but a "miracle."

Chapter 4   Languages and the Science of Language

1   The distinction between problems (tractable issues) and mysteries (issues that seem to be beyond our powers) has figured in Chomsky's work since at least *RL* in the mid-1970s. It is useful to keep in mind that in the background of the distinction is Chomsky's insistence that biology helps define the limits of human cognitive capacities.

2   I speak of semantics below; one conception of semantics outlined there (relations between words and things) is – while the 'standard' view – *not* Chomsky's conception of semantic in the context "semantic feature." If formal features of words include categorial features such as N and P, think of semantic features as additional features of words that distinguish between particular Ns – between the N "bank" and the N "horse," as well as between the N "bank" as in bank of a river and N "bank" as in financial institution. See the discussion below and in ch. 6.

3   Chomsky's grammars are "derivational," not "representational," meaning by the latter that a grammar starts with a representation of a sound or a meaning and moves towards the other, or perhaps with representations of both and decides whether they are compatible (*MP* 223). Chomsky's derivational grammars start with a set of elements (e.g., lexical items, categorial sets) and produce representations of both sound and meaning (and more too, perhaps). Nevertheless, he has always been tentative about his derivationalist approach and insisted that it is not clear that there is a substantive issue between derivationalists and representationalists. There are others in the field who are unwilling to be as tentative about the matter. And, *very* recently in "Minimalist Inquiries: The Framework" (1998), Chomsky seems to think that there might, after all, be empirical support for derivationalism.

4   I ignore phonology and phonetics ("sound") here, even though, as we find in ch. 6, for Chomsky there are strict parallels between how one should deal with issues of meaning (semantics as he reconceives it) and sound.

5   A verb with two obligatory argument positions demands that any expression in which it appears contain two nouns or noun phrases; the verb "says" how its arguments are (conceived to be) related and assigns its arguments "theta-roles" – Agent, Theme, Patient, for example. The list of theta-roles is not fully agreed upon.

6   So far as Chomsky is concerned, this can be a false dilemma. Meanings (and sounds) can be private – indeed, they *are* private in the sense that the sound I hear is in my head, and the meaning I associate with the sound is one that I have located in my mind – but there is communication anyway. Consider the case for sounds. He says, "you and I can talk to each other, though my (internal) sound system is not the same as yours. Presumably, when I meet you, my mind reacts reflexively by taking you to be identical to me modulo some modification M, and then works out M (reflexively, in simple cases; consciously and with hard work in others; impossible in still others). So the sounds are private, but there's no problem about accounting for communication (always a more-or-less affair). Same for

meanings. A lot of people have been misled about this" (personal communication, April 15, 1998). That said, it is worth keeping in mind that Chomsky lodges sound and meaning-specifying features (phonological, formal, and semantic features) in UG, a part of our biological heritage. So privacy is hardly going to pose a dilemma for him; he can appeal to innateness. Moreover, he can define, by appeal to I-languages, the specific differences in 'my' sounds and meanings and 'yours'. This story cannot be told for scientific languages, though; they have invented concepts and require a different account.

7   Davidson supposed at one time that it would be possible to construct a science of semantics, but seems now to have abandoned the project, just because a science seems to be impossible (see Davidson 1986). There are other variations on the basic theme of uniformity in semantics: Dummett (1986), for example, wants a "public language."

8   They might allow that what they are doing is dealing with the psychological states of speakers, but, in doing so, are ignoring individual variations. This is consistent with Chomsky's view of a theory of language as a theory of competence. But they also insist on going outside the head.

9   Frege seems to have held that the semantics on which the theoretician can get a grip is the semantics found in the 'languages' of mathematics and science. If his followers had respected this view, they would not have tried to apply Frege's efforts to natural languages, the use of which is inevitably free and creative. Chomsky (in lectures and *PP*: 46) has suggested that perhaps Frege's views really do suit the sciences. He, of course, deals with natural languages, where Frege's views fail.

10 Chomsky can appear to be of two minds about the extent to which such features are explicitly syntactic and linguistic. He sometimes speaks, as does Fodor, of words "expressing" their concepts, certainly suggesting that the concept could well be somewhere else in the mind and not therefore intrinsic to the word (lexical item) itself. On the other hand, he speaks of semantic features as simply included among the features that define a particular lexical item. These two claims can be made compatible, but it requires treating what Chomsky says about words expressing concepts as an informal expository effort that is better expressed in theoretical terms. This seems to be his policy: see ch. 6.

11 Remarkably, however, Bloomfield himself seems to have been an apostate at one time. In 1939 he published – under the title "Menomini Morphophonemics" and in a virtually hidden place (*Travaux du cercle linguistique de Prague*) – a generative account of morphophonemics that could just as well have been developed by the young Chomsky. The fact that virtually none of his followers were aware of this (Barsky 1997: 54–5, reporting Chomsky) and its complete lack of influence on them suggest that he would have been embarrassed by a rather obvious fall from behavioral orthodoxy. Chomsky reports that neither of his teachers Harris or Hoenigswald (who were friends and students of Bloomfield) mentioned to him that Bloomfield had done this work, even though they were very familiar with Chomsky's very similar early efforts. He remarks that this seemed to be an "illustration of the force of ideology in science, rather like

the effect of misunderstood logical positivism and of instrumentalism in psychology" (personal communication, April 15, 1998).

12   Many of Chomsky's attacks on philosophical efforts to understand language are attempts to dislodge these intuitions. His *RL*, e.g., is to a large extent devoted to this effort.

13   For an entertaining discussion of the normative dimension and its irrelevance to the theoretical study of language, see Pinker 1994b.

14   He does, however, speak about related matters. In *CL*, for example, he seems both puzzled and intrigued that Humboldt in his more romanticist moments was so attracted to the view that language and nation are linked; see the discussion of the "character" of a language, as opposed to its form.

15   There is more than a touch of irony in his choosing this terminology. Quine and other philosophers have prided themselves on naturalizing various domains – epistemology, in Quine's case. Chomsky criticizes Quine's behaviorist view of language as anti-naturalist dogma.

Chapter 5   How to Make an Expression

1   For the record, in the Extended Standard Theory's early stages, semantic interpretation proceeded over both deep and surface representations (they were by then called D-structure and S-structure).

2   Intuitively, a Markovian process is one that proceeds to a next step on the basis of what is the case at a particular step. It does not "look forward" or "look back." Incidentally, Chomsky was very successful in some cases: several of the mathematicians in his class became professional linguists. I do not know about the engineers.

3   A phrase structure grammar can be Markovian *as a rule system*. But that presupposes structure that none of the enthusiasts of finite state grammars at the time would have allowed.

4   So binding theory illustrates the structure dependence of the concepts a child (or adult) must have in order to be able to speak and understand others.

5   Chomsky cannot, and does not, define "r-expression" in terms of expressions that actually refer, hence the concept of quasi-reference (cf. *KL* 79). To rely on 'actual reference' would be to introduce semantic (in the traditional sense – in Chomsky's sense, pragmatic) considerations into a theory of binding that is, and must be, purely syntactic (internal, intrinsic, mental, etc.). It cannot have anything to do with how words are used, except in the sense that it helps outline the conditions that syntax imposes on the perspectives that language provides people for their use.

6   The class of clitics is broader than anaphors, but that fact is irrelevant here.

7   One measure of the independence of X-bar theory from the P&P framework is that those working in a rival system called Generalized Phrase Structure Grammar (GPSG) adopt and adapt X-bar theory too. The radical suggestion that X-bar theory can be absorbed into the operations of more fundamental principles is found only very late in the P&P framework.

8   He notes that Charles Fillmore made a similar suggestion in 1975.

9   This form of notation indicates that a label is nothing more than a lexical item (set of features), and that it is a member of a set that includes itself and the set of itself and the other lexical item with which it merges: minimal indeed.

10 Perhaps these a priori constraints on scientific inquiry include something like what Kant described as the regulative use of the metaphysical demands of completeness and finality *applied to particular domains*. For present purposes these might suggest that a theory *of language* tie in with other theories, so that the result is, if not a unified scientific picture of the world (*not* a complete picture – certainly both Kant and Chomsky reject that), at least one that is more unified than that provided by a scattered bunch of theories. For Chomsky, the most obvious domain to which to tie linguistics is biology, perhaps via some brain science.

Chapter 6   Meanings and Their Use

1   Chomsky spoke of a "use theory of meaning," but "meaning" should be read as "interpretation" in the usage I've been following. "Meaning" here is not the concept of meaning that one finds in Chomsky's later (still informal) terminology, where it is internal to the language faculty. At the time, "meaning" was a pragmatic notion (a matter of use); it included what we have seen Chomsky takes semantics other than his to be – reference and truth.

2   Recall that "wh" words as in "Who did Harry tell to paint the windows?" are often displaced from the positions where they are naturally 'interpreted': here, the position *x* in "*x* paint the windows."

3   Chomsky had noted almost ten years before that passive transformations do not preserve meaning: "we can describe circumstances in which a 'quantificational' sentence such as 'everyone in the room knows at least two languages' may be true, while the corresponding passive 'at least two languages are known by everyone in the room' is false" (*SyS* 101–2).

4   For Chomsky today, reference is undoubtedly involved in interpretation, not in meaning or content; in current terminology, meaning is a part of broad syntax, while reference is something that people do and is in pragmatics. But Chomsky in recent years has played with a technical concept of reference that he suggests might be placed in syntax. In 1982, in *LGB* (p. 324), for example, he suggests that a technical concept of reference might be defined entirely within the domain of syntax. This suggestion is pursued in *KL* and in more detail recently (1993) in his "Explaining Language Use." The idea, basically, is to allow that simply by assigning elements in a formal model to expressions in referring positions (e.g., subject) in a sentence, the result could be seen as a way to explore what a semantic interface contains. It could be thought of as a way to represent some structural 'knowledge' that a meaning or semantic interface contains. But my guess is that this suggestion is tongue-in-cheek. Chomsky does not need to introduce even a technical conception of reference to accomplish what he wants; feature specifications do the same. Perhaps he wanted to tease Quineans and Davidsonians who thought that reference to things in the world could constitute the core of a theory of meaning (or under-

standing, or content); perhaps he wanted to show that the term "reference" is up for grabs and that it does not need to be understood in the Quine–Davidson way. The informal use of "meanings" for his semantic interfaces seems to be differently motivated. He is quite serious: these interfaces, syntactically specified and defined, really can take the place of what the Fregeans did not manage to make the subject matter of a science – senses. That they can is because they are objective, well-defined entities in a science that is a branch of biology. And their position as interfaces that the organism can use helps make sense of how they are 'interpreted' by virtue of the fact that they guide interpretations.

5   It is still not entirely clear, even though these controversies have led to several books. In the 260 pages of Harris's highly readable *The Linguistic Wars* (1993), which goes into considerable detail about the arguments between Chomsky and his opponents during the generative semantics days, there is no clear indication of what semantics was supposed to be for any of the parties involved. In Huck and Goldsmith's more technical discussion of the generative semantic controversy in *Ideology and Linguistic Theory*, the only clear indication of what semantics was supposed to be for the generative semanticists was that it had something to do with logic (1995: 19) – presumably, then, with inference and truth. Perhaps this is supposed to ring Fregean bells, but the claim needs clarification.

On the matter of Chomsky ignoring semantics in favor of syntax, the reader can judge. My opinion is that his syntactic work has always been directed towards getting a theoretical grip on meaning and that what he once called "structural meaning" and now SEM ("syntactic meaning") represents a plausible way to do so that is consistent with the poverty and creativity observations. Most 'semantic theories' are not.

6   Chomsky prefers the former: "The optional features of a particular occurrence of "book" (say, [accusative], [plural]) are added by either [Numeration or Select] – presumably by [numeration], a decision that reduces reference sets and hence computability problems" (*MP* 236).

7   'Signal' is Chomsky's term. Cf. his draft paper, "Language from an Internalist Perspective" (1994).

8   While Cudworth did not think of his ideas as resident in language, he certainly seemed to think that the order of, and divisions in, language are quite close to the order and divisions of thought. Incidentally, Cudworth did not, as more modern philosophers might, distinguish between what might be called sentential concepts (<u>Keeping watch on the rhinoceros, Margo fell asleep</u>) and individual concepts (<u>house</u>). As with many others in the seventeenth century, though, "ideas" no doubt covered sentential concepts too.

Chapter 7   Anarchosyndicalism and the Intellectual

1   Classical liberalism had revolutionary implications too in the basic assumption that people act to fulfill inner needs. Cf. *DD* 398.

A shorthand way to make many of Chomsky's points here and below is to contrast a Madisonian democracy that assigns rights to individuals *and* to property with a Jeffersonian one that assigns rights to individuals alone. Current democracies (US, UK, Germany, Canada) are Madisonian in giving rights to property. Chomsky points out that Madisonian democracies, in giving private power (corporations, "legal persons") the 'right' to control the workplace, do not give these decisions to those who labor. The result is "wage slaves." Thus, these are not genuine democracies. They are also inherently unstable, unlike Jeffersonian democracies – those that more nearly satisfy the fundamental human need for freedom and creativity and thus more nearly suit Chomsky's anarchosyndicalist view of an ideal form of social organization. Madisonian democracies are unstable because they require the exercise of power; these 'democracies' are, in fact, autocracies. Unlike totalitarian systems that rely on direct threat and force, however, considerable private power in Madisonian states is directed towards control of government policy and (in part to effect this) towards a campaign of deception – a program of propaganda aimed at "manufacturing consent" among those who vote. In these corporate-run states, corporate media – particularly 'elite' media – are propaganda instruments. By (unthinkingly but effectively) filtering and skewing information and never questioning the presuppositions of the system (that the corporation has the 'right' to control) from which they benefit, media personnel ("intellectuals") manage the thoughts of others without the imposition of force. In a Jeffersonian democracy, in contrast, no "legal persons" or other forms of private power have rights, all individuals have as full access to information as possible, and all have the power to make decisions on anything that bears on their interests. A Jeffersonian democracy requires a different conception of media and of media's task, of course.

2 Very recent articles in *Time* critical of corporate welfare (but blaming it entirely on government) may signal a change of pace. Interestingly, Gingrich resigned in the same week as the first of these articles appeared, although not because anyone minded his participation in welfare, but for his failed attempt to use Clinton's sexual habits to gain more seats in the House and Senate for Republicans.

3 The term "communist anarchist" does not reappear in the interview or elsewhere in Chomsky's writing, so far as I know – no doubt because it suggests nothing not already implied by the other two and is liable to give rise to revulsion in some and visions of Leninist autocracy in others. Chomsky does, however, have considerable sympathy for Council Communism (Rosa Luxemburg and Anton Pannekoek).

4 Later in this interview, Chomsky shows his basic disagreement with Kropotkin's rather naive views.

Chapter 8 Human Nature and Ideal Social Organization

1 Chomsky signed a petition supporting the right of Robert Faurisson, a French professor of literature at the University of Lyon, to deny that the Nazi government in Germany massacred thousands of Jews during World War II (*LP* 308f; Barsky 1997: 179f). He also criticized the French judiciary's

effort to censure Faurisson and prevent him from continuing to perform his duties. His insistence on Faurisson's right to the free expression of his views, as well as his censure of the French attempt to deny Faurisson an audience, led to the fury of most Zionists and of the press in France – all of whom made the mistake of confusing defense of the right of someone to make a claim with defense of the claim itself. Chomsky's own view of the Holocaust, and of people who deny or defend it, is a matter of record: he has made it clear that the Holocaust was despicable and inhuman, and he thinks that anyone who tries to deny it is a moral monster, beyond the reach of reason. Furthermore, he has declared that he was once a left Zionist (at one time the mainstream) and is still attracted by policies (a binational state in Israel, for example) that were advocated by other left Zionists (Barsky 1997: 78, 171–2). He has also held, however, that the only reasonable immediate solution is the two-state solution, "the only viable alternative to continued oppression and war" (in an exchange on Chomsky's *Fateful Triangle*, printed in Otero 1994: iii. 392).

2   This strategy is found in many of Chomsky's writings, speeches, and discussions. One instance is an interview with David Barsamian in 1984 (*LP* 615): "[A]ny stance that one takes with regard to social issues, for example, advocacy of some kind of reform or advocacy of a revolutionary change, an institutional change, or advocacy of stability and maintaining structures as they are – any such position, assuming that it has any moral basis at all and is not simply based on personal self-interest, is ultimately based on some conception of human nature. That is, if you suggest things should be reformed in this or that fashion and there's a moral basis for it, you are in effect saying, 'Human beings are so constituted that this change is to their benefit. It somehow relates to their essential human needs.'"

3   It is printed in several places; my references are to *CR*.

4   The term is my choice; Chomsky might prefer "solidarity" because of the suggestions in its usage that association with others be close, involve mutual respect, and be directed towards a common goal. My choice has problems, in part because others – in particular, 'communitarians' such as Taylor and Walzer – have turned it to un-Chomskian ends. But it has the advantage of being the most widely applicable.

5   There seems to be a parallel between Chomsky's view that we perceive more clearly or understand more about our moral natures as civilization and "moral and cultural evolution" progress and his view that the history of the evolution of a science shows something about the nature of our minds and what they provide to scientific inquiry. In "any [scientific] field that has shown some progress, you find that at particular moments things converge. There is a certain level of understanding that is achieved and there's a certain range of problems that are alive and challenging and suddenly many people will get the same idea or similar ideas as to how to change perspective so as to reach a new level of understanding. This is sometimes called a scientific revolution." His explanation for convergence and the 'that looks right' effect in the sciences is that "we must be designed specifically to map our current problem situations into a certain small sub-

class of possible theories" (*LP* 467). If what Chomsky has in mind by moral progress, given his emphasis upon coming to perceive obligations and rights that have previously been ignored or denied – in the case under consideration, coming only fairly recently to recognize or understand that slavery cannot ever be justified – is like what he describes as progress in a science, perhaps one can think of the mind as imposing constraints on what people take to be right, in the same way as one can conceive of the mind imposing constraints on what a plausible hypothesis/theory is. This makes sense of the idea that in coming to recognize the universal application of moral principles we are coming to understand what is built into "natural morality" from the start. If so, slave-owners offering moral justifications for slavery were wrong all along from the standpoint of natural morality, even if it was not fully recognized at the time that they were. "We" did not have sufficient recognition of our moral natures but have now managed to at least reach a stage where we recognize that the slave-owner, in not applying to his slaves principles that he would apply to himself, his family, and his friends, was a moral monster. The picture has several problems, of course. But it does make partial sense of how to provide for emerging agreement and for moral progress – at least in the direction of universal application of principles. Not coincidentally, it also suggests that a science of human nature might have a bearing on the matter.

6 Perhaps this demand – like the demand for "social justice" and, more generally, justice and fairness – is an expression of the fundamental need for community. This seems plausible, and it may even be necessary for the argument to be complete, but pursuing the point would take us far afield.

7 The transcript to this and several other televised Netherlands debates is printed in Fons Elders's *Reflexive Waters*.

8 This is not a criticism. Chomsky, like anyone, has limited time and resources. As I remarked at the beginning of the book, though, his accomplishments may be unprecedented.

9 It does no good for apologists of Plato's anti-democratic and authoritarian picture of the republic to say that it represents the ideal state only. That is the point.

References

This bibliography contains only works to which reference is made. A full bibliography of Chomsky's works is a book in itself. Many hundreds of works by various authors that have influenced my study of Chomsky, and many of Chomsky's works to which I do not refer, do not appear below.

Arnauld, A. (1662). *La Logique, ou l'art de penser*. Tr. Dickoff & James, *The Art of Thinking*. Indianapolis: Bobbs-Merrill, 1965.

Austin, J. L. (1962). *How to Do Things with Words*. Cambridge, MA: Harvard University Press.

Barsky, Robert F. (1997). *Noam Chomsky: A Life of Dissent*. Toronto: ECW Press.

Beauzée, N. (1767). *Grammaire générale*.

Bloomfield, Leonard (1939). Menomini Morphophonemics. *Travaux du cercle linguistique de Prague*.

Bracken, Harry M. (1984). *Mind and Language: Essays on Descartes and Chomsky*. Dordrecht: Foris.

Brady, Robert (1943). *Business as a System of Power*. New York: Columbia University Press.

Buchanan, James (1975). *The Limits of Liberty: Between Anarchy and Leviathan*. Chicago: University of Chicago Press.

Burge, Tyler (1988). Cartesian Error and the Objectivity of Perception. In R. H. Crimm and D. D. Merrill (eds), *Contents of Thought*, Tucson: University of Arizona Press, 62–98.

—(1992). Philosophy of Language and Mind. *Philosophical Review* 101, 3–52.

Chomsky, Noam (1967). Review of B. F. Skinner, *Verbal Behavior*. Reprinted with added preface in Jakobovits and Miron (eds), *Readings in the Psychology of Language*. Englewood Cliffs, NJ: Prentice-Hall, 142–72.

—and Michel Foucault (debate) (1974). Human Nature: Justice versus Power. In Fons Elders (ed.), *Reflexive Waters*, Toronto: J. M. Dent, 135–97.

—(1992). Language and Interpretation. In J. Earman (ed.), *Inference, Explanation, and Other Frustrations: Essays in the Philosophy of Science*, Berkeley: University of California Press, 99–128.

—(1993). Explaining Language Use. In James E. Tomberlin (ed.), *Philosophical Topics* 20, 205–31.

—(1994a). Language from an Internalist Perspective. Draft copy, Lecture at King's College, London, May 24, 1994.

—(1994b). Naturalism and Dualism in the Study of Language and Mind. *International Journal of Philosophical Studies* 2, 181–209.

—(1995). Language and Nature. *Mind* 104, (413), 1–61.

—(1997). Internalist Explorations (MS). To appear in a volume of essays in honor of Tyler Burge.

—(1998). Minimalist Inquiries: The Framework. MS, Department of Linguistics, MIT.

Christophe, Anne, Emmanuel Dupoux, Josiane Bertoncini, and Jacques Mehler (1994). Do Infants Perceive Word Boundaries? An Empirical Study of the Bootstrapping of Lexical Acquisition. *Journal of the Acoustical Society of America* 95 (3), 1570–80.

Cinque, Guglielmo (1994). "On the Connections between Chomsky's Work in Linguistics and Cognitive Science, and His Social Views and Attitudes. In Carlos Otero (ed.), *Noam Chomsky: Critical Assessments*, London: Routledge, vol. 3, 333–46.

Clark, Austen (1993). *Sensory Qualities*. Oxford: Clarendon Press.

Cook, Vivian, and Mark Newsom (1996). *Chomsky's Universal Grammar*, 2nd edn. Cambridge, MA: Blackwell.

Cordemoy, Géraud de (1666). *Discours Physique de la Parole*. English trans. 1668.

Cudworth, Ralph (1731). *A Treatise Concerning Eternal and Immutable Morality*. Facsimile of original, New York: Garland Publishing, 1976.

Davidson, Donald (1980). Psychology as Philosophy. In Davidson, *Essays on Action and Events*, Oxford: Clarendon Press, 229–39.

—(1986). A Nice Derangement of Epitaphs. In E. LePore (ed.), *Truth and Interpretation*, Oxford: Blackwell, 433–46.

Descartes, René (1637). *Discourse on Method*, Tr. J. Cottingham et al., in *The Philosophical Writings of Descartes*, vol. 1, Cambridge: Cambridge University Press, 1985.

Du Marsais, C.C. (1729). *Véritables Principes de la grammaire*.

Dummett, Michael (1986). Comments on Davidson and Hacking. In E. Lepore (ed.), *Truth and Interpretation*, Oxford: Blackwell, 459–76.

Elders, Fons (1974). *Reflexive Waters*. Toronto: J.M. Dent.

Fodor, Jerry (1982). The Current Status of the Innateness Controversy. In Fodor, *Representations*. Cambridge, MA: MIT Press, 257–316.

Gleitman, Lila, C. Fisher, D.G. Hall, and S. Rakowitz (1994). When it is Better to Receive than to Give: Syntactic and Conceptual Constraints on Vocabulary Growth. *Lingua* 92, 333–75.

Goodman, Nelson (1952). On Likeness of Meaning. In L. Linsky (ed.), *Semantics and the Philosophy of Language*, Urbana: University of Illinois Press.

—(1961). About. *Mind* 70, 1–24.

—(1967). The Epistemological Argument. *Synthese* 17, pp. 23–8.

Goodman, Nelson (1968). *Languages of Art*. Indianapolis: Bobbs-Merrill.

Grice, Paul (1975). Logic and Conversation. In P. Cole and J. Morgan (eds), *Syntax and Semantics*, vol. 3. *Speech Acts*, New York: Academic Press, 41–58.

Harris, Randy Allen (1993). *The Linguistic Wars*. Oxford: Oxford University Press.

Henwood, Doug (1997). *Left Business Observer*, 80 (Nov. 17, 1997).

Huck, Geoffrey J. and John A. Goldsmith (1995). *Ideology and Linguistic Theory: Noam Chomsky and the Deep Structure Debates*. London: Routledge.

Jackendoff, Ray S. (1994). *Patterns in the Mind*. New York: Basic Books.

—(1997). *The Architecture of the Language Faculty*. Cambridge, MA: MIT Press.

Jackendoff, Ray S. and Fred Lerdahl (1983). *A Generative Theory of Tonal Music*. Cambridge, MA: MIT Press.

Lancelot, C. and A. Arnauld (1660). *Grammaire générale et raisonnée*.

Lyons, John (1970). *Noam Chomsky*. New York: Viking.

Marr, David (1982). *Vision*. San Francisco: Freeman.

Mehler, Jacques and Anne Christophe (1994). Language in the Infant's Mind. *Philosophical Transactions of the Royal Society of London Series B*, 346, 13–20.

Mishel, Lawrence and Jared Bernstein (1994). *The State of Working America 1994–95*. Armonk, N. Y.: N. E. Sharpe.

Moravcsik, Julius (1975). Aitia as Generative Factor in Aristotle's Philosophy of Language. *Dialogue* 14, 622–36.

—(1990). *Thought and Language*. London: Routledge.

Morris, Charles W. (1938). *Foundations of the Theory of Signs*. Chicago: University of Chicago Press.

Otero, Carlos P. (ed.) (1994). *Noam Chomsky: Critical Assessments*, 4 vols. London: Routledge.

Piatelli-Palmarini, Massimo (1980). *Language and Learning: The Debate between Jean Piaget and Noam Chomsky*. Cambridge, MA: Harvard University Press.

Pinker, Steven (1989). *Learnability and Cognition*. Cambridge, MA: MIT Press.

—(1994a). How Could a Child Use Verb Syntax to Learn Verb Semantics? *Lingua* 92, 377–410.

—(1994b). *The Language Instinct*. New York: William Morrow.

Pustejovsky, James (1995). *The Generative Lexicon*. Cambridge, MA: MIT Press.

Putnam, Hilary (1967). The Innateness Hypothesis and Explanatory Models in Linguistics. In Putnam, *Philosophical Papers*, Cambridge: Cambridge University Press, 1975.

—(1975). The Meaning of "Meaning." In K. Gunderson (ed.), *Language, Mind, and Knowledge*, Minnesota Studies in the Philosophy of Science, 7, Minneapolis: University of Minnesota Press.

—(1993). Replies. In James E. Tomberlin (ed.), *Philosophical Topics* 20, 347–408.

Samuelson, Paul A. (1970). *Economics*. New York: McGraw-Hill.

Scott, Dominic (1995). *Recollection and Experience*. Cambridge: Cambridge University Press.

Sellars, Wilfrid (1960a). Empiricism and the Philosophy of Mind. In Sellars, *Science, Perception, and Reality*, New York: Humanities Press, 127–96.

—(1960b). Philosophy and the Scientific Image of Man. In Sellars, *Science, Perception, and Reality*, New York: Humanities Press, 1–40.

Skinner, B. F. (1957). *Verbal Behavior*. Englewood Cliffs, NJ: Prentice-Hall.

Soames, Scott and D. Perlmutter (1979). *Syntactic Argumentation and the Structure of English*. Berkeley: University of California Press.

Sperber, Dan and Deirdre Wilson (1986). *Relevance: Communication and Cognition*. Oxford: Blackwell.

Strawson, Peter (1950). On Referring. *Mind* 49.

von Humboldt, Wilhelm (1836). *Über die Verschiedenheit des Menschlichen Sprachbaues*. Facsimile edition, F. Dummlers Verlag, Bonn, 1960.

Wittgenstein, Ludwig (1953). *Philosophical Investigations*. New York: Macmillan; Oxford: Blackwell.

Index

Achbar, Mark, 212
aesthetic judgment, 52, 53
agreement (for science), 57–60, 112–13
    see also convergence
analytic truths, 30, 58–9, 174–6
anaphor, 136–7
anarchosyndicalism/libertarian socialism,
    196–203, 221, 237–8, 248–9, 260n1
animal 'languages', 86–7, 91
appropriateness (of language use), 81–2,
    85, 94, 170–1, 173
Aristotle, 67, 77, 108
Arnauld, A., 2, 72
Attract/Move, 47, 157–8
Austin, J. L., 103

Bakunin, Mikhail, 216
bare output conditions, 97, 111, 126, 143,
    147, 157–8
base component, 126, 138
Beauzée, N., 72
behaviorism, 28–9, 250n1
binding theory, 134–7
Bloomfield, L., 107, 110
Brady, Robert, 195–6, 209
Buchanan, James, 196, 198, 202
Burge, Tyler, 40–1

capacities, 49–50, 51–5
Cartesian linguists, 2–3, 11–13, 70–2, 84
case theory, 134
cognitive powers (skills, etc.), 55–6

common sense understanding
    as basis for poverty and creativity
        observations, 82
    distinguished from scientific
        understanding, 5, 17–28, 42, 56–7
    enabled by faculties, 46, 52–3
    innateness of, 22–3, 54–5
    involves cooperation between vision,
        language, other faculties, 49
    of languages, 108–10
    as part of reason, 46, 49
    as problem solving capacity, 49–50
    role in Chomsky's constructivism,
        89–93, 174
    role in moral and political matters, 25,
        179–80, 204, 238, 242
communication
    not central aim of language, 87
    Chomsky on, 256n6
competence, linguistic, 48, 96
computational theory
    ch. 5
    of language faculty, 47, 254n9
    of mind, 38–9
    and recursion, 128
    and syntax, 102
    of vision, 46
concepts
    common sense and scientific conflict,
        21, 90
    innateness of shown by Plato, 63–4,
        67–8
    and knowledge of world, 89–93, 169–76
    within theory of language, 20, 169

connectionism, 253n17
constructivism
  Chomsky's as Goodmanian, 165,
    168–76, 253n15
  and properties and knowledge of
    world, 32, 89–93
  relation to internalism and nativism,
    5–6
  required by faculties of language and
    vision, 47
  supported by poverty of stimulus and
    creative aspect of language use, 17
convergence, in judgment, 232–8, 262n5
corporations
  control of media, 203–16, 220
  as "legal persons", 195–6
  role in democracies, 198, 260n1
  role in US government policy, 180–96
  and wage slavery, 201–33
  welfare for, 185–6
Cordemoy, Géraud de, 2, 70
creativity
  in language use: and appropriateness,
    81–2, 85; and Descartes' test for
    human minds, 79–89; role in
    determining adequate theories, 108,
    119; and stimulus freedom, 81;
    supports nativism, internalism, and
    constructivism, 6–7, 78; and
    unboundedness, 81
  in politics, 202, 226, 227–9
Cudworth, Ralph, 2, 59, 67, 70–8, 92, 229
  on internalist and nativist view of
    'interpretation', 168–78

Danchev, Vladimir, 204
Davidson, Donald, 42–3, 100
Deep Structure, 71, 126–7, 132, 153–6,
  259n3, 260n5
derivation, linguistic, 126, 132, 148, 256n3
Descartes, René, 15, 26–7, 33–4, 75, 78,
  82–9, 93, 169
Descartes' problem, 94
  see also creativity, internalism
descriptive adequacy, linguistic, 119–20,
  150
design problem, in minimalism, 147–50
discovery procedure, for language, 124
displacement property, 132
D-structure, 126–7, 132
domain of experience, 53–4
DuMarsais, C.C., 72
Dummett, Michael, 16

East Timor, 18, 211–14, 218
'economic man,' 181–2, 227, 231–5
E-language (approach), 106–11
eliminationism, 40–6
empiricism
  behaviorism as example of, 28–9
  and connectionism, 253n17
  distinguished from rationalism, 32
  and faculties, 88
  fails to explain acquisition, 68–9, 73–4
  and folk psychology, 43–6
  and generalized learning procedure,
    54–5
  and higher cognitive processes, 29–33
  and philosophers, 16
  relation to political coercion and
    control, 17, 57, 250n5
enabling
  defined, 52–3
  enablement by limitation, 60–1, 88–9
evaluation metric, 123, 133
evolution, 92, 252n13, 255n7
experience
  constituted (formed) by available
    concepts, 58, 92–3, 169–74
  domains of, 53
explanatory adequacy
  crucial for empirical justification, 72
  and grammars, 46, 127, 128–33
  and Minimalist Program, 150
  and P&P framework, 133–43
  in theories of language, 72, 119–24, 133
expression
  defined, 96–7
  output of language faculty, 120
  sound/meaning pair, 47, 97
  used in interpretation, 151–2
Extended Standard Theory, 133, 258n1

faculty (mental)
  distinct from capacity, 49–50, 51–3
  infinite but limited outputs, 88–9
  innately fixed, 51–2, 56
  modular, 48
  provide interfaces to other systems,
    50–1, 97, 150
  sensory, 50
  technical term, 39
  universal, 52
Faurisson, Robert, 261n1
Fodor, Jerry, 91, 153
folk psychology, 25, 27, 40, 43–6, 54
folk science, 25, 27, 45, 54

Index

formal features, 95–6, 104, 158–61
Foucault, Michel, 223, 235–7
freedom, 4:
  and Descartes' second test, 83–4
  and Descartes' test for mind, 81–2
  free labor as Enlightenment ideal, 184
  as fundamental human need, 224–35
  and linguistic actions, 7
  and limits on a science of language,
    101
Frege, Gottlob, 99–100, 103
Friedman, Thomas, 206

geometry (innateness of), 49
Gingrich, Newt, 184
Goodman, Nelson, 72–4, 162–3, 165,
    253n15
grammar
  defined, 96
  'chosen' by child, 122–3
  core, 96
  finite state inadequate, 127–9
  generative, 96, 127, 132
  pure phrase structure inadequate,
    129–31
  and recursion, 128–31
  see also Universal Grammar (UG)
Grand Area policy, 188–95
Grice, Paul, 103

Harris, Zellig, 110, 132
Herbert of Cherbury, 168–9
Herman, Edward, 204, 212, 214, 237
human nature
  fixed by innate faculties and capacities,
    56
  as part of general project, 12
  role in political discussion, 222–3,
    224–39, 261n2
  science of, 9, 223, 246, 248
Hume, David, 57, 92, 240, 242

ideas
  analytic connections between, 30
  general category for early Cartesian
    linguists, 169–70
  not necessarily conscious, 34
  as subject matter of science of
    language, 34, 169–70
  see also innate ideas
identity (of things), 93, 105–6
I-language
  defined, 97, 117

and Chomsky's individualism, 5
and Minimalist Program, 150
as object of natural science, 117
and UG, 102, 250n1
innate ideas
  argued for in Plato's *Meno*, 63–4, 67–8
  composed of innate features, 252n12
  condition for experience of a domain,
    53, 92, 170–4
  generated in the mind, 78, 159, 169–72,
    173–4
  inherent in rationalism, 32
  not consciously apprehended, 33–4
  objects of science of mental faculty,
    53–4
innateness
  biological basis of, 4
  of common sense concepts, 22–3, 77–8
  and creative aspect of language use,
    78–89
  and folk psychology, 43–5
  of language, 65–93
  of meaning, 4, 104–5, 162–3
  of moral concepts, 60, 231–3, 236, 262n5
  part of nativism, 4
  and poverty of stimulus observations,
    63–78, 121
  and syntax, 102
  see also innate ideas; Universal
    Grammar
intellectuals
  and corporate-run media, 204–5
  misrepresentations by, 204–8
  and Orwell's problem, 239–44
  as propagandists, 207, 209–16
  as recognizing responsibilities, 219–20
  responsibilities of, 204, 216–20, 241–2
  and telling the truth, 217–18, 238
  in totalitarian states, 209–10
  Western, greater culpability of, 220, 230
  see also Propaganda Model; social
    science (behavioral)
interface
  as set of instructions, 48
  output of faculty, 46
  as perspectives, 152, 156–8
  phonetic or PHON, 96
  provides tool to user, 152, 153, 169
  semantic or SEM, 96
  as sounds and meanings, 97
internalism, 3–4, 101–5, 151–2, 164–8, 171
  see also Descartes' problem; creativity;
    meaning

interpretation, 151–2, 168–74
and Deep Structure, 153–6
as use of a tool, 151–2, 165
of visual interface, 46
see also projection; constructivism
irony, 19–20, 25
comparison with Socratic, 244–5

Jackendoff, Ray, 53
Jay, Peter, 201
Jefferson, Thomas, 183, 198, 225, 260n1, 261n2
judgment-making capacities
common sense understanding as, 49
dependent on faculties' 'outputs,' 49–50
enabled by faculties, 52–4, 55–9
facial recognition as, 49
science as, 49
justification
empiricism's lack of, 62–3
of moral/political actions, 236–9
of moral/political vision, 221–4
and moral progress, 232–4
role of poverty and creativity observations in, 78
in science, 29, 118–19
in science of language, 147–50
see also descriptive adequacy; explanatory adequacy; naturalism; rationalism

Kant, Immanuel, 169, 228, 254n6
Kissinger, Henry, 189, 218, 250n5

language
acquisition, 68–70
and animals' communications systems, 86–7
common sense understanding of, 108–10, 112–18
E-language, 106–12
I-language, 106–8
individuation of, 106–18
and scientific symbol system, 20–8
structure dependent, 66
and Universal Grammar (UG)
see also language faculty
language acquisition device, 122
language faculty
as biological organ, 4
computational device, 39, 254n9
computational theory of, 47–57, 126–47
important source of concepts for common sense, 26

modular, 39, 48
produces sounds (PHONs) and meaning (SEMs), 47, 151–2, 156–68, 163–8
language of thought, 167, 176
language use
creative aspect of, 6–7, 78–89
guided by internal meanings and sounds, 57–9, 174–6
and internalism, 16–17
involved in reasoning, 37
and pragmatics, 100
no science of, 100–1
and unified project, 11
see also creativity; interpretation
LeMoyne, James, 191, 206–8
lexical items
connection with setting parameters, 121
features of, 158–62, 252n12
include semantic features, 103
list of in I-languages changes over time, 117
as mental dictionary, 95–6
and Minimalist Project, 143–7
and rewrite rules, 130
lexicology of in relatively primitive state, 103
and UG, 158–60
and X-bar theory, 138–47
see also Saussurean arbitrariness
lexical semantics, 78
LF, 161
see also SEM
liberalism (classical or Jeffersonian)
as anarchistic, 198
importance of creative labor for, 183–4
in Smith and Locke, 182–3
as traditional conservatism, 183
liberalism (new), 182–3
linguistic community, 108–11
linguistic processing not modifiable by, 38
not source of sound or meaning, 57, 68–70
support for by philosophers, 16
linguistics *see* science of language
Loebner prize, 85, 87

Madison, James, 182–3, 260n1, 261n2
'market discipline', 185, 195
Markovian computational system, 128–9, 258nn2,3

Marr, David, 34–5
mathematical linguistics, 14
　see also computational theory
mathematics (innateness of), 51, 53,
　63–4
meaning
　and common sense, 163
　embodied in SEMs or LFs, 47–8, 97
　guides use (interpretation), 174–6
　internal, 164–8
　and Minimalist Program, 156–62
　as natural 'object,' 162–8
　naturalized, 28
　part of syntax, 100–5
　SEMs as Fregean senses, 103–4
　subject matter of science, 105
　universal, 71, 104–5
Mehler, Jacques, 91
mental organ, 48, 88, 102
Merge, 47, 145–7
Mill, James, 209
mind
　access to, 34–5
　and body, 35
　Chomsky's view of, 36–40, 56, 87–9
　common sense concepts and, 40–6
　empiricists' view of, 28–33
　involves capacities and faculties,
　　50–1
　seen as plastic, 15–16
　and powers, 55–6
　as theory-constructing device, 30
mind/body problem, 35
Minimalist Program
　echoes of von Humboldt, 71
　and explanation, 124
　involves bare output conditions, 111,
　　143
　and lexical items, 143–7, 158–62
　and meaning, 156–62
　and optimality, 147–50
　and simplicity, 147–50
modularity, 4, 39
moral judgment, 52, 60, 231–7, 262n5
morphology, 95
morphophonemics, 130
Morris, Charles, 98–9
Move *see* Attract/Move
move-α, 137

nativism, 4–5, 17
　see also explanatory adequacy; innate
　　ideas; innateness; Plato's problem

naturalism
　empiricists not naturalistic (or
　　empirical), 32–3
　methodological term, 32–3, 111
　in science of meaning, 162–8
　in social/political matters, 223–4, 235–9
natural languages
　and common sense understanding, 20–1
　concepts in, 22–3
　conceptual structure provides domain
　　of experience, 57–60
　include possible languages, 114
　individuated by parameters, 114–17
　innate, 22, 23–4, 65–78
　and UG, 96, 127
needs, fundamental human, 222–35;
　262n4, 262–3n5, 263n6
Newton, Isaac, 35, 254n3
nominalism (Goodman and Chomsky),
　164–8
nouns, 23, 77, 106, 108, 139, 145, 160,
　256n2
Numeration/Select, 156, 160

optimality, 148–50
Orwell's problem, 209, 239–44

parameters, 73, 96, 114–15, 116, 121–4
Peirce, Charles Sanders, 54–5, 98
perspectives
　as internal meanings, 151–2
　as interfaces, 157
　involve human interests and concerns,
　　92
　as SEMs, 156–62
　as tools for use in interpretation, 152
　see also meaning; SEM
PF *see* PHON
PHON (phonetic interface), 47–8, 96–7,
　151, 156–7, 166–7
phonetics/phonology, 66, 95–6, 127,
　115–17, 158
phrase structure grammar, 21, 99, 127–32
　part of base component, 126
　replaced by X-bar theory, 137–43
Plato, 63–4, 67–8, 70
Plato's problem, 94, 121–4, 125–6, ch. 5
　see also explanatory adequacy; poverty
　　of the stimulus
Port-Royal grammarians, 71–2, 154
poverty of the stimulus observations
　as basis for deciding whether theory of
　　language correct, 16–17, 62–3, 78,
　　119–24

and Chomsky's unified project, 11
and language, 6, 63–78
and moral concepts, 232, 262–3n5
in P&P framework, 121–4, 134–44
theory of UG can explain, 13, 113–18
used by Plato for geometry, 63–5, 67–8
see also innate ideas; innateness; Plato's
problem; UG
powers (of mind), 55–6
pragmatics, 98–105
principles, 118, 121–4, 134–44
see also P&P framework
Principles and Parameters (P&P)
framework, 113–18, 121–4, 134–47
problem/mystery distinction, 94, 256n1
progress
in moral evaluation and justification,
232–4, 235, 262n5
in science of language, 118–24, 147–50
projection (constructivist), 89–93, 168–74
see also constructivism
projection (of lexical features), 138–43,
146
Propaganda Model (of media), 209–16,
240–3
Putnam, Hilary, 16, 72–4

Quine, W. V. O., 16

rationalism(ists)
biological, 33, 89–93
contributions to discussion of
innateness by early, 70–2
differences between Chomsky and
Descartes on mind, 84
distinguished from empiricism, 32–3
provides framework to relate
Chomsky's linguistic and political
work, 12, 248–9
understanding of mind only viable
one, 3, 32–3
see also constructivism; internalism;
nativism
reason, 36–9, 46–57, 240, 243–4
recursion (in theory of language), 128–31,
143, 146
reference
included in semantics, 99
in interpretation, 152, 259n1
involves agents (persons), 102, 104–5,
155, 258n5
normatively governed, 38
philosophers' view of, 37–8

part of pragmatics, 102, 104–5, 155,
258n5
quasi-reference, 135, 258n5, 259n4
not subject of science, 254n5
as tetradic relationship, 38
representation (internalist), 127
representationalism, 30
richness, 23, 67, 159
Ronat, Mitsou, 204
Rousseau, Jean-Jacques, 227
rule of language, 255n11
Russell, Bertrand, 18, 99

Samuelson, Paul, 180–1
Saussurean arbitrariness, 69–70, 117, 158
Schlegel, A. W., 2
science of language
chs. 4–6
and access to mind, 33–5
connection to Chomsky's politics, 9–13,
17, 222–3, 248–9
as developing, 11–13
does not deal with language use,
39–40, 101–2
evidence used, 13, 16–17, 18–19, 118–23
not social science, 37
reception of Chomsky's, 13–14
as syntax, 101–5
why Chomsky's theory is science,
94–124
see also creativity; internalism; poverty
of the stimulus observations; UG
scientific understanding
can remain undeveloped, 52
concepts of science, 20–5
constructivist, 61, 89–93
distinguished from common sense, 5,
19–28, 42–3, 56–7
enabled by faculties, 52–3
innateness (limited) of, 54–5, 255n7,
259n10
as problem-solving capacity, 49
provides (with common sense
understanding) human reason, 36, 46
sciences as artifacts, 21–2, 118–19
see also naturalism; theories, scientific
Sellars, Wilfrid, 40–1
SEM (semantic interface), 47–8, 96–7,
103–4, 105, 127, 147, 151–2, 156–7,
163–8, 169–74
see also meaning
semantic features, 95, 97, 104–5, 158–61,
256n2

semantics, 98–105, 257n7, 258n5, 259nn1, 4, 260n5
  see also lexical semantics
sense(s), 99–100, 103
sentence(s), 48, 58, 96–7, 127–47
  see also expressions
simplicity, 111, 121–3, 147–50, 246
Skinner, B. F., 28–9
Soames, Scott, 103
social cognition (capacity for), 52–3, 232
social science (behavioral), 179–80, 217, 238–9, 250n5
social science (Chomsky's new humanistic), 223–4, 237–9, 247–9
sociobiology, 250n1
Socrates, 63–4, 67–8, 244–7, 251–2
Spell-Out, 156
Sperber, Daniel, 103–10
Standard Theory, 126–33, 137
Steinberg, Joel, 1
stimulus freedom, 81
Strawson, Peter, 39
Surface Structure (and S-structure), 71, 126–7, 132, 153, 259n3
syntax, 98–105

theories, scientific, 20–2, 50–1, 62–3, 100–1, 112–13, 118–19, 119–24, 223, 246
theta-role, 103, 256n5
trace, 137, 142
transformation, 130–2, 137
  see also Attract/Move; displacement property
transformational grammar, 71–2, 127–33
triggering (in acquisition), 64, 90–3
truth
  aim of rational inquiry, 36
  analytic a priori, 57–60, 174–6
  component of semantics, 99, 105
  intellectual's moral obligation to tell, 216–20
  not necessarily the same for science and common sense, 36–7
  see also analytic truths
Turing, Alan, 84

Turing test, 84–7
  appropriateness as core of, 85

unboundedness, 81
  see also recursion
universal(s/ity/ism), 5, 74–5, 117–18, 123, 133–7
Universal Grammar (UG)
  contribution to theory of mind, 14
  and lexicon, 158–62
  naturalistic way of individuating languages, 11–18, 127–8
  natural languages deducible from, 96–7
  and Port-Royal grammarians, 70–8, 154
  presupposes innateness, 72–3
  in production of SEMs, 156–62
  provides a theory of language, 96, 119–24
  represents what child knows before acquiring a language, 96, 123
  requires experience and triggering to develop into a specific language, 116
  see also Minimalist Program; P&P framework; Standard Theory

verbal auxiliary structure, 130
verbs, 24, 57–8, 76, 174–5
vision (faculty), 34–5, 38–9, 46–8, 92–3, 116
von Humboldt, Wilhelm, 71, 173–4, 228–9, 258

Wilson, Deirdre, 103, 110
Wittgenstein, Ludwig, 111–12
Wittgensteinian language games, 87, 111
world
  constructed, 89–93
  different in science and common sense, 20, 27–8, 90–1, 252n8
  knowledge of, 89–93, 168–74
  supposed source of agreement in judgment, 44–5

X-bar theory, 137–47